Theatre in the Victorian Age

Theatre in the Victorian Age

MICHAEL R. BOOTH

CAMBRIDGE
UNIVERSITY PRESS

Published by the Press Syndicate of the University of Cambridge
The Pitt Building, Trumpington Street, Cambridge CB2 1RP
40 West 20th Street, New York, NY 10011–4211, USA
10 Stamford Road, Oakleigh, Melbourne 3166, Australia

First published 1991
Reprinted 1995

British Library cataloguing in publication data

Booth, Michael R. (Michael Richard), 1931–
Theatre in the Victorian age.
1. England. Theatre, history
1. Title
792.0942

Library of Congress cataloguing in publication data

Booth, Michael R.
Theatre in the Victorian Age / Michael R. Booth.
    p.   cm.
Includes bibliographical references and index.
ISBN 0–521–34351–8 (hard). – ISBN 0–521–34837–4 (pbk.)
1. Theater – Great Britain – Historical – 19th century. 2. English drama –
19th century – History and criticism. 1. Title.
PN2594.B58   1991
792'.0941'09034–dc20   90–21003   CIP

ISBN 0 521 34837 4 paperback

Transferred to digital printing 1999

To George Rowell

In Friendship

Contents

ix

Illustrations

xi

Preface

The purpose of this book is to provide the interested reader with a survey of the English drama and theatre within, approximately, the dates of Queen Victoria's reign, 1837–1901. To do this adequately it is necessary to look at the social background as well as the major fields of specifically theatrical endeavour – management, stage and auditorium design, production, acting and the job of the actor. No survey can be comprehensive enough or sufficiently detailed to include everything that should be said on the subject. For instance, nobody, perhaps, would wish the chapter on the drama longer, but it is not nearly long enough to be all-inclusive. However, all surveys face difficulties of selection. The topic of Victorian drama and theatre is a large one and I can only hope that what is offered here provides sufficient information and a reasonable number of insights to enable a reader at least to find his or her way into a complex and quite fascinating era in the history of theatre. More than a few competent historians and critics who have written before me will also be of help; some of their contributions are listed in a bibliographical commentary at the end of the book.

I would like to thank several colleagues for their expert advice on ticklish points in the manuscript or research assistance rendered: Alan Hughes, Barry Yzereef, Victor Emeljanow, and David Wilmore, whose patience and kindness in showing me, in every detail, the restored stage machinery at the Tyne Theatre, Newcastle, was invaluable in the research for chapter 3. I would also like to thank Christopher Robinson of the University of Bristol Theatre Collection, Marian Pringle of the Shakespeare Centre Library and Catherine Haill and the staff of the Theatre Museum in London for helping in the search for illustrations. Completing this book would have been impossible without the generous aid of the Social Sciences and Humanities Research Council of Canada and the continued support, both in terms of sabbatical leave and research grants, of the University of Victoria. Since I am quite possibly the last theatre historian in the world to do my research and writing by pen, I am deeply grateful to my wife Judy for her skill in making sense of my handwriting (no easy task) and producing an impeccable typescript.

Michael R. Booth
University of Victoria

Chronology

Date	Theatrical	Social and historical
1831	Vestris management of Olympic.	
1832	Select Committee on Dramatic Literature.	First parliamentary Reform Acts.
1833	Dramatic Copyright Act. Dramatic Authors' Society founded.	Abolition of slavery.
1834		Houses of Parliament destroyed by fire.
1835	Charles Mathews appears at Olympic.	
1837	Macready management of Covent Garden.	Death of William IV, accession of Queen Victoria. Euston Station opened.
1838		Proclamation of the People's Charter. National Gallery opened. Coronation of Queen Victoria. Paddington Station opened.
1839	Vestris–Mathews management of Covent Garden. Webster management of Haymarket. First theatrical use of limelight.	Chartist disturbances. Gold discovered in Australia. First Afghan War.
1840		Marriage of Victoria to Prince Albert. Institution of the penny post.
1841	Macready management of Drury Lane. Rachel appears at Her Majesty's.	Birth of the Prince of Wales (Edward VII).

Date	Theatrical	Social and historical
1842		Presentation of Chartist petition to Parliament. Massacre of British troops and British capture of the Khyber Pass.
1843	Theatre Regulation Act. Virginia Minstrels visit England. Macready leaves Drury Lane.	Thames Tunnel opened.
1844	Phelps management of Sadler's Wells. Webster management of Adelphi.	First electric telegraph line, Washington–Baltimore.
1845		Irish famine.
1846	Ethiopian Serenaders and Buckley Serenaders visit England.	Corn Laws repealed.
1847	Covent Garden opened as an opera house.	
1848	First theatrical use of electric carbon-arc. First proposal for a national theatre. Windsor Castle Command performances.	Revolution in Europe. Escape of Louis-Philippe of France to England. Chartist disturbances and final petition to Parliament. Waterloo Station opened. Gold discovered in California.
1850	Charles Kean management of Princess's.	
1851		Great Exhibition in London.
1852	Canterbury Hall opened in Lambeth, first purpose-built music hall.	Death of the Duke of Wellington. King's Cross Station opened.
1853	Buckstone management of Haymarket.	
1854		Crimean War. Crystal Palace opened.
1855	*Henry VIII* runs 100 nights at the Princess's.	Metropolitan Board of Works established.

1856	Covent Garden destroyed by fire. Henry Irving appears in Sunderland. Ellen Terry appears at the Princess's as a child actress.	End of Crimean War.
1857	Christy Minstrels visit England. Adelaide Ristori appears in London.	South Kensington Museum (Victoria and Albert in 1909) opened. British Museum Reading Room opened. Indian Mutiny and relief of Lucknow.
1858	New Covent Garden Opera opened. Swanborough management of the Strand.	
1859	Charles Kean leaves Princess's.	
1860		Victoria Station opened.
1861	Fechter plays Hamlet at the Princess's.	Death of Prince Albert. Civil War in America.
1862	Phelps leaves Sadler's Wells.	Cotton famine in Lancashire.
1863	The Ticket-of-Leave Man begins a run of 407 nights at the Olympic.	Underground Metropolitan Line opened.
1864		Charing Cross Station opened.
1865	Marie Wilton management of Prince of Wales's.	End of Civil War, assassination of Abraham Lincoln.
1866	Select Committee on Theatrical Licences and Regulations.	War between Prussia and Austria, defeat of Austria.
1867	Standard Theatre reopened under John Douglass management.	Parliamentary Reform Acts (England). Dominion of Canada established.
1868	Gaiety opened under Hollingshead management.	Parliamentary Reform Act (Scotland). St Pancras Station opened.
1869		Suez Canal opened.

Date	Theatrical	Social and historical
1870		Franco-Prussian War, defeat of the French and abdication of Napoleon III.
1871	Irving joins the Lyceum, appears in *The Bells*. First Gilbert and Sullivan opera, *Thespis*, at the Gaiety.	Paris Commune. Stanley meets Livingstone at Lake Tanganyika.
1874	Irving plays Hamlet at the Lyceum.	
1875	Tomasso Salvini plays Othello at Drury Lane. *Our Boys* begins a run of 1,366 performances at the Vaudeville.	
1876		Queen Victoria proclaimed Empress of India.
1878	Irving management of Lyceum.	Second Afghan War.
1879	Sarah Bernhardt appears at the Gaiety with the Comédie Française. Harris management of Drury Lane. Hare–Kendal management of St James's.	Tay Bridge disaster.
1880	Bancroft management of the Haymarket and first 'picture-frame' stage.	First Boer War.
1881	D'Oyly Carte opens fully electrified Savoy Theatre with *Patience*. Meininger Company appears at Drury Lane.	First telephone exchanges in London and the provinces. Natural History Museum opened.
1882		British military expedition to Egypt and occupation of Cairo.
1883	Benson Company formed. Alhambra music hall reopened.	Royal College of Music opened.

1884		Savoy Hotel opened.
1885	Music Hall Artists' Association formed. Bancrofts leave Haymarket.	Capture of Khartoum by the Mahdi and death of General Gordon. Burmese War. Parliamentary Redistribution Act.
1886		Colonial Exhibition in London.
1887	Empire Theatre of Varieties opened.	Queen Victoria's Jubilee. International Copyright Act.
1889	Ibsen's *A Doll's House* in London.	London County Council established.
1890	Alexander management of St James's.	
1891	Actors' Association formed. Independent Theatre Society founded by J. T. Grein; produces Ibsen's *Ghosts*. English Opera House (Palace Theatre) opened.	American Copyright Act.
1892	*Charley's Aunt* begins run of 1,492 performances at the Royalty. Select Committee on Theatres and Places of Entertainment.	
1893	Mrs Patrick Campbell plays Mrs Tanqueray at the St James's.	
1894	Elizabethan Stage Society founded by William Poel. Eleonora Duse appears in London.	Manchester Ship Canal opened.
1895	Irving knighted.	
1896	Last Gilbert and Sullivan opera, *The Grand Duke*, at the Savoy. Arthur Collins management of Drury Lane.	

Date	Theatrical	Social and historical
1897	Bancroft knighted. Beerbohm Tree management of Her Majesty's.	Queen Victoria's Diamond Jubilee.
1899	Irving management of Lyceum taken over by Lyceum Theatre Company. Stage Society founded.	Second Boer War.
1900	First production by Edward Gordon Craig, Purcell's *Dido and Aeneas*, at the Hampstead Conservatoire.	Relief of Ladysmith. Boxer Rebellion in China. Commonwealth of Australia established.
1901		Death of Queen Victoria, accession of Edward VII. Building of new Harrod's department store begins.

1

Theatre and society

The last time Queen Victoria went to the play before she was crowned in June 1838, was to Covent Garden Theatre, where she saw Edward Bulwer's popular new drama *The Lady of Lyons*, James Kenney's farce *The Irish Ambassador*, and another farce with a comic Irish character, *The Omnibus*, by Isaac Pocock. When she returned to the play some months after her coronation, after a long spell of opera-going, she saw at Drury Lane the pantomime *Harlequin and Jack Frost* and Van Amburgh's menagerie of lions, the first of seven royal visits to that monarch of beasts and its enterprising trainer. A week later at Covent Garden she saw Pocock's melodrama *Rob Roy McGregor* and another pantomime.[1] Thus in a few excursions to the theatre the Queen nicely spanned almost the whole spectrum of the Victorian popular theatre: farce, pantomime, melodrama and animals on stage. Add to this a penchant for opera, Shakespeare and comedy, and it can be seen that in her own person Victoria was the true embodiment of the theatrical taste of her subjects; the theatre was Victorian in this as well as in its name.

Victoria was, then, as representative an audience of one as she could be, and she stood at the apex of that vaster audience, her people. It is easy enough, since we know so much about her, to define Victoria's taste and assign causes for it, but harder to reconstruct that larger audience and its taste and to show how it changed over several generations of theatregoing. Yet without some understanding of that ever-shifting audience we shall understand neither the theatre itself nor the plays, actors, managers and spectacles that pleased or disappointed it. The theatre and the audience of any age is

[1] George Rowell, *Queen Victoria Goes to the Theatre* (London, 1978), p. 129.

1

a part of the society and culture of that age, indeed a creation of it, and it is not possible to comprehend that theatre and audience without some comprehension of what was happening economically, socially and culturally outside the theatre. The way through the Victorian and pre-Victorian audience to the theatre itself is as good an initial approach as any.

AUDIENCES AND SOCIAL CLASS

The hierarchical division of the Restoration and eighteenth-century auditorium into boxes, pit and gallery continued into the nineteenth century, and the theatre's solicitude for the better class of patron extended also to the provision of separate entrances for each section of the house, so that box holders would not have to rub shoulders at a common entrance with those headed for pit benches or gallery. Such divisions were class division rather than mere considerations of the pocketbook.

One of the most striking things about the Victorian theatre is its faithful reflection of social class, not only in the architectural disposition of its audiences but also in the content of its drama. It is interesting to see how theatre managers and others tended to look at theatre problems especially the problem of the box office, in class terms. Among the managers and proprietors giving evidence to the parliamentary Select Committee on Dramatic Literature in 1832 was Charles Kemble of Covent Garden, who complained that the late dinner hour took away the upper classes from the theatre. David Morris of the Haymarket believed that receipts for his boxes had been affected by the popularity of opera, which drew away 'persons in a higher class of society'.[2] When asked if nobility attended his theatre, George Davidge of the Coburg replied in the affirmative, and of the usual pattern of attendance said, 'On Monday nights I conceive we have the working classes generally, and in the middle of the week we have the better classes.' *His* profits came largely from the pit, unlike Kemble's, which should have – but did not – come from his boxes. Davidge regretted the fact that the drama had ceased to be 'a fashionable amusement' (1832 *Report*, pp. 79–85). The Keeper of the Crown Jewels, Edmund Lenthall Swift, remarked that in his opinion the audience of the minor theatres was composed of 'the lower part of the middle classes' (1832 *Report*, p.163).

Such concerns persisted throughout the Victorian period. The Examiner of Plays, William Bodham Donne, testifying to the 1866

[2] *Report from the Select Committee on Dramatic Literature* (London, 1832), p. 43.

Select Committee on Theatrical Licences and Regulations, agreed with the Committee member who asked him, 'Have you found that pieces are particularly popular among the lower classes which are founded on burglaries and robberies?'[3] The Lord Chamberlain, Spencer Ponsonby, told this Committee that pit and gallery audiences at theatres probably attended music halls as well – 'they are the same class of people' – where those who frequented boxes and stalls did not (1866 *Report*, p. 7). The great popularity of music halls and their competition with theatres led in 1892 to another Select Committee, this one on Theatres and Places of Entertainment, which heard much conflicting evidence on the question of which social class or classes attended the theatre and which the music hall and whether there was any overlap.

All this fuss and worry about categorising theatre and music-hall audiences by class is peculiarly Victorian (and immediately pre-Victorian), a theatrical manifestation of great social changes in the nineteenth century that as a matter of course produced significant changes in the composition of audiences. During the first half of the century society was being rapidly urbanised, a process whose speed is indicated by the fact that in 1850 about half the population still lived in the country but by 1900 only a fifth. But it was the generation after Waterloo that saw the major transition between a predominantly rural and agricultural society to a predominantly urban and industrial society. This meant not only the growth of the great industrial cities in the Midlands and the North – Birmingham, Sheffield, Leeds, Manchester, Glasgow – but also a vast increase in the population of London, from 900,000 in 1801 to 3,000,000 in 1851 to 6,000,000 in 1901. London itself was not primarily a heavy manufacturing city, but functioned as the service centre of the nation and the heart of the expanding import–export business. In 1801 London was the only city in the land with a population of over 100,000; by 1841 there were six, and by 1901 thirty. Such huge increases in urban population were a consequence of rural emigration, better health and diet, and a rising birthrate. The death rate also rose from 1810 to 1840 but declined for the rest of the century. By 1850 about 40 per cent of Londoners had been born elsewhere.

POPULATION GROWTH AND NEW THEATRES

The obvious social consequence of the population increase in London and other cities was an increase in the potential audience for theatre, an increase especially in the new industrial and working

[3] *Report from the Select Committee on Theatrical Licences and Regulations* (London, 1866), p. 88.

class. The 1851 Census states that 79 per cent of the population of London, including 2 per cent clerks, is working-class. The old eighteenth-century system of putting all classes under the roof of two or three central playhouses, harmoniously ordered within the traditional divisions of box, pit and gallery, was no longer possible. Not only did the pressure of numbers force the building of many more theatres (in the periods when the theatre business prospered) but also the location of the working-class population eventually dictated the building of neighbourhood playhouses far from the West End and from middle-class patronage: theatres in the East End, across the Thames on the Surrey side of the river, and on the northern fringes of the West End – theatres that catered primarily to their local populations, which were very largely working and lower middle-class.

Population growth of this magnitude was the consequence of changes in the shape of London that affected the theatre as much as did the sheer pressure of numbers. The East End of London began developing after the building of the London docks: the West India Dock in 1799, the London Dock in 1802, the Surrey Dock in 1804, and the East India Dock in 1805. This initial phase of London dock-building was completed by 1828 with the St Katharine Dock, and enabled London to serve as the nation's principal trade centre. Naturally, the docks and the river attracted a wide variety of businesses related to exports and imports, factories, and workshops, all clustered east of the City of London. In the Victorian period a growing population, almost entirely working-class, settled densely in the proliferating mean streets of the East End to man the work-places, load and unload the ships and do the dirty jobs of the sprawling and filthy metropolis. By 1901 the East End was the largest working-class conglomeration in the world, a great city in its own right, with its own network of entertainment, unvisited and virtu-ally unrecognised by the rest of London.[4]

The building of theatres in the East End properly began in 1828 with the reopening of the East London (formerly the Royalty) as the ill-fated Brunswick Theatre.[5] The City Theatre in Cripplegate and the Garrick in Leman Street followed in 1831, the Standard in Shore-ditch in 1835, and the City of London in Norton Folgate in 1837. The Grecian and the Britannia in Hoxton and the Effingham in

---

[4] Charles Booth says in 1889 that the population of the East End is 909,000, but he does not include West Ham, East Ham, Stratford, Clapton, Stoke Newington, etc., which, if included and allowing for a population increase in a decade, was nearly 2,000,000 in 1900, according to Walter Besant. See Charles Booth, *Life and Labour of the People in London: First Series* (London, 1902), p. 32, and Walter Besant, *East London* (New York, 1901), p. 8.

[5] It collapsed during a rehearsal three days after it opened, killing fifteen.

Whitechapel opened as saloon theatres between 1834 and 1843, and
by the fifties were operating in conventional theatre buildings. All
these theatres except the City remained open, frequently renovated
and rebuilt, until the late 1860s, when one by one they began to
close. However, in 1866, the year of the *Report from the Select
Committee on Theatrical Licences and Regulations*, the East End entertainment industry was considerable. The *Report* states that the
capacity of six East End theatres amounted to 17,600 places nightly
or 34.3 per cent of the total audience capacity of London theatres
excluding Covent Garden and Her Majesty's, which were opera
houses. Indeed, 63.7 per cent of that total capacity is taken up by
theatres outside the West End (1866 *Report*, p. 295). Not listed in this
report are the audience capacities of music halls and the numerous
penny gaffs in the East End, or of the large saloon theatres like the
Albion in Whitechapel. From the evidence of these figures it is quite
wrong to think of the audience experience of London theatre and
drama solely as a West End experience. If the Queen were the apex
of the English audience, the working class was its broad, strong base.

Although East Enders still travelled West to sit in the galleries of
middle-class theatres, and although some East End theatres made a
great effort, especially when they opened or reopened, to attract a
clientele from outside the immediate neighbourhood, the East End
community essentially attended its own theatres, which did not
draw an outside audience. It was the exceptional middle-class critic
or writer who made the journey to an East End theatre, usually in
search of a colour story, and usually to patronise what he saw. The
lack of attention East End theatres received was not merely a matter
of geographical remoteness; as an urban entity the whole of the East
End was beyond the social and cultural pale for the middle-class
Londoner from the West, and his ignorance of it was profound. In
1882 the eminent drama critic of the *Daily Telegraph*, Clement Scott,
complained of a dearth of amusement in the East End. At the time he
wrote there were still four major theatres open and at least eight
music halls. Testimony to the 1892 Select Committee indicates that
witnesses passionately concerned with the relationship between
theatres and music halls knew nothing of theatres and music halls in
East London. Their lack of interest in, if not contempt for, the forms
of popular theatre appealing to a lower class made performances of
this kind of theatre of no consequence to the state of the theatre as
comprehended by a West End vision, and it is the West End,
middle-class point of view that we find in the few extant accounts
of working-class theatre and drama on which modern theatre
historians rely. They are mostly to be taken with a grain of salt,

especially when given to moralising. The life of the Victorian urban theatre in poorer districts, carried on though it was in critical darkness, was extraordinarily vigorous and not the less interesting and significant for being a manifestation of popular taste and working-class culture.

AUDIENCE COMPOSITION

The map of London theatres and the audience was then, even by the early Victorian period, nothing like what it was at the end of the eighteenth century, when the first manifestations of radical social change began to appear in the theatre. Eighteenth-century theatrical culture had been essentially dominated by the aristocrats of the business in London, Drury Lane and Covent Garden, and, in the second half of the century in the provinces, by a small network of Theatres Royal and leading circuits. By 1843 this traditional and stable theatre structure had fragmented. In that year the Theatre Regulation Act, finally passed after years of agitation from the 'minor' theatres and the anti-monopoly interests, abolished the privileged position of the 'majors', the theatres holding letters patent from the crown (Drury Lane and Covent Garden again) and threw open to all theatres the opportunity of performing the so-called 'legitimate' drama: farce, tragedy, and comedy. Previously a handful of minor theatres, some licensed by the Lord Chamberlain and some by local magistrates, distributed around the West End and on the Surrey side of the Thames, had challenged the majors by playing the 'illegitimate' drama (these terms were contentious in definition) – light comedies with songs, burlesques, melodramas – and sometimes poaching the dramatic fare of their alleged oppressors. These minor theatres attracted audiences supposedly a cut below the audiences of Drury Lane, Covent Garden, and the summer operation of the Theatre Royal in the Haymarket, but the precise composition of the audience at any one of them was a matter of the particular neighbourhood and particular dramatic attraction. If the latter were especially novel and interesting it drew, as one witness told the 1832 Select Committee, 'people from all parts of the town, and even from the country, to witness it' (1832 *Report*, p. 122). If not, the audience tended to be mostly local and reflected the social makeup of its area, if outside the narrow limits of the West End, such as at the Pavilion in Whitechapel or the Coburg on Waterloo Road on the Surrey side. Minor theatres in the West End drew more miscellaneous audiences, or even a fashionable one, as in the case of Madame Vestris's up-market Olympic Theatre of the 1830s.

After 1843 the new theatrical freedoms did not translate into another wave of theatre building. Apart from renovations and refurbishments, the construction of theatre in London stopped entirely between 1843 and 1866. The reasons for this cessation are to be found outside the theatre, in the depressed economy and the preponderance of slumps over booms. The period from 1815 to the 1860s was financially difficult for theatres, with many closures and bankruptcies, and with desperate attempts to find new revenue by a general lowering of seat prices. The lower prices, notably at Drury Lane and at Covent Garden (which went over to opera in 1847), were designed not only to keep present audiences but also to attract new ones at a lower level of class and income. This undoubtedly had effects upon the repertory, moving several theatres firmly in the direction of gratifying popular taste in melodrama, farce and spectacle entertainment. The gradual accumulation of public wealth and the new national prosperity led to a building boom in the West End theatre that started in 1866 and lasted till the end of the century. This would not have happened without the promise, or at least the well-grounded hope, of profits from the box office; the greater prosperity meant that people had more money in their pockets for entertainment. This was especially true of the middle class, which reaped most of the benefits of national affluence and bestowed their favours upon the West End theatres.

As late as the 1880s and 1890s, nevertheless, certain West End theatres, like the Adelphi, the Princess's and Drury Lane had a strong element of lower middle-class and working-class patronage, confined to the pit and gallery perhaps but still an influence on the choice of repertory. To some extent the benefits of prosperity spread socially downwards, for real wages generally rose during the second half of the century and the cost of living declined, largely due to the availability from about 1870 to 1900 of cheap imported food.

Even before the 1860s thoroughly respectable middle-class audiences were attending Charles Kean's seasons of Shakespeare, gentlemanly melodrama and refined comedy at the Princess's Theatre in the 1850s, stimulated in part by the Queens' patronage of Kean at court theatricals in Windsor Castle and her regular attendance at the Princess's. And before that again there had been the Olympic audience in the 1830s – elegantly turned out patrons in an elegantly decorated auditorium – and firm intellectual and middle-class support for William Charles Macready's two ventures into management at Covent Garden 1837–39 and at Drury Lane 1841–43, not to mention the audiences for Samuel Phelps's Shake-

Plate 1 'Pit, Boxes, and Gallery': the Surrey Theatre, 1836. Print by George Cruikshank. By courtesy of the Trustees of the Victoria and Albert Museum.

Plate 2 'The Pit, Sadler's Wells,' 1850. Drawing by Charles Green. By courtesy of the Trustees of the Victoria and Albert Museum.

speare at Sadler's Wells in the forties and fifties and Alfred Wigan's well-bred management of the Olympic from 1853 to 1857.

While the West End theatre was undoubtedly moving inexorably towards greater and greater respectability of management and patronage, it is a serious over-simplification to picture the nineteenth-century theatre, as some still do, as climbing slowly out of a swamp of mob rule and working-class domination in the earlier part of the century to reach an eminence of profound Victorian decorum and middle-class and fashionable patronage of the theatre. After 1815, however, the latter was not substantial enough to fill the boxes of the patent theatres, and the former contained unruly elements that created disturbances in the auditorium, such as the Old Price riots at the reopened Covent Garden in 1809. Audience behaviour in the major theatres, possibly because of their great size and poor acoustics, tended to restlessness and boisterousness in the Regency period. Such behaviour was mostly, but not entirely, confined to the galleries, whose occupants were badly placed. A German visitor to England in 1826, Prince Pückler-Muskau, recorded his disgust at the behaviour of gallery spectators at the opera in the King's Theatre, who interrupted the singers with shouts and tossed orange peel and other food substances onto the heads of the pit.[6] Seeing Macready as Macbeth at Drury Lane, the Prince noted, despite his fine acting, that 'the interest was generally so slight, the noise and mischief so incessant' that it puzzles him to understand how artists could form themselves before 'so brutal, indifferent, and ignorant an audience'.[7] This sort of behaviour improved in the London theatres in the early Victorian period, although there were signal exceptions like the patriotic riots against the French actors playing *Monte Cristo* at Drury Lane in 1848. Inevitably, as manners and society changed, so did conduct in the audience.

Drury Lane, Covent Garden, and the Haymarket had never been theatres where the urban working class obtained any sort of control; in any case they could not have afforded to sit anywhere but in the gallery, which had always been the territory of the journeyman, the apprentice, the domestic servant, the sailor and the soldier. Later in the century, even when the theatre was more soberly attended in conformity with general social trends, and certainly more lavishly patronised by the middle class, the working class by no means disappeared from the theatre, even from the West End. There was also still a basic core of East End and transpontine theatres largely patronised by the working and lower middle class. In the provinces

[6] *A Regency Visitor*, ed. E. M. Butler (London, 1957), p. 83.   [7] *Ibid.*, p. 275.

the industrial manufacturing class still went to the theatre in large numbers. After all, even in central London in the 1890s, 80 per cent of the resident population was working-class. It would have been surprising if none of them went to the theatre.

The theatre must also have benefited from the shortening of working hours among all classes of the theatregoing public in employment. Work hours fell in the 1870s, and this shortening – a fifty-four hour week was typical of the last quarter of the century – made it theoretically possible for an employee to attend a whole evening's entertainment. The disappearance of 'half-price' admission at 9 p.m. and the truncation of the playbill from two, three, or four pieces to only one must have had a direct relationship to the length of the working day. It was no longer necessary to prolong the evening to midnight or 1 a.m. to ensure that those who stopped work at 8 or 9 p.m. could get their money's worth, and perhaps it was no longer crucial to the box office.

Generalising about nineteenth-century audiences is, in the absence of a great deal more evidence than is presently available, a risky business, especially when it also leads to possibly unwarranted conclusions about the drama and public taste. It is also difficult to generalise about the conventional divisions between the audience in box, pit and gallery, because at different prices and in different locations the social composition of the audience could differ widely. Nevertheless, the social and cultural implications of a play performed at a Victorian theatre, and therefore the play itself, cannot be completely comprehended unless one is aware of the audience for which it was performed, and that audience will change, theatre by theatre, district by district, decade by decade. This is so in the West End as in the East, or in any theatre district. The Victorian audience lived in its own culture and its own network of economic and social relationships; it did not exist only in auditoriums for the benefit of the scholar. It lived in a wider society of which the theatre was a small part; fully to understand it means knowing something of its social and cultural habits, jobs, wages, cost of living, places of residence, class status, means of transportation, patterns of migration and settlement, moral and political outlook – anything that goes to make up complete human beings living at a chosen moment in history who came together for the collective but usually incidental purpose of seeing a play.

The social range of the Victorian audience extended from the Queen to the meanest of her subjects who possessed the price of admission to a theatre gallery or penny gaff. By the end of the century the range of theatrical entertainment available to all classes, and the number of locations where they could enjoy it, had vastly increased. The theatre and music-hall business had taken on the proportions of a mass entertainment industry. According to figures supplied to the 1892 Select Committee, there were then 550 places of amusement in London, fifty of which were theatres, the remainder being music halls, concert halls, and other places of amusement. All these venues together offered accommodation for half a million people nightly.[8] In addition, thirty-nine music halls held licences for music and dancing (1892 *Report*, p. 366). A third set of figures put the number of music halls at thirty-five, providing accommodation for 45,000 spectators nightly (p. 461). It was estimated that outside London there were 200 theatres and 160 music halls (p. 79).

THE MUSIC HALL

Any account of the Victorian theatre would have to at least acknowledge the fact of the music hall and the competition it offered the theatre. One of the interesting aspects of the Select Committee hearings into theatrical matters, aside from their function as touch-stones of contemporary concern (collectively, the three major Select Committee reports contain an enormous amount of information about the theatre, each conveniently spaced a generation apart) is the increasing presence of the music hall in the deliberations, a presence that matched its growth in the social and cultural life of the Victorian city. Victorian music hall developed from the saloon entertainments, all-male drinking clubs and music clubs of the first half of the nineteenth century; these proliferated in the 1830s and 1840s. In the 1850s several important halls opened in London, either adapted from the older concert rooms in a tavern setup or built for the purpose, such as the Canterbury in Lambeth, the Middlesex in Drury Lane, Wilton's in Whitechapel (still in existence), and Weston's in Holborn. A further wave of music-hall building occurred in the sixties. Like the theatres, music halls in the West End slowly became more 'respectable' and middle-class; halls like the Alhambra and the Empire in Leicester Square (with its notorious promenade) also had an audience of fashionable and bohemian young men in evening dress.

In 1866, however – half-way through our period – music halls were still primarily drinking houses with entertainment provided as an added attraction, still with tables and chairs and a chairman and still very much male working and lower middle-class in audience

[8] *Report from the Select Committee on Theatres and Places of Entertainment* (London, 1892), p. 79.

composition. Some witnesses at the Select Committee hearings that year complained that the new popularity of the music halls was depleting gallery audiences at the theatres. The taste of the public was more for music halls than theatres, claimed one witness, 'because a man can sit down and drink his glass of grog, and blow his pipe, and enjoy himself there, not caring for anybody.' The same witness, E. T. Smith, then lessee of Astley's, defined a theatre, as distinct from a music hall, as 'a place where there is scenery and performance in costume, and so on, and where there is no drinking, and it is under proper censorship' (1866 *Report*, pp. 129–32). The contention between theatres and music halls intensified in the years leading up to the 1892 Select Committee, which was concerned with the opposition of the theatre to dramatic sketches in the halls, the licensing and inspection of theatres and music halls, the question of drinking and smoking in the auditorium (not allowed in theatres) and the revenue in the halls arising from the sale of drink as compared with money taken in admission charges. Theatre managers argued vigorously that it would be inartistic and offensive to actors and audiences if drinking accompanied dramatic performances, recalling a question put to a witness in 1866, 'Do you think, then, that brandy-and-water with Shakespeare will make a man more drunk than brandy-and-water without?' (p. 22). However, their arguments were convincing; the Committee did not recommend changes in the law on this point. But it could not, and did not wish to, legislate to protect theatres from the encroaching popularity of the halls, and there is much evidence to suggest that a not inconsiderable proportion of the lower class of audience largely deserted the theatre for the music hall in the second half of the century, finding both the entertainment and the easy social freedom of the halls more to its liking – a secession which may also have hastened the transformation of the lively, bustling, occasionally riotous, and fully illuminated pre-Victorian theatre auditorium into the generally quiet, passive, and darkened West End house of the late Victorian and Edwardian eras.

What the London theatre lost to the halls must have been more than made up by the presence in the metropolis, for the first time in large numbers, of an audience from the provinces. As early as 1832 one of the Select Committee's witnesses was asked, 'Is it not generally supposed that the theatres are principally filled by visitors passing to and fro through London?' (1832 *Report*, p. 27). The answer was in the negative, although other witnesses had the opposite opinion. There are no statistics on the subject, but by 1866 witnesses were willing to elaborate. John Hollingshead, later manager of the Gaiety, believed that the London audience was 'largely composed of country people; the old metropolitan playgoer lives out of town, and does not go so much to the theatre as he used to do; the provincial people come to town, and fresh audiences are created every night' (1866 *Report*, p. 191). Horace Wigan, the manager of the Olympic, told the Committee that the playgoing public had much increased, that the class of playgoer in London was different, and that theatres were 'in very great proportion' supported by the travelling population (p. 163). Writing in 1871, the dramatic critic of the *Athenaeum* declared that among 'the chief supporters of our theatres are country people, incited by the advertisements and criticism they have seen in the London papers'.[9]

If one examines runs of plays, one sees that the 1850s are a watershed dividing the Victorian theatre from the old practice of operating a full or partial repertory system and that distinctive feature of the commercial theatre today, the long run. A theatre can sustain the long run of a play only when the box office takes in enough money to pay off the production and running costs and turn a sufficient profit; this cannot happen and cannot be attempted unless there is a potential audience large enough to allow management and backers to take the financial risk. The great increase in the population of London was certainly one factor producing the long run in West End theatres, which did not occur until the population passed 3,000,000. Another factor was the tourist audience. A modest but growing number of this audience came from overseas when the transatlantic steamship made the voyage from North America so much quicker. Charles Pascoe's *A London Directory for American Travellers* (1874) lists twenty-three London theatres, all of them in the West End. However, the great majority of visitors in the mid and late Victorian period were from the provinces. In the 1850s only thirteen productions in the West End ran for 100 consecutive nights or more; this figure rose to forty-five in the sixties and 107 in the seventies. Charles Kean's *The Winter's Tale* ran at the Princess's for 102 nights in 1856. These seem to have been the first occasions in the English theatre when a mainpiece on the bill had a run of such length. Yet in the 1860s the drama *The Ticket-of-Leave Man* ran for 407 nights; in the 1870s the comedy *Our Boys* for 1,362. The increasing frequency of the long run and its increasing length can be attributed to the enlarged population, greater public and notably middle-class affluence, and significant numbers of provincial visitors.

[9] Thomas Purnell, *Dramatists of the Present Day* (London, 1871), p. 14.

RAILWAYS

Their way of getting to London was by train. The development of the railway system much affected the structure and practices of the Victorian theatre. The Great Exhibition of 1851 saw the first mass invasion of London by rail. John Cole calculated of that Exhibition summer, 'At least five-sixths of the [theatre] audiences were composed of foreigners and holiday excursionists from the country',[10] and many theatres extended their seasons. By that date several major railway termini had been built in London: Euston, Paddington, London Bridge and Waterloo. King's Cross followed in 1852 and St Pancras and Liverpool Street were completed in the 1860s. By 1900 there were ten main-line termini in the metropolis and visitors to London could arrive conveniently from all parts of the country. Since the volume of rail passenger travel in England trebled between 1850 and 1870, it seems reasonable to assume that the number of visitors from the provinces to London increased greatly in the same period. Such visits could be made for the day from suburban stations or country stations near London, as well as from much farther away. E. T. Smith told the 1866 Committee that he tried to conclude his entertainment at a reasonable hour so that people coming up to town for the theatre 'can go back by the 11 o'clock train' (1866 *Report*, p. 140). J. B. Buckstone, manager of the Haymarket, said, 'I can always tell when a quantity of people have come from the surrounding districts; at a certain time you can see them moving away to catch the trains to go home' (p. 124).

The railway, which was responsible for the growth of the middle-class suburb, also served to bring its residents back into town for an evening's entertainment if they did not choose to go instead to the cheaper and more accessible new suburban theatres and music halls that marked the theatrical topography of the 1890s and 1900s. The spread and steady improvement of gas street lighting in the metropolis since the early Victorian period helped to make going to the theatre safer, and the invention of the incandescent gas mantle in 1895, with its immediate application to street lighting, was the culmination of this process before the arrival of electric street lighting. The decline of street crime after the big garrotting scare of the early 1860s also made the streets much more secure for the theatre-goer, whether he took a cab or walked from his flat, lodgings, or omnibus stop. By the 1870s and 1880s the suburbs were fully served by the railways. In central London the Metropolitan Railway

[10] J. W. Cole, *The Life and Theatrical Times of Charles Kean, F.S.A.*, 2nd edn (London, 1859), vol. II, p. 11.

opened in 1863 and, running initially between Paddington and Farringdon Street, was the first attempt to avoid urban congestion by providing fast underground transport; the Inner Circle was completed in 1884. This congestion was increased by the large numbers of horse-drawn omnibus services springing up from 1829 to serve the Londoner as well as the suburban commuter and the provincial visitor arriving at a rail terminus. Nevertheless, such services (including the new hackney carriage, or cab) got people to the theatre, and no longer did the Londoner have to live within walking distance of the theatre in order to see a play, if he could not afford a private carriage. This fact alone enlarged the potential audience.

In 1906 Mario Borsa noticed the elegance of many passengers alighting at London train stations and heading for the theatre:

> Each evening these ... trains disgorge hundreds and thousands of fair ladies elegantly attired, accompanied by their well-groomed male escorts. Beneath the lofty, massive, and gloomy station roof, between the slimy, blackened walls, among the tireless, panting engines – grimy with soot and ruddy with the glow of furnace doors – through the foul, smoky, suffocating atmosphere of the station, they thread their way – delicate visions of white, pale blue, or pink, in hoods or wraps of Japanese silk, embroidered slippers and fleecy boas, wrapped in their brocaded opera cloaks, beneath which stray glimpses are caught of the lace and chiffon of evening bodices – or they flit, with a fantastic shimmer of pearls and diamonds, with a soft rustle of silks, satins, and tulle.[11]

Such people, Borsa remarked, were on their way to the stalls and boxes of West End theatres and would finish the evening drinking champagne in the best hotels. It is true that these observations were made in the middle of an increasingly ostentatious Edwardian age rather than at the end of Victoria's reign, a few years earlier, but at the very least they show how important the railways were in bringing the well-off middle and fashionable class to the theatre; much of this was happening before 1901.

Borsa also noticed another audience, which had clearly walked or taken the omnibus or the tube to the West End, in the long queues that formed patiently outside the theatres in all weathers for the unbookable pit and gallery seats. From the point of view of social composition it was 'a mixed crowd: formed for the most part of small parties and courting couples. There are shopmen, clerks and spinsters in pince-nez, but more numerous still are the shopgirls, milliners, dressmakers, typists, stenographers, cashiers of large and

[11] Mario Borsa, *The English Stage of To-Day* (London, 1908), p. 3.

small houses of business, telegraph and telephone girls, and the thousands of other girls whose place in the social scale is as hard to guess as to define.'[12]

PROVINCIAL THEATRES

The railway network that brought the provincial or suburban theatregoer to London also finally determined the system of theatrical organisation outside the metropolis. By the end of the eighteenth century a flexible and stable structure had evolved. At its head stood the provincial Theatres Royal, either operating directly under letters patent granted by the crown or a licence issued by the Lord Chamberlain, including Edinburgh, Bath, Norwich, York, Hull, Liverpool, Manchester, Bristol, Newcastle, Brighton and Dublin (considered a part of the British theatre system). These theatres had their own stock companies and, in some cases, were the headquarters of their own circuits. More Theatres Royal were established in the nineteenth century. From the best of them, such as Bath and York, promising actors graduated to a permanent berth at Drury Lane or Covent Garden. In turn, touring actors from the London patent theatres would appear at the provincial Theatres Royal to star with the local company while Drury Lane and Covent Garden were closed for the summer. The second tier in the provincial theatre was the circuit, a loose collection of towns, numbering from two to fifteen or sixteen, among which a single company (occasionally subdivided) moved with geographical convenience at appropriate times of the year, whenever potential audiences might be gathered in some numbers – at race meetings, fairs, assizes and other major social events. Each circuit had a home base – like York, at a Theatre Royal – and played its longest season there. There was a hierarchical order among circuits, the prominent ones playing the larger towns, the lesser a smaller, more rural network. The passing in 1788 of an act enabling justices of the peace outside London and outside towns containing Theatres Royal to license theatrical representations greatly increased the number of provincial theatres in the circuit system.

By the 1820s there were over forty circuits, but they had already begun a rapid decline from the peak of their health and profitability in the first decade of the new century. Social change, population shifts, new patterns of transportation and easier provincial access to London theatres, the exorbitant fees paid to touring stars – these may

[12] *Ibid.*, pp. 4–5.

have been factors contributing to the decline. The opening years of Victoria's reign saw the circuit system at its last gasp; by about mid-century it was dead and the stock companies had retreated to the larger towns and cities.

Outside the circuit system and at the bottom of the provincial hierarchy lay the strolling companies, still dividing the receipts the same way that Elizabethan sharing companies did, while the circuits paid their actors a weekly wage. These companies visited villages and small towns that the circuit companies missed; sometimes they played without scripts and followed rough scenarios of melodramas. The booth or portable theatres that set up at the numerous provincial fairs were a cut above most strolling companies, and the bigger ones, like Richardson's, which also appeared, as did others, at the London fairs, were well organised. Their repertory was melodrama, pantomime, farce and some Shakespeare, and their large audiences mainly from the industrial working and agricultural labouring classes. For a significant segment of the population the strolling company and the booth offered the only theatre they ever saw. An important part of the Victorian theatre experience, especially in the early period, was entirely divorced from conventional theatre buildings.

The audience for the provincial theatre was as variable as that in London. However, because in many centres the audience was gathered under the roof of one or two playhouses – like the situation in the eighteenth-century London theatre – and not too dispersed according to neighbourhood, class and repertory, as in London, its social composition was probably more centrally representative. Evidence suggests that the backbone of the provincial audience was the pit and gallery, and that at least until half-way through Victoria's reign the box audience, fashionably present in the earlier years of the century, had so dwindled that many theatres had a hard time making ends meet: the boxes, after all, were the most expensive seats. In the larger industrial towns the artisan and labouring classes figured prominently, especially in the gallery, which they jammed on Saturday and Monday nights. Their behaviour, while rarely riotous, was sufficiently lively and uninhibited – there are many descriptions of audience behaviour in local newspapers – to be a deterrent to the more decorous sections of the middle class, but liveliness does not mean that they did not follow the play with keen appreciation and understanding. The pit audience probably contained a much greater proportion of clerks, shopmen, and their families than the gallery, but depending upon the fluctuation of seat prices – and their trend, as in London, was downward in the early Victorian period – there could be a considerable admixture of artisans. Rural and small-town theatres had quite different audiences, but the dramatic fare of both large and small provincial theatres was much inclined toward melodrama and pantomime, the former a particular delight of working-class audiences, with a goodly quantity of Shakespeare, which appealed to all classes. Pantomime, 'the sheet-anchor of the drama at the present time' (1866 *Report*, p. 233), as one provincial proprietor put it, was not merely popular: it was absolutely essential for a profitable season (which is often the case today). The ubiquitous Christmas pantomime saved many a struggling provincial management from bankruptcy and in the late Victorian period was strongly represented in the provinces while declining in London.

TOURING COMPANIES

In the last thirty years of the nineteenth century the provincial stock company, which had survived the disappearance of the circuits, fell victim to another offshoot of the railway age, the touring company. There had always been touring actors: the eighteenth- and early nineteenth-century stars who took over the major roles when they appeared with the local company, and the strolling players who travelled in the reign of Queen Victoria much as they had in the reign of Queen Anne and Queen Elizabeth, on foot or by cart, and who acted in barns, halls, taverns and any place both convenient and sanctioned by the law. In a sense, a circuit company that moved from town to town and played a fixed season in each was also a kind of touring company.

The company that toured by rail was quite different, and of two kinds. One sort was structured to tour the latest West End hit and travelled with a single comedy, comic opera, or drama until the tour was over, then disbanded. This practice probably began in 1868 with a tour of Tom Robertson's comedy *Caste*; the same organisation sent out further tours of Robertson successes for fourteen years. (The 1860s also seem to have seen the beginnings of the out-of-town opening. The Prince of Wales's company tried out Robertson's *Ours* in Liverpool and Manchester before opening it in London in 1866, and in 1869 the Haymarket company performed Tom Taylor's comedy *New Men and Old Acres* in Manchester before its London première.) The other kind of company toured with a repertory of several pieces, whether melodrama, comedy, Irish drama, Shakespeare, farce or a mixture, and it remained in existence as long as finances and management permitted. Some of these companies also played in London, like the Shakespeare companies of Frank Benson and Ben Greet at the end of our period; others made forays from their London bases, like Henry Irving's from the Lyceum and Beerbohm Tree's from Her Majesty's. Most stuck to the provinces, and year after year travelled their appointed rounds, ranging in quality from first-rank companies with established stars and excellent ensemble (the Compton Comedy Company was one of these, with a touring life of thirty-five years) to mediocre groups of failing and poorly managed actors. Some leading actors in touring companies, such as Benson, Barry Sullivan and John Martin-Harvey had enormous reputations in the provinces but could be coolly received in London. The big touring companies, like the Lyceum, took their scenery with them, which would have been quite impossible without rail facilities.

Whether the tour was of a single play or a repertory, the local stock company was doomed. Even before the days of company touring, the 1866 Select Committee was told that the number of provincial theatres was being reduced:

> There are many theatres in small towns which are going back and are disappearing. For instance, in many places where there are no railroads, and which places are at a great distance from London, the population does not support a theatre. The audiences occasionally see London pieces, or see pieces in Manchester or Birmingham, and they are not satisfied with the performances that can be given in those very small theatres ... The theatres decay in those towns, but they are improving vastly in the large towns.   (1866 *Report*, p. 210)

The question of audience expectation is important here. Although there were arguments on both sides, faced with a choice between local stock company acting standards and the standards of a well-rehearsed West End hit or of a good company touring with a repertory, audiences seem to have abandoned their patronage of the stock company, which in some parts of the country uneasily shared the same theatre with tours. They may not have had much choice in the matter. The death of the stock company was really a matter of economic inevitability. Gradually the better and larger provincial theatres, especially in the bigger centres, were leased or bought up by speculators and eventually corporate theatre chains. Splendid new theatres, built solely for touring, were opened as number one venues for tours out of the West End. Lesser tours, depending on size or box-office potential, would be designated as number two, number three or number four venues, and it sometimes happened that a smash West End hit would be toured by three or four companies simultaneously, each performing in an appropriate venue and each with acting talent appropriate to its ranking. In 1893 there were actually seven companies touring the smash West End hit farce, *Charley's Aunt*, in the provinces. Some touring companies divided up the provinces geographically, and sent out North, South, East and West companies. The profound change in the organisation and structure of the Victorian theatre which the touring system effected also changed the acting profession and forever destroyed the tradi- tional ways in which the actor learned his job – a subject to be examined in the fourth chapter. In 1871 a dozen touring companies were on the road;[13] the *Era* of 28 March 1896, lists 158. Clearly this particular area of employment for actors was sizeable, and touring itself a major subdivision of the theatre industry.

There was a larger dimension to the late Victorian phenomenon of touring than the provincial. In 1882 a writer for the *Theatre* remarked that 'the theatrical life of the present day might be described as a round of glorified strolling. The "circuits" of Bristol, Norwich and York of the last century are now replaced by those of the United States, South Africa, India and Australia, and a modern actor thinks as little of a season in Melbourne or New York as his grandfather did of a week's "starring" in Edinburgh.'[14] Ever since the replacement of sail by steam, the opportunities for a much expanded scale of overseas touring became available for both the star and the company. Transport by steamship reduced even the longest voyages from Britain to Australia and New Zealand and across the Pacific, from months to weeks. The big companies, led by star actor-managers, profited most from steamships. Henry Irving's Lyceum company, for instance, crossed to North America eight times between 1882 and 1903. These tours, lasting several months each, were on a large scale, with a fair-sized repertory and a full complement of sets, but they were all profitable and helped to sustain Irving at the Lyceum in his later years.

Besides the theatrical market in the United States, it was the Empire that made touring possible and desirable for British com- panies. The expansion of theatrical horizons to comprehend the whole globe was a remarkable feature of Victorian cultural imperial- ism. Some companies spent almost all their time abroad, and the length of the longer tours, especially if the company visited the Antipodes or went round the world, can be imagined. The conven- tional trade and export routes for the touring company were well established by the 1890s. A tour to North America would usually include Eastern Canada, and if the company reached California sometimes Vancouver and Victoria, British Columbia. A company

[13] George Rowell and Anthony Jackson, *The Repertory Movement* (Cambridge, 1984), p. 12.
[14] Evelyn Ballantyne, 'Some Impressions of the Australian Stage', *Theatre* (April 1892), 186.

that travelled westward to San Francisco could either recross America by a different route and revisit Philadelphia, Boston and New York before sailing back across the Atlantic, or it could continue its journey westward across the Pacific to New Zealand and Australia; most chose the former course and many never reached the west coast at all. Within the Empire, companies sailed from England to the West Indies, going on to America or returning home. They also sailed to South Africa and undertook an extensive tour before coming back. Or they did not return to England, but proceeded to India, landing in Bombay, playing a season there, and then taking the long train journey to Calcutta, from which, after further appearances, they could travel to Australia and New Zealand by means of brief visits to the Far Eastern colonial outposts, as well as to the settlements of foreign nationals in Shanghai and Peking, and occasionally to the small but growing group of British and American traders in a port city like Yokohama, if it were a convenient place to break the voyage and change ships; so much depended on steamship routes and a careful avoidance of spending too many idle days in a port while waiting for the onward steamer. It was a lot simpler to sail to Australia directly from England, and after some months in the major cities sail to New Zealand, either returning home the same way or continuing to San Francisco via Honolulu and touring North America before finally sailing home across the Atlantic.

To have a chance of success, tours had to be very carefully planned in advance, and much reliance was placed on local organisers, agents and producers. Even the most careful planning could be undermined by illness, unpredictable accidents and civil disturbances, and conditions in the country visited could vary from pleasant to appalling. After the necessary theatrical abilities, the most important qualities for touring performers to possess were adventurousness, perseverance and adaptability. They also had to confront and learn to cope with all kinds of minor irritants like strange and unfamiliar insects, climatic extremes, indifferent food, wearying train or coach travel and uncomfortable hotels. Nevertheless, companies persisted, for the rewards could be substantial.

RELIGIOUS ATTITUDES TO THEATRE

Audience support for large-scale touring seemed, by all the evidence of the 1890s and the Edwardian period, to be assured for many years, and in general at this time in Britain the loyalty of the whole social spectrum to the theatre was both heartening and profitable. It was not always so. Witnesses at the 1832 Select Committee hearings, assigning reasons for the alleged decline of the drama and of theatre attendance, dwelt on possible social causes like the later dinner hour in fashionable society, the habit of reading at home, prostitutes in the theatres, and sometimes mentioned, as did Charles Kemble, that 'religious prejudice is very much increased, evangelical feeling, and so on; and they take away a great number of persons from the theatre who formerly used to frequent it' (1832 *Report*, p. 43). Since the Elizabethans the theatre had been a subject of execration for Puritan writers and divines and the evangelical revival of the eighteenth and early nineteenth century was no kinder. There is no doubt that for moral and religious reasons a significant but unmeasurable proportion of the adult population would not go near a theatre, although many were content to attend dramatic readings of plays anywhere else, the objection here being to the building and not the drama as a whole. Large sections of the clergy were particularly hostile, and sermons were often preached against the theatre; one Anglican clergyman in Sheffield, for example, preached a sermon attacking theatrical entertainment every year from 1817 to 1864.[15] Such hostility could extend to the wider population without necessarily involving a moral point of view based on religious belief. The alleged immorality of actresses was a notorious aspect of this hostility.

Towards the end of the nineteenth century, religious feeling against the theatre abated but by no means disappeared. For one thing, owing to the determined efforts of mid and late Victorian theatre managers in the West End, the theatre became more 'respectable'. Not only were its audiences much quieter, better behaved and – in the stalls and dress circle – better dressed, but its leading actors as well as its managers made themselves as middle class and as utterly respectable as possible, projecting an image that deliberately counteracted the (at morally best) raffish figure of the actor and manager in the popular consciousness. Charles Kean and William Charles Macready, at the beginning of our period, were quite certain that they were gentlemen and conducted themselves accordingly. Macready made his farewell to the theatre on the stage of Drury Lane in 1851, having discarded the dress of Macbeth, the clothes of an actor, and addressed the audience in a suit of sober black, the clothes of a gentleman. Charles Kean, reacting strongly against the dissolute life of his father Edmund, behaved with the utmost propriety as actor and manager; had he not done so the Queen would not have put him in charge of supervising the Windsor Castle

[15] Kathleen Barker, 'Thirty Years of Struggle: Entertainment in Provincial Towns between 1840 and 1870. I', *Theatre Notebook*, vol. 39 (no. 1, 1985), 26.

theatricals. Gradually, the poor public image of the theatre began to change, faster in London, perhaps, than in the provinces, and by 1895 Henry Irving could receive at the hands of his sovereign the first knighthood given to an actor. Significantly, it took another thirty years for an actress to receive the equivalent honour.[16]

Irving's management of the Lyceum was deemed so morally estimable that it was extensively patronised by the socially fearful and by clergymen. W. H. Hudson declared in 1886 that 'men and women are found in the Lyceum to-day who, a few years ago, would have been shocked at the thought of being seen in a theatre ... As a consequence the Lyceum pit is nightly visited by those who would be unwilling to enter any other London theatre.'[17] Other managements, like John Hare's at the Garrick and George Alexander's at the St James's, were in the same general class of respectability, though Alexander produced 'daring' plays like *The Second Mrs Tanqueray*. As for the Church, its patronage of the Lyceum was well known. A correspondent to the *Church Review* in 1896 said, 'At the Lyceum may be seen frequently thirty or forty clergy' (5 March). Another correspondent, identifying himself as a 'Professional Actor', claimed that 'we see priests crowd into the theatres at the popular seaside resorts in the summer vacation who would never dream of entering a theatre in their own town' (27 February). There was still, however, much clerical opposition to the theatre. Cardinal Manning was an inveterate foe and the stage was still denounced from the pulpit. Nevertheless, it was a sign of the times that in the late 1880s and in the 1890s clergymen became central figures in melodrama and the new 'problem play'. Henry Arthur Jones made ministers the heroes of *Judah* (1890) and *Michael and His Lost Angel* (1896). The hero of *The Golden Ladder* (1889), by Wilson Barrett and George Sims, is a missionary, and an adaptation of Hall Caine's popular novel *The Christian*, whose hero is a tormented minister in Soho, was given three productions in the West End between 1899 and 1915.

One production in particular met with immense clerical favour, and its reception was a striking episode in the history of ecclesiastical attitudes to the theatre. Wilson Barrett's religious spectacle melodrama *The Sign of the Cross*, first performed at the Lyric in 1896, was a sensational tale of the attraction of a dissipated Roman prefect under Nero to a female Christian prisoner. Unable to persuade her to renounce Christianity in order to save herself from a terrible

---

[16] Geneviève Ward and Ellen Terry were made Dames of the British Empire in 1921 and 1925 respectively.
[17] *The Dramatic Review*, 9 January 1886.

death, he accepts her faith and walks with her into the arena to face the lions. The play is full of splendidly theatrical protestations and demonstrations of the virtue of the Christian faith and contrasts between Christian piety and pagan corruption. The dice are morally loaded, to say the least. One critic, who called the play 'a Salvation Army tragedy', noticed how different the audience was from the usual West End audience:

> It seemed to be the emptying of the churches and chapels of London. Most of the people appeared to be unused to such surroundings. They walked as though they were advancing to pews, and took their seats with an air of reverential expectation. Clericals, too, were present in remarkable attendance. There were parsons to right of me, parsons to left of me, parsons in front of me ... When the lights were turned very low in the auditorium, and pious opinions were ejaculated on the stage, it was remarkably like a religious exercise. 'Ahs' and 'hear, hears' were distinctly audible, and I should not have been surprised at an 'amen' or a 'hallelujah.'[18]

The Sign of the Cross was praised from the pulpit and recommended to congregations ('in fact a sermon such as few among us could preach');[19] the Dean of Rochester, the Archdeacon of Singapore, and other church figures both distinguished and undistinguished wrote to the papers and to Barrett lauding the play and urging Christians to attend.

The success of *The Sign of the Cross*, which even won over Nonconformists, provoked a lengthy and often excited correspondence in the *Church Review* that on the whole focussed upon the general question of religion and the stage rather than on Barrett's production. One especially determined opponent of the production itself, however, Father Ignatius (Joseph Lyne) wrote several times and also preached a sermon against it. His argument is to some extent usefully if eccentrically representative of religious hostility to the theatre. The play is not to be approved, because it is in a theatre, where Christians should not go. The actress playing the heroine is scantily dressed, as are the ladies in the dress circle. A woman plays a male role. The (faintly) orgiastic banquet scene in the prefect's palace is too detailed in staging, 'because for Christian children to see such things would cause them to ask questions that it is best they should not ask until they are more prepared for physiological studies'.[20]

After three months and sixty-nine letters, fairly evenly divided for and against the stage, the editor of the *Church Review* closed the

[18] G. W. Foote, *The Sign of the Cross* (London, 1896), pp. 8–9.
[19] *Church Times*, 10 January 1896.
[20] *The Theatre: with Special Reference to 'The Sign of the Cross'* (London, 1896), p. 25.

correspondence with an editorial entitled 'The Ethical Aspect of the Stage' (2 April 1896), which decided in favour of *The Sign of the Cross* and of any play that appealed to the religious instinct.

By 1900 the theatre's battle for respectability had been won, and a rather grudging religious acceptance upon occasion transformed itself into enthusiastic approval. One could hardly speak of a clerical audience for late Victorian theatre – a clergyman in the *Church Review* correspondence suggested (perhaps facetiously, but it is hard to tell) that every Church paper should have its own dramatic critic whose prime duty would be to inform churchmen of which plays to see and which to avoid – but clearly increasing numbers of the clergy felt that they could go to the theatre without either incurring public disapproval or offending their own moral and religious principles. Indeed, as early as 1879 the Rev. Stuart Headlam founded the Church and Stage Guild to bring the clergy and the acting profession closer together.

Thus by the year of Queen Victoria's death in 1901 the theatre had greatly altered since 1837. Many of these changes were the consequence of social and cultural change which did not originate in the theatre but naturally included it. Moral and religious attitudes to the stage are a part of this change. The softening of previously harsh evangelical views is not a development merely interesting in the abstract but one that had practical social consequences in directly adding undetermined numbers to the theatre audience, both in the clergy and more significantly in the population at large. The new railways had also greatly augmented the London audience and permitted the introduction of the long run, as had the increase in the urban population. The predominantly working-class neighbourhood playhouses were also a consequence of this increase, as well as being a by-product of the industrial revolution. The Victorian theatre never operated free of censorship and licensing restrictions, but it did see, in 1843, the freeing of London theatres from the monopoly restrictions imposed on them by the Licensing Act of 1737 and the placing of all theatres, at least theoretically, on an equal legal footing. The multiplication of West End theatres in the mid and late century had a lot to do with economic prosperity, and the massive changeover in the provincial theatre from circuit stock company to touring company was also an aspect of economic development and technological change.

Most of these changes have a distinct chronology, and their development, though complex, can be easily followed. It will not do – as must by now be obvious – to assume any sort of homogeneity for Victorian theatre: the 1840s were not the same as the 1850s, the

1870s were not the 1880s. The theatre was just too lively and changeable to be categorised in that way. Its growth in the Victorian market for mass entertainment (in itself a significant cultural development) was an industrial success story in terms of output and employment, but it must be remembered that like any business endeavour it had all kinds of vigorous competition. The theatre was by no means the only available entertainment. Not only did it try to fight off the music hall, but also contended for its share of the private purse with lectures, panoramas and dioramas, magicians, minstrel shows, mesmerists, magic lantern presentations, circuses, menageries and a whole host of specialist showmen and entertainers who lived by pleasing the public. That the theatre succeeded in doing this, in appealing to all classes of society, and becoming solidly established and generally profitable, is no small measure of its achievement. The sheer *popularity* of Victorian theatre is a lesson of a kind to the theatre of our own day.

2

Management

At the apex of the Victorian theatrical hierarchy stood the manager. He (or she, since there were women managers) was often an actor as well; sometimes he was a business speculator who had come lately to the theatre as a likely source of profit. Whatever his origins he was in today's terminology – anachronistic if applied to the nineteenth century – both the artistic and administrative director of his company, as well as carrying financial responsibility. The Victorian theatre received no subsidy, governmental or municipal; the manager financed his operation entirely out of his own pocket or that of his backer, or from borrowed money. He took the risk and also the profits, if they materialised.

Nineteenth-century theatre was by no means a sure thing financially. Between Waterloo in 1815 and the accession of Victoria in 1837 times had been bad for the theatre. In London Drury Lane and Covent Garden ruined a succession of managements; in the provinces the circuit system was collapsing. In the 1840s matters were not much improved. William Charles Macready failed at Drury Lane as he had at Covent Garden, and the latter became an opera house in 1847. Provincial theatre continued to contract. The whole business of theatre in the nineteenth century was, as we know, intimately connected with the economic health of the nation. When the nation was poorly so was the theatre, and an understanding of economic context is necessary to explain the sudden slumps in theatre attendance and profitability, which occurred in the thirties, forties, fifties and even in the much more prosperous late Victorian period. Managers could certainly run theatres badly, and often did so, but they are not to blame for the wider financial misfortunes that afflicted them; it required good theatrical husbandry to stand out against hard times and sudden depressions.

MANAGERIAL RESPONSIBILITIES

The manager rarely owned his theatre, but leased it from the owner of the building, who in turn paid ground rent to the landholder. The terms of the manager's lease usually obliged him to maintain the building, pay rates, taxes and insurance, and leave all fixtures and a stock of scenery, costumes and properties behind him when the lease was terminated. The lessee took a big gamble, the landlord far less of one. By the end of the century, in the theatrical good times of the 1880s and the 1890s, the building and leasing of theatres became a speculative boom of its own. 'Any local tradesman can now run a theatre at a profit without the least theatrical experience',[1] was one acidulous comment on the mushrooming surburban theatre, and, writing more generally of theatre business, John Hollingshead, who had successfully managed the Gaiety for many years, said, 'The return for this *maximum* of security and the *minimum* of risk is a percentage that would make a house-owner's mouth water. It varies from 10 to 20 per cent *per annum*, the average probably being about 15 per cent. When a tenant breaks down or finishes his tenancy, there is no difficulty in finding another, and an unusual closure of a few weeks, or even months, is amply covered by "solid deposits".'[2] Other evidence exists, however, to suggest that speculation in theatre building at the end of the century was somewhat riskier than this, and that syndicates were concerned in these speculations, sometimes with the financial involvement of the manager.

In addition to financial obligations to the landlord, the manager had all the burden of running his company and putting on plays. Here his duties were manifold. He chose actors and cast them in each play; he selected key administrative, backstage and front-of-house staff. He was responsible for the weekly salary bill for all personnel before and behind the curtain (though some technical staff were paid off by sub-contractors). He decided which plays were to be performed and scheduled them, frequently cutting and rearranging the texts to suit the exigencies of production and the acting capabilities of his company. He usually superintended rehearsals, and if he were an actor performed leading roles in a large part of the repertory. A myriad of major and minor matters, both artistic and administrative, occupied his attention. He read new plays, dealt with rejected

[1] Leopold Wagner, *How to Get on the Stage* (London, 1899), p. 68.
[2] John Hollingshead, *Gaiety Chronicles* (London, 1898), pp. 29–30.

authors, interviewed acting applicants, kept an eye on the door-keepers and the box-office staff, machinery, and auditorium and, in the last quarter of the century, might well plan and participate in provincial and overseas tours.

Thus the manager's daily workload was a heavy one, and even when the theatre was closed in the summer time was taken to prepare for the next season. It was not unknown for managers to run more than one theatre at the same time. One who did this was John Coleman, who in the second half of the century managed, at varying times, several provincial theatres as well as Drury Lane and the Queen's in London. He describes a typical day in his managing life:

> The entire arrangements of my theatres were organised by my head and controlled by my hands. The day was occupied (unless when travelling) thus: up at seven; at eight, morning's post, reading and answering letters; breakfast at nine; at ten, consultation with prompter, scene painter, carpenter, and property man for arrangements of scenery and properties for night's performance; at eleven, rehearsal; (in prosperous times) a drive or a gallop for an hour; at three, dinner; at four, *The Times* and a snooze; at five, a cup of tea; at six, theatre, to act twice or thrice during the week (or every night, if necessary!); home at eleven – a light supper; from twelve to two, study – study – words – words! Then to bed ... This was the routine day after day, week after week, month after month, year after year.[3]

The manager's life was rendered busier at pantomime time. If he managed a provincial theatre, or a London theatre with a policy of annual pantomime production like Drury Lane or the Britannia in the East End, a failure at Christmas could not even, for crucial financial reasons, be contemplated. Arrangements for the pantomime started months before Christmas, and intensified frantically as Boxing Night – the traditional pantomime opening night – neared. The manager was not just caught up in all this activity, but in fact generated it. Augustus Harris, the manager of Drury Lane from 1879 to 1896, has left an account of his own industry in the production of *Mother Goose* in 1880:

> How can I put down all that has to be done – of my hundred daily interviews with property men, costumiers, scenic artists, ironsmiths, musicians, with clowns, shoemakers, acting managers and advertisers, with drapers, carpenters, ropemakers, and supers; how everything has to be ordered, everyone to be drilled? ... Constantly besieged from morning till night, at least twenty people always waiting to see me, each one on different business. Rushing, for forty-eight hours at a time, to Newcastle, Birmingham, and Paris, driving from one place to another,

---

[3] John Coleman, *Fifty Years of an Actor's Life* (London, 1904), vol. II, p. 684.

ordering goods worth thousands of pounds, returning to the hotel only
to find a score of telegrams calling for my immediate return to London,
where on arriving besieged as before by acrobats, chorus, money-takers,
columbines, and more people than I can remember. And to think that this
life was led for ten weeks, without one moment's peace, without time for
eating, drinking, or even sleeping.[4]

Harris may have become more systematic in his arrangements for
later pantomimes, but he increased his labours by also rehearsing the
Drury Lane pantomime, inevitably a huge production with an
enormous cast and all kinds of theatrical complexities. Sometimes he
sat in the stalls bawling instructions to those on stage; when he lost
his voice an aide would shout Harris's directives through a paste-
board trumpet. When on the stage, he rehearsed furiously:

> With his cloak floating loosely about him, and giving him the semblance
> of a pantomime demon, he darts from one end of the stage to the other
> like a globule of quicksilver ... He is, indeed, ubiquitous, and not content
> with directing everything and everybody, acts and attitudinises every
> part played. Now he is instructing a principal as to his entry, and going
> through it for his edification with emphatic gesticulation. Now he
> interrupts a leading lady with 'No, my dear, that's not it', and proceeds to
> illustrate how the words are to be uttered and the action performed that is
> to accompany them. Now he takes another by the hand, and leads her
> along, and postures her and poses her till she acquits herself to his
> satisfaction. Now he is demonstrating to an attendant the right use of her
> fan, or to a guard that of his weapon. Now with a bound he pounces on a
> member of a procession and leads him along in the way in which he
> should go. Now he indicates to a pantomimist that he must get through
> his work higher up or lower down the stage. Now he comes to the rescue
> of Mr. Barrett with 'That will not do at all' and insists on words being
> sung out and music kept time to. Now he is turning over the pages of a
> bundle of papers which he carries in his hand, and rapidly scoring
> alterations thereon. Now he is hastily scribbling messages and instructions
> on scraps of paper, rumpling these up into balls, and flinging them at
> some satellite in the stalls. Anon he is in the stalls themselves studying the
> effect of a coloured light or of a grouping from the front, and hoarsely
> issuing instructions for its modification. Anon he flops for a moment as
> though exhausted, into an armchair, placed with a table at one of the
> wings, but only to spring up again like Antaeus five seconds later.
> Occasionally he soliloquises somewhat forcibly on the stupidity of the
> human race in general, and of Drury Lane supers in particular.[5]

[4] Augustus Harris, 'My First Drury Lane Pantomime', *Old Drury Lane Christmas Annual*
(London, 1882–83), p. 5.
[5] *Illustrated Sporting and Dramatic News*, 2 January 1886.

MOTIVATION AND CAPITAL INVESTMENT

Being a manager was, clearly, not an easy life. Becoming one required strong motivation as well as capital. Although management was a risky business, the incentives were powerful. Managers could and did amass fortunes, especially in the last quarter of the nineteenth century. Just as strong an incentive, however, was the desire to advance ahead of the throng, to stand out with distinction above one's peers. This was notably true of actors. Even though actors who became managers recognised the onerous nature of the task they were assuming and the consequent diffusion of their interests, hitherto solely focussed upon acting, their ambition usually triumphed over the obstacles. Johnston Forbes-Robertson, who went into management in 1895, declared that 'several actors, younger than I, had taken up management very much earlier in their careers [he was forty-two], and there was nothing for it but to take a theatre if I was to maintain my place'.[6] John Martin-Harvey, whose first venture into management was in 1899, said much the same thing:

> When an actor has reached a certain point in his development – a certain limit (so he imagines) in the opportunities for self-expression which engagements at various theatres have given him – it seems to me that he must become his own manager. He cannot remain stationary. Unless further and (a far more difficult condition to achieve) *better* opportunities are presented to him he must decline both in prestige and development, or at least oscillate between good and bad parts, which is a doubtful way of preserving what reputation an actor may have.[7]

Of course the actor-manager was entirely in control of his own parts; he could appear when he liked and how he liked, cast himself to the very best advantage in relation to a weaker company or, as Beerbohm Tree did, build up a strong company with himself as the star. In fact, a West End actor-manager was automatically a star, and that in itself was a compelling motive for taking on the job.

Martin-Harvey went into management with *The Only Way* (an adaptation of *A Tale of Two Cities*) on borrowed capital of £2,000, which comprised £900 for three weeks rent in advance, £1,000 for production expenses, and £100 for incidentals. This meant that the running costs of the play had to be paid for out of box-office revenue. These costs amounted to £770 a week and for only one week of the run could they be met out of revenue. Luckily, the

[6] J. Forbes-Robertson, *A Player under Three Reigns* (London, 1925), pp. 164–65.
[7] *The Autobiography of Sir John Martin-Harvey* (London, 1933), pp. 253–54.

backer who had lent Martin-Harvey the £2,000 also paid the losses out of his own pocket. Thus one of the most successful plays of Edwardian England lost £4,000 on its first appearance, despite a London run and a provincial tour. It was, incidentally, the 1890s that saw the real emergence of the financial backer, whether City speculator, ambitious playwright or good friend, and this backer might support a single production rather than subsidise a full-scale management.

Martin-Harvey recovered his fortunes quickly, although he began badly; *The Only Way* was succeeded by other failures. Nevertheless, what forcibly strikes a later theatrical age is the relatively small sum needed for an initial managerial venture. Martin-Harvey had borrowed £2,000. In 1865 Marie Wilton opened the Prince of Wales's Theatre on £1,000 from her brother-in-law. For that amount the theatre was renovated and redecorated, and £150 was left over to pay for the first production, a triple bill of a one-act comedy, a farce and an operatic burlesque. In 1868 Hollingshead, a journalist rather than an actor, began management of the Gaiety with £200 of his own money and £5,000 raised by a syndicate organised by the owner of the new theatre, which was built as a speculation. In the 1860s, as in any other decade, the rent a manager had to pay for a leading West End theatre varied. The Princess's was £3,800 a year, the Lyceum £4,000, the Haymarket £4,400, and Drury Lane £7,800.[8] Rent was usually paid quarterly and only the first quarter came out of the money a prospective manager had to raise. Augustus Harris took Drury Lane in 1879 with £3 15s. in his pocket, raising £2,750 in order to open the biggest theatre in the West End, the graveyard of so many managements. (The previous manager, F. B. Chatterton, had failed in the middle of the run of *Cinderella*, owing £40,000.) Irving borrowed an undisclosed sum to open the Lyceum; more fortunate than Martin-Harvey, he was able to pay this back fairly quickly out of his striking early successes and the profits of provincial touring. Few managers could raise the capital to build or buy their own theatres outright. However, Charles Wyndham built, furnished, and decorated Wyndham's Theatre in 1899 for £37,000, which came from the profits of his management of the Criterion. Tree put £10,000 of his Haymarket profits into the building of the grandly elaborate Her Majesty's in 1898; the rest of the capital required was provided by a syndicate. The theatre was built for £55,000. (In 1849 the new Olympic – admittedly a far less splendid theatre, rebuilt when costs were lower – opened for £10,000.)

[8] Letter by Dion Boucicault to the *Times*, 2 October 1862.

COMPANY ORGANISATION AND EXPENSES

A manager spent his money not only on a lease and a building, but also upon a company. The Victorian theatre company was structured in much the same way as a Georgian company, except that the technical and backstage staff had grown in number because of the greater complexity and increasing elaboration of production and lighting, especially in the larger and better equipped theatres. As soon as he entered upon his lease, the manager needed to appoint a business manager (the treasurer, in early Victorian theatre), who looked after advertising and printing. He also supervised the front-of-house staff, money-takers, check-takers, attendants and the box office. A fairly large operation would probably need a deputy, the acting manager. The size and nature of the acting company to be employed depended upon the theatre taken, the budget and the repertory or long-run policy to be adopted. These considerations also determined the number and composition of the technical personnel, which would consist of stage carpenters (or scene shifters), machinists, gasmen, limelight operators, property men and wardrobe staff. In a theatre with a sizeable technical staff, each area would have a chief answerable directly to the stage manager. The Victorian stage manager did not exercise quite the same functions as the modern stage manager, but on the production side he was the manager's right-hand man. In the later Victorian period the prompter assisted the stage manager as well as going about his own duties; his function had changed and diminished somewhat over the years, but he was still an important member of the production team. Earlier in the century, before the long run and the lengthier rehearsal period that accompanied it, there was a real necessity in the repertory system for the prompter's voice. The large numbers of supernumerary actors, or supers, on the stage in spectacle productions, necessitated the appointment of a super master to rehearse them; sometimes this job was done by the stage manager or prompter. Specialist instructors like a singing master and a ballet master were always in place for the Christmas pantomime and were retained for other kinds of production which included singing and dancing. A chief scene-painter was a necessity, and in a large operation he had assistants. However, scene-painting, like costuming and furnishing, was increasingly jobbed out to studios and other commercial establishments. Another significant post was the conductor and musical director of the orchestra, for no Victorian theatre, no matter how humble, was without its musicians, even if only two or three in number. A West End theatre might have an orchestra of thirty or even larger; Irving, for instance, had an orchestra of thirty-five or thirty-seven for *Faust* at the Lyceum in 1885. Other theatre staff included dressers, a stage doorkeeper, a call boy, a housekeeper and sometimes a fireman and a policeman.

In small provincial theatres the total size of the company would be modest and the number of positions accordingly reduced, but in London it was a different matter. Earlier in the century the major companies at Drury Lane and Covent Garden were swollen in size because of the varied demands of a complete repertory system; virtually separate companies were kept for tragedy and comedy, and sometimes opera as well. In the mid and late Victorian period the necessities of spectacle drama, whether melodrama, pantomime, or Shakespeare, expanded company numbers. The legitimate drama's last stand at Covent Garden was the management of Madame Vestris and Charles Mathews; in the 1839–40 season they had 684 employees on the payroll, including 80 actors, 89 supers, 116 in wardrobe, and 199 technical staff.[9] Charles Kean at the Princess's in the 1850s staged fewer productions annually than Vestris and Mathews, trying for runs whenever possible, but because of his policy of large-scale Shakespeare mounted along archaeologically recreative lines he found his expenses heavy and his company large. In some of the Shakespeare revivals it numbered nearly 550. Irving in 1881 was using thirty gasmen and ninety stage carpenters for his revival of *The Corsican Brothers*, and the total company for *Robespierre* at the Lyceum in 1899 amounted to 639, divided into 48 administrative and front-of-house staff, 236 backstage and technical staff and 355 actors (including supers) and musicians.[10] In 1902 the Lyceum was employing 500 on a daily basis, His Majesty's 400.[11]

The use of great numbers of supers to make up stage crowds frequently enlarged the Victorian acting company, at least in theatres where managers put on that kind of show. Macready utilised between 100 and 200 senators in his Covent Garden *Coriolanus* in 1838, Charles Kean at least 250 citizens for the triumphal entry of Bolingbroke into London in *Richard II* (1857), and Irving 165 soldiers in *Macbeth* in 1888. These numbers were considerably exceeded in late Victorian theatres like Drury Lane and the Standard

[9] William W. Appleton, *Madame Vestris and the London Stage* (New York, 1974), p. 128.

[10] Alan Hughes, 'The Lyceum Staff: A Victorian Theatrical Organization', *Theatre Notebook*, vol. 28 (no. 1, 1974), pp. 15–16.

[11] Georges Bourdon, formerly stage manager at the Odéon in Paris, undertook a comparative study of French and English staging. He lamented the superiority of English staging to the French, partly attributing it to the larger number of scene-shifters and other backstage staff. 'Staging in the French and English Theatres', *Fortnightly Review*, vol. 71 (January 1902), pp. 154–69.

in the East End – not that leading provincial managers did not also make a splendid and heavily populated spectacle of their pantomimes. The large numbers employed in pantomime were exceptional compared to those required in even the most lavish productions with historical or contemporary settings, but they were annually exceptional. The staff for *Little King Pipkin* at Drury Lane in 1865 was nearly 900, with 48 seamstresses and wardrobe staff, 45 dressers, 17 gasmen, 200 child performers and 60 in the ballet.[12] The 1881 *Robinson Crusoe* included 260 children and supers and 150 dancers.[13] Augustus Harris was particularly fond of enormous processional entries: the mustering of the Thieves and their followers in the Cave in *The Forty Thieves* of 1886 numbered nearly 500 and the processions of the Kings and Queens of England and their retinues in the 1882 *Sinbad the Sailor* totalled 650.

There was only one way of paying for and profiting from productions of this magnitude of expenditure and that was, of course, the long run. The gradual West End changeover from a repertory system, with the evening or weekly bill frequently changing, to a system geared to produce only one play at a time, and that, it was hoped, for a long run, took a good thirty or forty years. By the end of this changeover, also, the provincial stock company had almost disappeared and was replaced by the touring company.

Both these changes were as significant for managers as for actors and audiences. A West End manager no longer had to run a season balanced in the old way between new plays and revivals, between tragedy and comedy, between melodrama and farce and so forth. Such a balance was designed to keep new entertainments continually before a relatively small potential audience so that they would (ideally) maintain a steady and enthusiastic patronage. Now that this audience had grown so much larger the manager could afford to specialise in the kind of drama that he felt would be successful and would keep his name and theatre favourably before the public, so that the good will accruing from one success to the next would (ideally) build a large and loyal audience eager to see anything he did. This meant finding a distinctive identity for his theatre and play policy, not an easy matter with keen competitors and a sometimes saturated market. The late Victorian and Edwardian actor-managers were especially good at doing this, but earlier Phelps at Sadler's Wells (1844–62), Kean at the Princess's (1850–59), the Bancrofts at the Prince of Wales's (1865–79), the Swanboroughs at the Strand (1858–87) and Hollingshead at the Gaiety (1868–86) all ran popular

[12] John Doran, *In and About Drury Lane* (London, 1881), vol. 1, p. 3.
[13] A. G. Bowie, 'Some Notes on Pantomime', *Theatre* (January 1882), p. 27.

managements individually distinctive in repertory and production styles which built up faithful audiences over a period of years.

If a management were responsible for sending out a tour of a hit play from the West End, then it was merely a matter of finding a cast to do it, or perhaps three or four casts, depending on the size of the hit and whether it was worthwhile to play the 'smalls' as well as the number one and two venues. Artistic decisions were virtually unnecessary; in most cases the touring production was a carbon copy of the West End original. As we know, a popular actor-manager could also tour with his own small but carefully selected repertory or his own hit; such touring, both provincial and international, could be more lucrative than playing in London.

London managers like Harris at Drury Lane, John Douglass at the Standard and Sara Lane at the Britannia, played Christmas pantomimes as a matter of policy and ran them for as long as four months, which meant in effect that up to a third of the annual total of performances at such a theatre was taken up with pantomime – a kind of annual long run. In the provinces, where pantomime was more generally popular, the profits of Christmas were likewise absolutely crucial to the financial health of the theatre and a vital instrument of managerial policy. For some reason pantomimes were almost always successful; if they had not been, and if going to the pantomime had not become a family tradition, provincial theatre in the Victorian period could hardly have existed. This success had little to do with quality. 'There is a certain sum to be got in a certain time, and no increased pressure, either in outlay, ornament or supplementary attraction; no interpolated adjuncts, whether in the shape of acrobats, aeronauts, funambulists, elephants, horses, dancing dogs or monkeys; of duplicate harlequins and columbines, multiplied clowns and incalculable sprites, can swell that sum beyond the average amount. The case reduces itself to a matter of arithmetic. So many holiday visitors for a given number of weeks, give so much and no more.'[14]

To take only one provincial example: Wilson Barrett had operated the Grand Theatre in Leeds at a loss during 1886, most of the productions being touring shows, but was rescued by the Grand's own pantomime, *Sinbad the Sailor*. It ran for ten and a half weeks, or about 20 per cent of the theatre's weeks of performance for the year. By the end of the run 200,000 people had come into Leeds by special excursion trains to see *Sinbad*, in addition to the city audience (Leeds then had a population of 300,000). The final profit on the panto-

[14] *The Life and Theatrical Times of Charles Kean*, vol. II, pp. 38–39.

mime was £1,766; that year Barrett told his landlords that his average annual profit for the eight years to 1886 had been £2,067. If the return from *Sinbad* were at all typical, this meant that Christmas pantomime had over the years been providing the manager of the Grand with roughly 85 per cent of his profit.[15]

Without profits or the hope of obtaining them there would have been no pantomime and no Victorian theatre, so there is little need to apologise for spending some time on financial facts and figures. A manager's expenses had to be precisely calculated before he even opened his doors. Rates, taxes and insurance were his responsibility under the terms of his lease, which itself cost several thousand pounds annually. Then he would have to bear the charges of gas and limelight (and electricity after the electrification of many West End theatres in the 1880s). Before the manager hired his company, then, his expenses were already considerable. It was estimated in 1885 that these might amount, in an average-sized West End theatre in a good position, to about £80 a week. The size and makeup of his acting company would depend upon the artistic policy adopted, whether the dramatic fare was to be melodrama, burlesque, comedy, farce or comic opera. In terms of weekly acting salaries, some of these genres were more expensive than others. Pantomime was the most expensive of all, but pantomime was produced only once a year. In 1885, at least, comic opera was twice as costly as comedy, farce or melodrama, perhaps £240 a week compared to £120.[16] Then there were the salaries of the production, administrative and miscellaneous staff as previously identified; after that the costs of production – costumes, properties, furniture, lumber, canvas, paint, authors' fees, etc. A manager kept two accounts: Production and Preliminary, for all costs leading up to opening night, and then the Daily or Weekly account listing expenses after opening night, including weekly salaries. Payments to authors came under Production and Preliminary, while advertising was an expense straddling both accounts. Advertisements appeared in newspapers, on playbills in shop windows and public houses, and later in the century as coloured posters on walls and hoardings, and on the boards of sandwich-men roaming the streets. Large sums could be spent upon advertising, especially in advance of a big touring production. It was said that nearly £20,000

[15] Anthony Field, 'Wilson Barrett at the Leeds Grand Theatre, 1886', *Journal of Arts Policy and Management*, vol. 1 (February 1984), pp. 14–15.

[16] 'The Theatrical Business', *St James's Gazette*, 10 January 1885. Six articles by 'An Old Lessee' appeared under this heading between 10 January and 13 February. They are a valuable source of information for the business operations of a late Victorian West End theatre. For a summary of this information see Michael R. Booth, 'Theatrical Business in the 1880s', *Theatre Notebook*, vol. 61 (no. 2, 1987), pp. 51–56.

were spent on poster advertising for each provincial tour of two West End melodrama hits of the early eighties, *The Lights o' London* and *The Silver King*.[17] Although advertising was a heavy expense, it could be much reduced after a few months if a piece were playing to good houses. Free orders, or 'paper', a way of making a theatre look full in the absence of heavy box-office sales, was really a form of advertising and required good judgment on the part of the business manager.

REVENUE AND PRICING POLICY

The sources of revenue for a manager were well defined. A small but regular income could be derived from the rental of bars and refreshment areas to an outside contractor, who provided catering staff, crockery, cutlery and glasses. Sometimes managements operated their own refreshment services. The rental was larger if the contractor also had the right to sell programmes and charge cloakroom fees. Before the days of programmes, which were not widely used before the 1870s, playbills were sold in the auditorium. The refinement of bars and coffee lounges was a mid and late Victorian development. Respectable but fairly incidental sums could also be made by selling off properties and costumes to other theatres, or they could be used for a provincial tour. Because of heavy wear and tear, sales of this kind were usually not possible for sets. The disposal of pantomime properties and costumes meant an annual income; there was always a market for them.

The box office was a manager's major source of revenue. It was not until the 1880s that an efficient system of selling tickets was devised for West End theatres, with counterfoils attached to tickets, and seat number, area of auditorium, date and price printed on the ticket. The old system, in which tickets were laboriously written out by hand, led to mistakes and corruption on the part of box-office and front-of-house staff. The mid-Victorian development of the 'libraries', or booking agents, meant that tickets were sold outside the theatre box office; the libraries paid the management weekly and received a 25 per cent discount. The box-office capacity of the average-size West End theatre in the mid-eighties was £160 to £200, which translated into a weekly revenue of over £1,000, excluding matinées, if the theatre were playing to full houses.[18]

[17] 'Some Curiosities of Theatrical Advertising', *Theatre* (November 1890), p. 222.
[18] By the 1880s new West End theatres were getting smaller. In the 1850s Charles Kean's Princess's held £250, and though he regarded it as a 'small' theatre, its seating capacity was, according to the 1866 Select Committee *Report*, 1,579. Irving's Lyceum in the 1880s

Matinées had been tried in the 1860s and were a regular feature of Christmas pantomimes during the school holiday, but did not become widespread until the next decade. They were then frequently used as tryouts for new plays, sometimes by the management itself, sometimes by ambitious playwrights or speculators; a manager could usefully rent out his theatre for the (usually single) performance at £25 or £30. In this manner several Ibsen plays were introduced to London. By the end of the century matinées were mostly used as they are today, to provide additional performances of the evening's attraction.

The box-office capacity of a theatre, and the box-office income a manager received, was a consequence of seat pricing, a matter of social as well as financial policy. Early in the century prices at Covent Garden after the rebuilding of 1809 stood at 7s.6d. for the boxes, 4s. for the pit, and 2s. and 1s. for the lower and upper galleries. The Old Price riots at the reopening forced a reduction of some prices, but they were as much an expression of class and political antagonisms as hostility to raised prices. From that point, and especially in the early Victorian period, prices slid steadily downward. During Osbaldiston's Covent Garden management of 1835–37, boxes were 4s., pit 2s, and galleries 1s.; E. T. Smith at Drury Lane charged the same in 1852. These were major theatres; at the minors prices were even lower. It cost 6d. to enter the pit at the Victoria and Britannia in 1850, and 3d. for the galleries.

At the same time the patent theatres were reducing prices, the fashionable class did not at all mind paying half a guinea for a pit seat at the opera. This was a social phenomenon; seat pricing for the theatre and the opera was merely a manifestation of that phenomenon. The choice of repertory, the nature of the audience and of public taste, were matters closely related to seat pricing policy and the social position of the manager and his theatre. For instance, with his low prices E. T. Smith was deliberately aiming at a popular audience with a taste for spectacle and thrilling melodrama. Since it was difficult to attract the upper classes to the more expensive seats, the answer from managers of this stamp was to lower prices in an attempt to attract a different class with different tastes and less money to spend on the theatre. The final abolition of the old custom of half-price was also social in its implications. In the previous century the public was admitted to the theatre for half the price of admission at the end of the third act; from 1825 half-price was taken about 9 p.m. The audience attracted by half-price in the Victorian

could seat about 1,800 spectators and £420, but that capacity had been increased since 1878, when it was £228.

period was mostly a pit and gallery audience and it included young men about town who did not want to spend the whole evening at the theatre, which then started at 6.30 or 7 p.m. and could go to midnight or later. However, half-price was principally directed at clerks, shop assistants and other persons in employment who did not finish their working day until 7 or 8 or 9 p.m., and these were generally lower middle class. The first managements to abolish half-price – there had been previous unsuccessful attempts – were those catering to more elevated audiences, notably Madame Vestris at the Lyceum and the Bancrofts at the Prince of Wales's.

After years of low prices, the managers of the 1860s and 1870s began to raise them. This too was a social as well as financial calculation. The potential middle-class audience was becoming more prosperous and new theatres were being built. The 'return' of the so-called intellectual and socially respectable classes to the theatre – in fact, as we have seen, they had never been absent – was much praised in the press. More specifically, managers wanted to cash in on what was happening socially. The 6s. West End stall became 7s. and in the 1870s went up to 10s. and 10s.6d. The dress circle (a socially significant new term) went from 5s. to 6s. and then 7s. These were considerable increases, given the decline in the cost of living, but they are perfectly understandable from the social as well as the economic point of view. Managers wanted a respectable social image for their theatres as well as larger profits, and they acted quickly to tailor their entertainments as well as their prices to what they perceived as the changing audience, an audience they helped to change by artistic policy and seat pricing. By 1879 thirteen theatres in the West End were charging at least 10s. for a stall; in 1873 there were ten. By contrast some prices in the East End had come down even from their low levels of the 1850s: the Britannia, the East London, and the Pavilion were asking only a shilling for a stall and the top stall price outside the West End was 5s. at the Surrey.[19]

With the increase in prices came a reduction in the length of performances and a later starting time. The attempt by some managers in the thirties, forties and fifties to attract the widest possible audience by running long programmes was reversed by those who wished to attract the class of people who liked to come to the theatre relatively late and leave early. Such a class did not exist in sufficient numbers in an earlier generation to support any theatre with this policy. The later dinner hour for this class also helped to push back the starting hour from 6.30 to 7 p.m. in the 1860s and

[19] John Pick, *The West End* (Eastbourne, 1983), p. 53.

eventually to 8.00 and 8.30. The number of pieces on the bill was correspondingly lessened from the three or four of the early Victorian Haymarket and Adelphi, to mention only two examples, to a short curtain-raiser and a mainpiece. The audiences of the eighties and nineties were commonly offered, as we are today, only the one play of an evening, and they did not protest.

The reason for the prosperity of the late Victorian West End manager was a combination of good profits from a newly moneyed or reasonably paid and socially conscious audience and the low cost of operating his theatre. Rentals were not yet exorbitant; wages, except for star actors, were modest, and the economic situation was stable. In 1885, 'if the house averages two-thirds full, the manager will clear £40 a night, but only £10 a night if half-full'.[20] These figures did not include front-of-house revenue or production costs, but they show that the break-even point could be low in percentage terms, and profits on a long run of good houses satisfactorily high. One of the big hits of the 1880s was *Faust* at the Lyceum, a play with heavy initial Production and Preliminary expenses of nearly £12,000. It ran 187 nights in its first season, 1885–86. Not only did Irving pay off all the production costs on that first run but also made a profit of £16,000 on a box-office average of 82 per cent capacity. By 1902, at the end of its production career at the Lyceum, in the provinces and in America, *Faust* had taken in over £250,000 at the box office.[21] At the other end of the scale, George Alexander at the St James's Theatre in 1900 ran *A Debt of Honour* and *Rupert of Hentzau* for only eighty-five and fifty-one performances respectively, to houses less than half filled, and still made a slight profit on each play.[22]

MACREADY

In his long tenure of the St James's from 1891 to 1918, Alexander was the epitome of the *fin-de-siècle* actor-manager, polished, elegant, successful and the recipient of a knighthood. Very different was the early Victorian William Charles Macready, who assumed his tenancy of Covent Garden only a month after the Queen had come to the throne. Macready was then a man of forty-four and the unchallenged head of his profession. He had been on the London stage for over twenty years, and, much given to worry about the financial security of his family, was determined to capitalise upon his

[20] *St James's Gazette*, 19 January 1885.
[21] Michael R. Booth, *Victorian Spectacular Theatre* (London, 1981), pp. 123–24.
[22] A. E. W. Mason, *Sir George Alexander and the St James's Theatre* (London, 1935), p. 150.

attractions as an actor by going into management. He also had the honourable motive of advancing the interests of the legitimate drama, which he saw as virtually moribund in a decade of disastrous managements at Drury Lane and Covent Garden increasingly dominated by what he deemed degraded and meretricious spectacle. Macready was temperamentally unsuited to working under another manager for any length of time; indeed, his pride, sense of superiority, and short temper too often overcame him with unfortunate consequences even during the course of his own management.

In spite of these difficulties, which were largely a matter of personality, Macready in his two periods of management at Covent Garden (1837–39) and Drury Lane (1841–43) proved to be as distinguished a manager as he was an actor. As far as was possible with a fair-sized repertory he rehearsed his company carefully and at length, often, rather surprisingly, displaying endless patience with individual actors and technical staff. He had a strong sense of a production's unity and coherence, used large numbers of actors intelligently and paid a great deal of attention to scenic harmony and scenic 'illustration' of a text. Like Charles Kean and Henry Irving he anticipated the twentieth-century director in many ways, assuming the overall role of coordinator of all aspects of production as well as rehearsing. None of this meant that he sacrificed one jot of his acting perquisites as a star. When Macready was on stage – he assumed the leading roles in most of his productions – the focus of attention was always upon him. In the days of the star actor, even in such well-run, directorially advanced companies as Macready's, Kean's and Irving's, the art of ensemble went so far and no farther.

When it came to repertory, Macready was a stout supporter of the old order. In four seasons of management he performed eighteen of Shakespeare's plays, eleven of them in his first Covent Garden season. His respect for Shakespeare extended to restoring the text of *King Lear* (and the Fool along with it), which had not been performed since Nahum Tate's adaptation captured the stage in 1681. He tended to be overfond of the old-fashioned literary play with little stage attraction, sometimes producing it out of a sense of duty to the legitimate and to the literary circle that surrounded him (Forster, Browning, Dickens, Talfourd) than out of genuine enthusiasm. Several of these plays were utter disasters, such as Darley's *Plighted Troth* (1842) and Browning's *A Blot in the Scutcheon* (1843). On the other hand, two plays by a new dramatist (but well-known novelist), Edward Bulwer, were great successes: *The Lady of Lyons* (1838) and *Richelieu* (1839). Much of this success must be attributed to Macready's editorial efforts as well as his acting and management; he worked closely with Bulwer on the acting texts. Quite understandably, given his self-assumed position as defender of the best interests of the English drama, Macready disliked the popular drama and had no truck with melodrama, even declining to consider an offer from Dickens of a stage version of *Oliver Twist*. Macready was also devoted to the repertory system, and refused to countenance longer runs of undoubted successes like *Henry V, The Tempest* and the opera *Acis and Galatea*. This was an admirable expression of principle, but it denied him much-needed revenue at the box office.

Macready lost money in his two managerial stints, but how much is not known, and it appears that he simply tired of management rather than collapsed under a burden of debt. He also worried – as did other actor-managers – about the cumulative effect of the multifarious chores of management upon his art as an actor. Certainly he was very busy, as entries from his diary reveal:

> Went to the theatre, and sent for Robertson to speak about the accounts. Mentioned the fact of the bills I had twice before spoken of being continued despite of my complaints ... My dresser thought he could undertake the office of regulating the coals and candles for twelve shillings, which saves me at once eighteen shillings per week. Went over Bradwell's accounts with Willmott and Robertson; the latter is *not* the man for such a duty in such a time ... A letter from Mr. Phillips to Bartley, refusing to act Rashley in to-morrow night's bill, threw us into embarrassment. This fellow, who never attracts individually one sixpence, will now receive a week's salary – £35 – for playing in one farce – and perhaps not that. Miss Shirreff was affecting nerves and hysterics, and to pacify her I was obliged to change *Artaxerxes*, announced for Tuesday. So much for these knavish singers. Went over the *Novice* in the saloon. Messrs. Paine, of the *Morning Gazette*, called for advertisements and orders. Bagnall called for an engagement; I heard him speak and dismissed him civilly. Wrote several notes. Spoke with Head about Othello's dresses. Coming home, tried to read an adaptation of *Volpone*, but fell asleep, overpowered with fatigue of mind and body.[23]

Preparations for the Covent Garden season of 1838–39 showed Macready involved in their every aspect:

> Much business was before, and occupied me variously throughout the day; the price of work was settled; the ladies' rooms appointed and settled; the private boxes, lobbies, and whole part of the theatre inspected and finally settled as to its cleaning, etc. The expenses of the men's wardrobe reduced, and alteration made as to the lighting; to reduce still

[23] *The Diaries of William Charles Macready*, ed. William Toynbee (London, 1912), vol. I, pp. 416–17.

> more the expenses, questions about the laundry work – still, still impo-
> sition! Scene-room, wardrobe, carpenter's room; business with all; cast
> pieces and made out the bill for the first night.   (I, 470)

The search for good new plays – for no company could live on
revivals alone – endlessly occupied a weary Macready. 'Finished *Blot*
[*in the Scutcheon*]. Went over *Athelwold* – will not do at present.
Wrote to Serle for *Honest Man's Fortune*. Received and read it – *not
do*. Searched, hunted, ruminated; could find nothing' (II, 193).

Despite Macready's often haughty and arrogant treatment of
actors, many stuck by him loyally and transferred with him from
Covent Garden to Drury Lane, an indication of their respect for his
art and their knowledge that they were performing in the company
with the highest standards in England. However, his private opinion
of actors was rarely favourable. 'These players,' he wrote when he
was rehearsing *Cymbeline*, 'oh! how well they merit all the indignity
that can be heaped upon them. The greater part are miserable
wretches' (II, 192). Singers were worse. 'I wish they were all tied in a
sack together! They wear my heart out' (I, 442).

Carrying separate companies for drama and opera, engaging
comedians who did not act in tragedies and tragedians who did not
act in comedies, and trying successfully to operate a huge enterprise
in two theatres already notorious as graveyards of hopeful managements, with theatrical competition increasing around him, it is not
surprising that Macready failed to profit financially and tired of the
struggle. He was too much a perfectionist and stood too much on his
professional dignity to make the sort of compromises that might
have helped him at the box office. Yet that was his nature, and the
wonder is that he succeeded as well as he did. Although he managed
only briefly compared to others, his management is one of the most
important of Victoria's reign. Coming early as it did, it set high
standards in production and artistic integrity that all later managements of quality followed, influencing them particularly in the
staging of Shakespeare, the use of stage crowds, the conduct of
rehearsals, the illustrative value of scenery and spectacle and, in the
largest sense, the sheer dedication to what was best in theatre.

VESTRIS

Macready's ventures were bracketed by two other significant
managements, that of Madame Vestris at the Olympic, Covent
Garden and the Lyceum, and of Samuel Phelps at Sadler's Wells.
Lucia Vestris was the first of the notable female managers of the
nineteenth century, one of the very few occupations in which a

woman could compete on equal terms with a man and even control him economically by taking him into her employment. A comedienne, singer and dancer with a previously notorious private life, Vestris reopened the Olympic in 1831 with a policy in part determined by the legal situation: the Olympic was a minor theatre which had no right to play the legitimate drama. Eschewing melo-drama, the standard fare of the minors, Vestris resolved to make the illegitimate repertory which she selected – musical pieces, little comedies, extravaganzas, farces and burlesques – as entertaining and fashionable as possible. She redecorated her theatre tastefully, dressed and furnished her stage richly, shortened the length of her bill and rehearsed with care.

Vestris's eight-year management of the Olympic was not a splen-did financial success, but she succeeded in attracting fashionable and respectable audiences, thus giving the lie to those who declared gloomily that patrons of this class had deserted the theatre entirely. She and her new husband, the comedian Charles James Mathews, took Covent Garden from 1839 to 1842 and moved into the legiti-mate drama. They did as well as could possibly be expected with that white elephant of a theatre, restoring *Love's Labour's Lost* to the stage (the first production since the seventeenth century), putting on an important production of *A Midsummer Night's Dream*, a play pre-viously thought almost unstageable and dreadfully hacked about in presentation, and achieving a dazzling success with Boucicault's comedy *London Assurance*. The company was, given the talents of its two stars, naturally stronger in comedy than tragedy, and so it also proved with the last Vestris–Mathews management at the Lyceum from 1847 to 1855. Here, although they again drew the respectable and the fashionable, they were less successful and financially very hard-pressed. Except for the spectacle extravaganzas of J. R. Planché in which Vestris starred, the repertory was undistinguished, depend-ing largely upon adaptations from the French. After 1843 any theatre could produce what it liked, subject to the censorship powers of the Examiner of Plays, but abolition of Drury Lane's and Covent Garden's monopoly on the legitimate drama did not help the Lyceum. Illness and financial difficulties added to the burden of the managers and, toward the end of their lease, the Lyceum was moribund. However, Vestris and Mathews had bequeathed much to their successors. They shared with Macready an attention to detail and thorough rehearsal, and they knew how to make the *petite* both attractive and elegant. The relative success of the Olympic, a small London theatre by early Victorian standards (about 1,300 capacity), pointed the way to the success of the even smaller theatres of several later managements. Vestris herself had shown that it was possible for a woman to take on a major theatrical enterprise and acquit herself with distinction.

PHELPS

Like Vestris and Mathews, Samuel Phelps could play more legitimate drama after the monopoly ended. An actor under Macready, Phelps learned from his manager; he also understood the defects of the Macready management and resolved not to allow them at Sadler's Wells. Initially he went into management in partnership with the actress Mrs Warner in 1844, but she withdrew after two seasons, leaving Phelps as sole manager until he gave up Sadler's Wells in 1862. The theatre itself, in north-east London, was remote from the West End for the actors and audience of the day, and it was a daring move to attempt a major theatre in Islington. However, the move succeeded: Phelps built up a loyal local audience and attracted at least some patronage from spectators who normally attended West End theatres only. It was the nineteenth century's single endeavour to decentralise London theatre and produce a legitimate repertory outside the West End. After Phelps – who himself went back to the West End to act – the concentration of theatrical forces in the West End strengthened and the area outside the centre was given over to the old working-class theatres and the new suburban playhouses – both of them, by the end of the century, merely staging posts for shows touring out of the West End.

Phelps's management was especially distinguished by his fealty to Shakespeare: in eighteen years he put on thirty-one of the plays. In the season of 1856–57 fourteen plays by Shakespeare appeared at Sadler's Wells; in the same season Charles Kean did three. Phelps was operating what was essentially a repertory theatre and Kean was not, but the record is nevertheless impressive. Phelps also revived Elizabethan, Jacobean, and eighteenth-century plays, many of which had been theatrically dormant for generations, and did his best to put on good work by contemporary dramatists. Although he was the star, he ran his company along ensemble lines, and was not, unlike Macready, jealous of potential rivals. He continued Macready's practice of painstaking rehearsals and unified productions. Phelps was not an archaeologist like Kean and did not spend as lavishly upon his productions, but they were always aesthetically pleasing; sometimes, as in the case of *Pericles* and *A Midsummer Night's Dream*, scenically outstanding. Through Phelps, the best in Macready's practice was passed on to the next generation, not in a smooth continuity, but as a valuable bequest to be used when most needed; this bequest included his young actors.

Another actor-manager much influenced by Macready (although they were personal enemies) was Charles Kean. In reaction to the flagrant immorality of his father Edmund, Kean was – like Macready – determined to be a gentleman, even though he went on the stage as a young man. He had, after all, been to Eton, as Macready had been to Rugby, but he did not possess the latter's fundamental distaste for his profession. Beginning his nine-year management of the Princess's Theatre in 1850 (in partnership with the comedian Robert Keeley for one season), Kean was well aware of what Macready had achieved. He went into management to make money, no doubt, but also to 'revive public taste and restore the stage, generally supposed to be on the decline, to its former elevation', as his biographer claimed, with a nod in the direction of Phelps, who 'was making a manly stand, but his scene of action was too far east, and too much circumscribed by its locality to divert into unwonted channels the antagonistic tide of fashion'.[24] No fringe locality for Kean: the Princess's on Oxford Street was acceptably within the boundaries of the West End.

Like Macready and Phelps, Kean made Shakespeare the cornerstone of his enterprise, producing fifteen of his plays altogether; in the season of 1857–58, for instance, only forty-two out of the 269 acting nights were not given over to Shakespeare. Kean's attitude to Shakespeare was an extension of Macready's. Whereas the latter had seen the value of spectacle as a means of historical illustration in Shakespeare and as a pictorial expansion of the text, Kean saw it (despite his claims to the contrary) as theatrically attractive in its own right and as a way of recreating Shakespeare's historical settings as fully as possible – even if it meant putting on stage scenes only described in Shakespeare, as in *Richard II* and *Henry V*. In this aim he was aided by a team of fine romantic scene painters, perhaps the strongest assembled by any nineteenth-century manager. Such recreation was archaeological in intent; it was not for nothing that Kean was made a Fellow of the Society of Antiquaries during the run of *Richard II* in 1857. His basis for producing Shakespeare lay in his own pictorial, archaeological and educational theory. He was the first manager to develop these theories fully (if not always consisten-

[24] *The Life and Theatrical Times of Charles Kean*, vol. II, p. 2.

tly) in doing Shakespeare, thus setting important precedents for later managers to follow. Victorian progressivism regarded Kean's methods as a positive theatrical advance. His biographer declared that thirty or forty years ago 'there was no succession of pictures, no resuscitation of actual manners and persons as they existed in bygone times'. The spectators of this period, as well as of Shakespeare's own time, alas, 'had no perception of the power with which pictorial and mechanical art could be called in to relieve, vary, and enhance the effect of impressive acting'. Thus, in Kean's *Richard II*, 'the veritable Richard stood, moved, and spoke before us' (II, 212–13). For Kean and many Victorians Shakespeare was both a historian and an educator and the best way to teach history was to do it from the stage by reanimating the actual historical past of the plays. This doctrine lasted a long time in the theatre. Managers from the Bancrofts to Beerbohm Tree subscribed to and practised it and Tree's *Henry VIII* in 1910 was as much an attempt to teach through living historical pictures as was Irving's *Henry VIII* in 1892, as was Kean's in 1855.

Kean was not, of course, entirely dependent on Shakespeare. Like all managers he looked for good new plays, and found two adaptations from the French by Boucicault that admirably suited his own acting style: *The Corsican Brothers* (1852) – a big hit with the Queen, who saw it eight times – and *Louis XI* (1855). The former, in which Kean played the double role of a Corsican of ancient family and his twin whose death in a duel the brother is implacably bent on revenging, combined manly honour with exciting swordplay and established a short-lived school of so-called 'gentlemanly melodrama' on the stage. The latter, in which Kean assumed the character of a remorseless tyrant terrified by death and retribution, was one of those one-part romantic historical melodramas so essential to the Victorian star system and the box office. The fact that the part of Louis XI was in both Phelp's and Irving's repertory was not a coincidence. Macready's Cardinal Richelieu was another star role of this kind, also played by Phelps and Irving.

Macready and Kean intended the combination of star acting, scrupulous production and sound management to be irresistible at the box office. Both failed in their objective, Macready in part because of the sheer size of his theatre and his operation, Kean, as he alleged, because of the limited box-office capacity of the Princess's. He spent handsomely on his theatre, but could never make a consistent profit. In his first seven seasons there was a total profit of £2,627, or just over 1 per cent return for an outlay of nearly £250,000.[25] Later

---

[25] M. Glen Wilson, 'Charles Kean: A Financial Report', *Nineteenth Century Theatre*, ed. Kenneth Richards and Peter Thomson (London, 1971), p. 44.

seasons made money and lost it; the slump of 1857 coincided with a deficit of £4,000 on the season of 1857–58. Like Macready at the end of his tenure Kean was left empty-handed. Both men had during their managerial years foregone a certain and substantial income from star acting appearances in London and the provinces.

CALVERT AND SAKER

One aspect of Kean's management most influential in the provinces was his method of producing Shakespeare. First Charles Calvert at the Prince's Theatre in Manchester from 1864 to 1877 and then Edward Saker at the Alexandra in Liverpool did their best to replicate Kean's archaeology and illustrative spectacle in a notable series of productions. Like Kean, Calvert went to Venice to prepare for his *Merchant of Venice* (1871), exceeding even Kean's archaeological enthusiasm by bringing back a gondola for the production. His *Henry V* of 1872 repeated Kean's interpolated triumphal entry of the victorious monarch into London, a scene only touched on by five lines of the Chorus at the beginning of Act V. This scene lingered in the mind of Alfred Darbyshire, who was responsible for the archaeological accuracy of the production:

> To me it was the realisation of an ideal: it represented all that art and stagecraft could do to illustrate a great historical poem. Those who saw the scene will not have forgotten the crowd of citizens, artizans, youths, maidens and nobles of the land who filled the streets and temporary balconies hung with tapestries, and who with eager expectation awaited the arrival of the young King-hero at the entrance to London Bridge. One remembers the distant hum of voices, and how the volume of sound swelled as the little army approached on its march from Blackheath; how the sound burst into a mighty shout as the hero of Agincourt rode through the triumphal archway, the 'Deo gratias Anglia redde pro victoria' and other hymns of praise filled the air, showers of gold dust fell from the turrets, red roses of Lancaster covered the rude pavements, the bells clashed out, and a great thanksgiving went up to heaven for the preservation of the gallant King and his little army of heroes. The curtain descended on a perfect picture of mediaeval England.[26]

Calvert's *Sardanapalus* of 1875 seems to have been very like Kean's of 1853, especially in respect to the final conflagration. Saker, too, imitated Kean, and for his *Winter's Tale* of 1876 probably borrowed the prompt book from Kean's widow as well as the music and

---

[26] Alfred Darbyshire, *The Art of the Victorian Stage* (London, 1907), pp. 44–45. Like Kean, Calvert published acting versions of his revivals accompanied by quotations from scholarly authorities in a preface.

Plate 3   The English Fleet at Southampton. Charles Calvert's *Henry V*, Prince's
Theatre, Manchester, 1872. Design by Thomas Grieve. By courtesy of the
Shakespeare Centre Library.

designs of furniture and properties,[27] since Kean had done a most
scholarly production in 1856.

   Imitative or not, Calvert's and Saker's productions of Shakespeare
were up to high metropolitan standards, and exemplify the good
production work being done in the provinces in the mid-Victorian
period. Previously, provincial theatres were best known for strong
acting companies whose leading graduates moved to London. Such
companies rapidly decreased in number and the provinces developed
their mid and late Victorian reputation for production rather than
acting, for pantomime and Shakespeare rather than an Edmund
Kean, a Macready or a Phelps.

[27] M. Glen Wilson, 'Edward Saker's Revivals and Charles Kean: An Addendum', *Theatre
Notebook*, vol. 34 (no. 1, 1980), pp. 18–19. This article also discusses Kean's influence upon
provincial production.

Plate 4   Henry V returning in triumph to London. Charles Calvert's *Henry V*,
Prince's Theatre, Manchester. Design by Walter Hann. By courtesy of the
Shakespeare Centre Library.

Charles Kean's management ended in 1859, Phelps's in 1862. The
lapse of time between these dates and the opening of the next
illustrious management, that of the Bancrofts at the Prince of
Wales's Theatre was only brief, and clearly much had been done
under Vestris, Macready, Phelps and Kean to raise standards of
production and exalt the occupation of manager. Yet it was
common among critics and writers of the 1880s and 1890s looking
back upon the start of the Prince of Wales's management in 1865 and
the years before it to claim that stage art had been in a primitive and
degraded condition, and that managers had been heedless of their
charge. This is hardly true when the achievements of the generation
before 1865 are considered. Writing in 1885, Clement Scott declared
that indeed these achievements were considerable, but that in a very
few years they faded. He pointed to the fairly lax managements of
Benjamin Webster at the Adelphi and Buckstone at the Haymarket
in the fifties and sixties: 'Stars shone in the dramatic firmament, but
guiding spirit there was none . . . The stage was not destitute of good

actors, but the method of management was careless and indifferent.'[28] Undoubtedly the application of polish and detail to modern drawing-room drama and comedy was still to come by the early sixties, and undoubtedly Shakespeare had all but disappeared from the London stage. The so-called 'new realism' of the Prince of Wales's style was believed by such commentators to be the dawn of an era, but in any case the content of the drama was changing and necessitated new methods. These methods, however, had their antecedents in the attention to detail of the best early Victorian managers, even though the kind of drama they produced was different. Nowhere in the history of Victorian theatre is there a break in continuity, a completely new beginning.

WILTON AND BANCROFT

Marie Wilton, the second important female manager of the century, tired of being typecast as a boy in saucy burlesque parts, saw no escape but management. She took on the run-down low-class Queen's on a small borrowed capital, renamed it, redecorated it prettily and made a deliberate pitch for the carriage trade, despite her fears that its location north of Soho was too far from the West End and, from her own middle-class point of view, in too insalubrious a district. She was not encouraged by the Queen's audience: 'My heart sank! Some of the occupants of the stalls (the price of admission was, I think, a shilling) were engaged between the acts in devouring oranges (their faces being buried in them), and drinking ginger-beer. Babies were being rocked to sleep, or smacked to be quiet, which proceeding, in many cases, had an opposite effect!'[29] It was precisely this sort of popular audience that Marie Wilton deliberately excluded from her renovated theatre with her decorations (the stall seats had white lace anti-macassars), her repertory, and her prices; the price of stalls immediately rose 600 per cent. In 1867 she married Squire Bancroft, an actor in her company, and thereafter he assumed most of the burden of management. The burlesques and comediettas with which the theatre opened were replaced by the comedies of Tom Robertson, which sustained the Bancrofts to an extraordinary degree for twenty years, both at the Prince of Wales's and at the Haymarket. In these years approximately 2,900 performances of six

[28] *Theatre* (July 1885), p. 50. Scott idolised Tom Robertson. His views on this matter have been convincingly refuted in some detail by Ernest Bradlee Watson in *Sheridan to Robertson* (Cambridge, Mass., 1926), pp. 293–401.

[29] Squire and Marie Bancroft, *Mr and Mrs Bancroft On and Off the Stage*, 4th edn (London, 1888), vol. I, pp. 178–79.

comedies by Robertson were given, or about 145 a year, almost half the total number of performances for the whole period. Never was a Victorian management more dependent upon the work of one writer.

The Prince of Wales's was by mid-Victorian urban criteria a small theatre, with a seating capacity of about 800. The Bancrofts stayed there for fourteen years, admirably successful with their policy of attracting audiences to a comfortable, well-run house performing well-rehearsed and well-acted comedies and dramas with a strong emphasis on the drawing-room. The *Times*, reviewing Robertson's *M.P.* in 1870, noted that the actors are 'almost at arm's length of an audience who sit, as in a drawing-room, to hear drawing-room pleasantries, interchanged by drawing-room personages' (25 April 1870). Henry James, who liked neither the Bancrofts' style nor their principal dramatist, remarked of their 'little theatre' that 'the pieces produced there dealt mainly with little things – presupposing a great many chairs and tables, carpets, curtains, and knick-knacks, and an audience placed close to the stage. They might, for the most part, have been written by a cleverish visitor at a country house, and acted in the drawing-room by his fellow inmates.'[30] The littleness of the Prince of Wales's with its relatively small box-office capacity, even combined with high prices, persuaded the Bancrofts to take a larger and more central theatre, the Haymarket, with double the seating capacity.

Here they prospered even more greatly, to such an extent that they were able to retire in 1885, after only five years at the Haymarket, with a net profit for their twenty years of management of £180,000. Part of this profit came from Squire Bancroft's hotly contested decision to turn all the 2s. Haymarket pit seats into 10s. stalls. Before alterations, there had been only sixty stall seats. The displaced pittites protested long and loud on the opening night of the new management; critics complained, and the *Theatre* ran a special symposium on the question, 'Is the Pit an Institution or an Excrescence?' Contributing to this symposium, Clement Scott, a strong supporter of popular theatre, stated that the new company should be 'acceptable to the public at large and not only to the upholders of a fashionable and fastidious exclusiveness' (March 1880, p. 139). All to no avail. The Bancrofts had set the prices and the precedent; it was they, at the Prince of Wales's, who introduced the 10s. stall. Other managers followed. Fashionable and fastidious exclusiveness in a smallish central theatre, with a good and well-rehearsed company

[30] 'The London Theatres', *Scribner's Monthly*, vol. 21 (January 1881), p. 363.

playing middle-class drawing-room drama and comedy tinged with aristocratic and fashionable colouring to middle-class audiences with aristocratic and fashionable aspirations, became the keystone of West End managerial policy in the 1880s and 1890s. There were exceptions, of course. Theatres like the Princess's and the Adelphi still pursued a policy of domestic, sensational and spectacle melodrama for popular audiences, and Drury Lane under Augustus Harris was famous for its spectacular Autumn Drama as well as its annual pantomime. Irving's Lyceum, while especially fashionable on its setpiece opening nights by invitation, was a good-sized theatre given over to a broader style of drama and acting and a grander scale of production.

IRVING

Henry Irving's management of the Lyceum lasted from 1878 to 1899. Much more so than Squire or Marie Bancroft, Irving was a star actor as well as a manager; the whole weight of the Lyceum enterprise rested upon his ability to take the leading male parts in almost all the plays in the theatre's repertory. This repertory consisted mainly of romantic and historical melodrama and Shakespeare – Irving produced twelve of his plays at the Lyceum – with some works commissioned from contemporary dramatists. In spite of the urgings and ragings of Shaw, Irving refused to venture into the territory of Ibsen and Shaw himself. Neither he nor his co-star Ellen Terry were actors of realistic psychological parts in domestic dramas; more to the point, the Lyceum audience, loyal for many years to Irving's own kind of theatre, would have rejected him in such parts, and the plays as well. As we have seen, he toured extensively, both in the provinces and in America; his successful tours to that country handsomely subsidised the Lyceum and showed other managers that international touring was desirable and lucrative. The Lyceum was the first English company to be acclaimed internationally. At the beginning of his management Irving built up a remarkably stable and faithful group that complemented and supported his own acting. Some of them stayed with him for a long time, Ellen Terry for the duration, Martin-Harvey for fourteen years. His business manager, stage manager, and prompter were with him from beginning to end.

Like the Bancrofts, Irving generally operated a long-run system, which meant that he usually had a lot of time to prepare and rehearse a new production. His most successful Shakespeare, *The Merchant of Venice* in 1879, ran for 250 nights and his *Hamlet* of 1878 for 100. (He had earlier played Hamlet under the previous Lyceum management in 1874 for 200 nights – a great strain for an actor.) Indeed, the Achilles heel of the actor-manager system was the durability and good health of the actor-manager himself. Irving's health finally broke down after years of overwork, and this, combined with an ageing company, a declining box office and a disastrous fire in 1898 that destroyed most of the theatre's stock of scenery and thereby reduced the repertory to a minimum, persuaded Irving to turn over the Lyceum and his business affairs to a syndicate. The syndicate failed and Irving had to spend his last years plodding round the provinces. He died on tour, in 1905. An anti-climactic end to a glorious career, perhaps, but he had already achieved all his goals except that of a tidy sum for his retirement. The goal of social recognition and status for the acting profession was, in his own eyes, one of the most important, and this was officially obtained by the touch of a sword in 1895, when Irving was knighted. Well before this, however, the Lyceum auditorium was a place of resort for distinguished figures from artistic, social and political life. Irving also entertained handsomely, even royally in his private rooms at the Lyceum and on the stage after performances. At these state dinners – that is what they really were – given by command of the undisputed chief of the theatrical profession, Irving played host to the Prince of Wales, the Duke of Teck, the Sultan of Perak, the Crown Prince of Siam, the Abbé Liszt, Indian maharajahs and hosts of explorers, poets, novelists, ambassadors, scientists, historians, divines and inventors. These dinners, the fashionable first nights, the manager's reputation as an artist, the respectability and high standing of the Lyceum, all contributed to place Irving at the apogee of late Victorian theatre management.

DOMINANCE OF THE ACTOR-MANAGER

By the end of the nineteenth century the actor-manager entirely dominated the London stage. Irving at the Lyceum, Tree at Her Majesty's, Alexander at the St James's, Charles Wyndham at Wyndham's, Charles Hawtrey at the Comedy, Cyril Maude at the Haymarket, Arthur Bourchier at the Garrick, Mrs Patrick Campbell at the Royalty – all were installed in West End theatres, all with established reputations as actors or managers, or both, with identifiable artistic policies that over the years built up for most of them audiences loyal in the same way that consumers are loyal to traditional brand-name products.

It has been argued that these managers were socially elitist, that above all they coveted status and social standing and catered in their prices, their repertory, and their auditorium arrangements to a middle- and upper middle-class audience with money to spend on the now socially fashionable theatre.[31] There is undoubtedly some truth in this. Irving and other managers positively revelled in social luxuries and loved hobnobbing with the titled, the famous and the privileged. However, one can hardly blame them, in the entirely commercial Victorian theatre, for capitalising on their advantages and designing a product that would sell well in a market eager to buy. A manager lived and died at the box office. If that failed, he and his business failed; there were no grants to help him. Why not make more money rather than less, if that were possible in fair competition and if one offered value for the money? Additionally, the whole direction of upper-class social life in London was toward the fashionable and the ostentatious, and the theatres, inevitably a part of that life, were at least reaping a harvest of profit such as had never filled their stores earlier in the century. It would be difficult to deny them that, or to blame the managers for taking advantage of a favourable situation.

The leading actor-managers not only held a supremely dominant position in the late Victorian West End, but they were also at the head of touring. By this time provincial theatres, like Wilson Barrett's Grand at Leeds, originated nothing or very little of their own with the major exception of the Christmas pantomime, and each of them existed by taking in touring companies – perhaps forty a year. Despite improvements in quality, only a handful of these were of the first class. A provincial manager could not fill his theatre all year with Irving, Hare, Tree, Alexander, Benson and the like; neither could he afford to. When such companies came, however, they were considerable attractions, and they did not follow the practice of other managements which toured a single West End play in hiring lesser actors with instructions to mimic the originals. Not only did the star actor-managers perform on tour, but the full London company, except for supers who were recruited locally, would also appear, complete with the West End sets, costumes, properties and many of the technical staff. Prices might be raised for these leading companies, but few minded. The tours of the best companies resembled royal progresses, with special trains full of actors and scenery crisscrossing Britain. Or crossing the Atlantic by ship. Forbes-Robertson recalled his tour of America in 1913, when conditions were much the same as they had been at the end of the previous

---

[31] John Pick in *The West End* argues this case in some detail.

century: 'I took the same repertoire that had served me at Drury Lane, and practically the same company, and all the scenery, dresses, and the properties of the eight plays, which when on the move filled eight freight cars each forty feet long, and for the company two passenger cars.'[32] Such grand touring could start from humble beginnings. George Alexander's first tour of five weeks with the St James's company in 1891 earned a profit of £49. By the end of the nineties his provincial autumn tours of twelve to fourteen weeks were bringing in regular profits of over £4,000.[33]

The golden age of the actor-manager did not long endure. The passing of Irving's Lyceum into the hands of a syndicate was a sign of the times, of investment in theatre as a pure business speculation. The upheaval of the First War and the ubiquitous demand for light entertainment disrupted the equilibrium of the actor-manager system and destroyed the individual appeal of the manager's repertory. The cost of theatre rentals mushroomed, as did all the costs of running a theatre: it took a much higher percentage of box-office capacity and longer runs to break even. A new period of inflation further disturbed the stability of costs. By the end of the war most of the old actor-managers were dead or in retirement. While they flourished, however, Victorian theatre management expressed important aspects of public taste and of mid and late Victorian society as well as new techniques of business operation. It disappeared because society changed, and when society changes the theatre changes. Writing in 1935, A. E. W. Mason, Alexander's biographer, noted this change. His comments can serve as an *adieu* to late Victorian actor-management:

> A first night at a theatre in the year 1900 was an event in the social life of the town. There are too many of them in 1935 to arouse more than a languid interest . . . Also there are too few men and women acting in their own theatres. The theatre is now accommodation for a play. In 1900 it was that and a good deal more. It was definitely associated with someone, an old friend as it were, who for good or ill had chosen the play which the audience was now to see, who would himself or herself shortly appear upon the boards. It was more vital on that account. It was less of a lodging-house. There was a thrill in the air as the auditorium filled. Would the old firm do it again?   (pp. 132–33)

---

[32] *A Player under Three Reigns* (London, 1925), p. 270. In a later tour of America Forbes-Robertson was forced to drop Shaw's *Caesar and Cleopatra* from his repertory because of the cost of transporting its three freight cars of sets and properties. Despite the heartbreak of the carpenters, all the scenery and properties were burnt on the California seashore.

[33] *Sir George Alexander and the St James's Theatre*, p. 214.

3

Playhouse and production

In writing fondly of the past glories of the actor-manager system,
A. E. W. Mason also draws attention to the way in which the
relationship of the audience to that system manifested itself in the
theatre. The 'thrill in the air' he explains as 'expectation, even a
trifle of excitement before the lights went out and the adventure
began. The horseshoe of the auditorium contributed to produce
that rapport between the actors behind the footlights and the spectators in front of them, which is essential to the enjoyment of a
play. There were people everywhere – people and warm colours. A
spark passed from one to another and established a sort of fellow-
ship which would last the evening through' (p. 133). Clearly the
auditorium of the St James's Theatre under George Alexander – or
of any other late Victorian West-End theatre – was both a social
and an architectural forum, an expression of social interaction within
the audience and between audience and actors, as well as an architectural shape dictated by space and business considerations and the
necessities of performance. Percy Fitzgerald commented that in
Irving's Lyceum 'the whole has an air of drawing-room comfort . . .
The spaces in front and behind the footlights seem to blend.'[1]
Entering the auditorium of the Lyceum, H. A. Saintsbury declared
that 'the spirit gripped you: it had enveloped you before you took
your seat, gas-lit candles in their wine-coloured shades glowed
softly on the myrtle-green and cream and purple with its gilt mouldings and frescoes and medallions . . . You were in the picture,

[1] Percy Fitzgerald, *The World behind the Scenes* (London, 1881), p. 42.

58

beholding, yet part of it.'[2] The act of going into a theatre and seating oneself to watch a play was an important part of Victorian theatregoing, especially in the atmosphere of luxury and refinement in the West End theatre in its glory. The unity between architectural space, interior decoration, the formal attire of the audience in the boxes, stalls and dress circle, and the pictorial richness of the stage was social and cultural as well as theatrical.

There was nothing new about this. The theatre forms of every age are an expression of social and cultural determinants as well as of production methods, architectural fashion and business policy. Such an expression is especially noticeable in the Victorian theatre. The Regency theatre auditorium, despite a vast increase in size in the two rebuildings of Drury Lane (1794 and 1812) and in the new Covent Garden (1809), followed the same architectural practice as the English theatres of the previous hundred and fifty years. An audience seated in a raked pit, facing a stage projecting beyond the proscenium, was surrounded on three sides by an audience seated in boxes. Above the box audience in the lowest tier sat more spectators in one, two or three shallow balconies divided into further boxes or galleries, depending upon the size and status of the theatre. The boxes nearest the stage on both sides went right up to the proscenium arch and thus directly abutted the forestage. The auditorium was rectangular, fan-shaped or U-shaped, and the pit ended at the back below the front boxes. Except for the boxes, seating was unreserved and spectators sat on backless benches; chairs and backed benches were often provided in the boxes. Whether the auditorium was lit by candles, or later by gas, it was never dark, and a play was viewed by spectators sitting in full or partially reduced light.

Changes in the architecture of the nineteenth-century auditorium occurred well before the accession of Queen Victoria. When structural iron was introduced into late eighteenth-century building methods, it was not long before its advantages became obvious in theatre construction. Previously the only way of increasing audience capacity in new theatres was to have a larger site so that the pit could be made wider and deeper and the boxes and galleries stacked up one above the other. Such a solution is obvious in Henry Holland's new Drury Lane of 1794 and Benjamin Wyatt's rebuilding of the same theatre in 1812. Audience capacity, exclusive of standees, was extended to 3,600 and 3,000 respectively, and many aspects of performance were lost, both visually and acoustically, in the vast new spaces. The first theatre building to take a different approach

[2] 'Irving as Stage Manager', *We Saw Him Act*, ed. H. A. Saintsbury and Cecil Palmer (London, 1939), p. 396.

Plate 5   Auditorium of the Surrey Theatre, 1849. *Illustrated London News.*
By courtesy of the Trustees of the Victoria and Albert Museum.

seems to have been a much smaller minor theatre, the Sans Pareil (later the Adelphi) in 1806, when either at its initial construction or at some time afterward the pit was extended under what used to be the first balcony level, thus eliminating the lowest row of boxes but providing a good deal of extra space for benches. This could be done because of the use of iron in the balconies and support posts. It was a modest development that spread to other theatres, although not fully implemented on a commercial scale until the Victorian period, when the rising cost of land and other economic pressures prevented investors from purchasing large sites and building considerable free-standing structures like Drury Lane and Covent Garden. Not until the end of the century and after it were such structures again built, such as D'Oyly Carte's English Opera House (1891), now the Palace, the Hippodrome (1899) and the Coliseum (1904).

Plate 6   Auditorium of the new Surrey Theatre, 1866, during a pantomime.
Illustrated London News. By courtesy of the Trustees of the Victoria and Albert
Museum.

Nevertheless, the Victorians built some very large theatres. The
3,600 seating capacity of Holland's Drury Lane was exceeded by the
3,900 of the Britannia and the 3,800 of Astley's, a theatre containing
a circus ring. The Pavilion at 3,500, the Standard at 3,400, and the
Victoria at 3,000 complete the 1866 Select Committee's list (*Report*,
p. 295) of London theatres with a capacity of over 3,000. Drury Lane
is listed at 3,800. Interestingly, Drury Lane is the only West End
theatre in this list, the other large theatres being built well away from
the fashionable areas to accommodate the sizeable popular audience
from the lower middle and working class. The pressure of population and urban growth and the expectation on the part of investors
of ever-enlarging audiences were responsible for such increases in
size and audience capacity, which could not have been achieved

without the deepening of balconies and their extension over the pit made possible by new construction methods. These involved the use of iron trusses, stanchions and girders. With the application of steel construction to theatres in the 1880s and 1890s, the old supporting posts could be eliminated entirely and the cantilevered balconies made still deeper. By this time, however, the tendency was to build smaller theatres for the spoken word, not larger, and the architectural emphasis was on intimacy rather than scale. Whether small or large, theatres displayed the same general auditorium shape: a lower floor of stalls and pit extending under the dress circle to the back and side walls, with the circle and additional balconies wrapped around and above the lower floor in the graceful curves of a horseshoe (favoured for acoustics), a bell or a semi-circle.

Thus the audiences of the Victorian theatre, like earlier audiences, could be seen as well as see, a particularly important point to the beautifully dressed and jewelled ladies in the boxes and the front of the dress circle in the late nineteenth century. There was no use in dressing like this for a dark auditorium; both self-display and the observation of other members of the audience were possible only in a good light. This may explain the hostile reaction to darkening the house during the first London stagings of Wagner's *Ring* cycle in 1882 and 1892, for an opera audience was notably well dressed. And it may also explain the very leisurely adoption of the modern practice of virtually blacking out the auditorium while the play is in progress, a custom that did not become general in the West End until after the First War. There was certainly no technical reason why it could not be done, even with gaslight. The explanation was social and not technical: the Victorian theatre was a place of social resort as well as a facility for the performance of a play. This was especially true earlier in our period (and well before that, of course); as time passed and manners changed audiences became quieter and more decorous, and people commonly went to the theatre for the sole purpose of seeing a play – a purpose admirably fulfilled, for better or worse, in our own darkened proscenium-arch theatres, where we sit facing front in religious silence, our only dim view of other members of the audience being the backs of their heads. It is difficult to be noisy in a dark auditorium or quiet in a bright one, and a constant source of complaint even near the end of the nineteenth century was the conversational zeal of many members of the audience and their habit of ignoring the stage for minutes on end in order to indulge in private chatter well above the level of a whisper. That this chatter was social and not about the performance tells us something of the nature of the late Victorian theatre experience.

Audiences that dressed better and more fashionably were likely to insist on appropriate standards of decoration and comfort and these the managers of West End and the classier provincial theatres were happy to provide. The elegant neo-classical mouldings, delicate designs, and light colours of the Georgian theatre – the golds, the creams, the pale greens – were gradually replaced by heavier and more ornate plaster reliefs and darker colours. In 1876, for example, the Bancrofts redecorated the Prince of Wales's, replacing the light blue of the old scheme with amber satin and dark red 'and, to harmonize with a peacock frieze over the proscenium, which was very elaborately painted on a gold ground, handsome fans made of peacock's feathers were attached to each of the private boxes by gilt chains'.[3] Auditoriums became decoratively fussy (as did contemporary living-rooms) with much emphasis on richly coloured hangings. Not all theatres went this way, but by 1900 the dark golds and heavy crimsons of the Edwardian theatre were prominent.

Standards of comfort were also changing, in the theatre as much as in the home. That ubiquitous staple of theatre seating for nearly two centuries, the backless bench, was no longer acceptable to an age that also rejected long hours in the theatre. The placing of backs on benches was one small step in the right social direction; more significant was the introduction of chairs in the pit in the form of stall seats. The orchestra stall seems to have been introduced either at the Lyceum during the visit of a French company in 1828, or at the opera (the King's Theatre) in 1829, and confined to a few rows at the front of the pit. Benjamin Webster at the Haymarket put in stalls in 1843, as well as adding backs to his pit benches. Slowly the stalls pushed these benches farther and farther back, although a glance at illustrations of mid-Victorian theatres like the Gaiety and the new Adelphi show that half the lower floor was still given over to pit benches, backed or not. The 1866 Select Committee *Report* shows that in terms of capacity the pit at all West End theatres except the Adelphi and Her Majesty's opera house could take many more spectators than the stalls; even the Prince of Wales's had only 90 stalls to 300 pit places. The climax of this trend was reached when Bancroft laid out the whole floor of the Haymarket with stall seats in 1880. In less daring theatres the pit was eventually banished to a few dark and airless rows of benches beneath the overhang of the dress circle, where it languished until the 1950s and final abolition. Rather later than the introduction of stalls was the designation of the first balcony as the dress circle – where, as in the stalls, one had to wear

---

[3] *Mr and Mrs Bancroft On and Off the Stage*, vol. II, p. 73.

formal evening dress – and here too chairs rather than benches were provided. The boxes remained but became fewer in number and ultimately survived only next to the proscenium, with the worst sightlines in the house but the best position for seeing and being seen.

The division of an audience into box, pit and gallery had been distinguishing features of auditorium design since the Restoration. These categories roughly corresponded to status and income levels among the patrons: the aristocracy and the fashionable in the boxes; the lawyer, critic, student and tradesman in the pit; the servant, apprentice and journeyman in the gallery. During the reign of Victoria these divisions continued to reflect class structure; indeed, they were intensified in many theatres by the careful provision of separate payboxes, entrances and refreshment spaces for the different classes of audience, so that well-dressed holders of stalls, boxes and dress circle seats would not have to rub shoulders with humble pittites, who in turn would be protected from contact with the denizens of the gallery. When the new Her Majesty's Theatre in the Haymarket opened in 1897, it was furnished with discrete entrances for the boxes, stalls and dress circle, for the pit, for the upper circle and for the gallery. Not only this: there were also separate *exits* for the stalls, for the dress circle, for the pit and for the gallery. Four segregated bars served the gallery and upper circle, the dress circle, the stalls and boxes and the pit.

One class of patron was not especially popular in the Victorian theatre – prostitutes. Early in the century they swarmed in corridors and certain poorly lit sections of the Drury Lane and Covent Garden auditoriums and were much resented, not only by the morally censorious but also by many members of the audience who did not want to expose their womenfolk to such insalubrious sights and presences. Managers must have had mixed feelings, for prostitutes paid their way and attracted a clientele of their own into the theatre. Macready seems to have been the first manager to have made a determined effort to keep out prostitutes, for which he was commended in the press, and the problem gradually ceased to be a matter of much concern, at least for the theatre, if not for the music hall and the penny gaff.[4] However, since parts of the West End – especially the Haymarket – were notorious haunts of prostitutes all through

[4] Penny gaffs were small theatres in working-class districts, usually converted shops, patronised mostly by juveniles. They were the 'lowest' form of urban theatre; in the early and mid-Victorian periods there were scores of them in London and many more in the larger industrial cities. Their repertory consisted mostly of cut-down melodramas and pantomimes and comic songs.

Plate 7 The gallery at a Drury Lane pantomime, 1893. *Illustrated London News*. By courtesy of the Trustees of the Victoria and Albert Museum.

the mid and late Victorian periods, there would have been no avoiding them in the streets, for they made a practice of congregating outside, if not inside, theatres. In this respect the East End was as bad as the West.

The separation of the classes by seating divisions was a business as well as a social matter, and we have already seen how the spread of the stalls and the sharp increase in their price was calculated to raise box-office revenue from an increasingly prosperous and increasingly theatre-minded middle class. Business practice, in fact, determined the structure and nature of Victorian theatre. It started with the building: affordable land was not commonly available on main urban thoroughfares, so that investors and builders either used very narrow frontages for their theatres or gave the public access to them by mean narrow alleyways or courts running from principal streets. Since a theatre's profits came firstly from the sale of seats and secondly from refreshment areas, seats were jammed as closely together as possible and foyer space was sacrificed to bar space. Dressing-rooms and other facilities for performers were usually quite inadequate and sometimes downright dangerous.

SANITATION

There might, therefore, be an air of luxury and refinement out front, but elsewhere it was a different matter. In this regard John Hollingshead is witheringly critical of the theatres of the 1860s, 'nearly all badly built, badly lighted, badly seated, with inconvenient entrances, narrow winding passages, and the most defective sanitary arrangements. They smelt of escaped gas, orange peel, tom-cats, and mephitic vapours.'[5] Such conditions did not improve until the authorities began to pay attention. Cyril Maude was positive that his wife Winifred Emery caught typhoid in a dressing-room at the Comedy Theatre (opened in 1881) because of faulty drainage, and was horrified at the sanitary conditions of the Vaudeville in 1888 (opened in 1870):

> The smell of bad drainage was so noisome underneath the stage that when one had to cross from left to right below (our only means of crossing, as the stage was small and overcrowded with scenery mostly), one had very carefully to hold one's breath and smother one's nose in one's pocket-handkerchief. The passage up to the Vaudeville stage door from the Strand was a miserably dirty court with the lowest of the low inhabiting filthy doss-houses on the side opposite to the stage door ... The dressing-

[5] *Gaiety Chronicles*, p. 6.

room accommodation was very meagre and sordid, and the stench everywhere was *abominable*.[6]

The erstwhile Chairman of the London County Council's Theatres and Music Halls Committee was even more specific in his testimony to the 1892 Select Committee, drawing his material from an authoritative report in the *Times*:

> Little care has been bestowed upon the sanitary arrangements, especially below the stage and behind the scenes, as well as in the cloak-rooms, &c. of the auditorium ... Dressing-rooms are often quite inadequate, faulty in situation, in air space, in ventilation, in the number of windows, and in water supply. Water-closets and urinals are frequently placed in improper situations, bad forms are used, and sometimes the workmanship is at fault. They are often ventilated into dressing-rooms, refreshment-rooms, lobbies, staircases, and even on to the stage. Ventilation is frequently unprovided for in rooms behind the scenes ... The majority of the defects are of structural origin, and hence it is impossible to prevent these from being constant sources of danger. The effects produced on the health of the audience were theatre headache and theatre diarrhoea; and of the actors were sore throats, loss of voice, typhoid fever, so called rheumatism, and habits of intemperance. Certain theatres are recognised in the theatrical profession as risky places to play in, from the liability of illness being engendered.   (1892 *Report*, pp. 10–11)

Another witness told the Select Committee that none of the dressing-rooms at Covent Garden, by then a lavishly appointed opera house, were ventilated, and that it had one W.C. for the entire cast of principals, supers and ballet (p. 181).

SAFETY AND FIRE PROTECTION

Such a state of affairs could not be allowed to continue, and indeed for some time past theatre safety, particularly fire safety, had been a matter of public concern. A French critic of the English way of doing things had complained in 1867 that 'the particular mode of construction for the interior and the stage is left an open question, no apparatus in case of fire is fixed upon, heating and ventilation are not obligatory, workshops are not interdicted, neither are there any stringent regulations relating to the comfortable seating of the public'.[7] The problem was partly that the statutory authority over theatres (since the Act of 1843), the Lord Chamberlain, did not bother much with matters of sanitation, comfort or even fire protec-

---

[6] *Behind the Scenes with Cyril Maude* (London, 1927), pp. 72–74.
[7] M. G. Davioud, 'A French Survey of English Theatres', *Builder* (June 1867). Quoted in Richard Leacroft, *The Development of the English Playhouse* (London, 1973), p. 226.

tion. He licensed all London theatres (but not music halls) except Drury Lane and Covent Garden, which still operated under royal patents. From the 1850s his officials did undertake inspections, complete with written reports submitted to the managers, inspections which at first did not even include the area behind the stage. In 1878, however, an act of Parliament gave the new Metropolitan Board of Works authority over the construction of London theatres and music halls – previously the Lord Chamberlain's office would inspect theatre plans – with special emphasis on fireproofing and adequate exits. Ten years later the Local Government Act gave county councils the responsibility of licensing buildings for stage plays. The London County Council, also a new authority, established the aforementioned Theatres and Music Halls Committee for this purpose; it also had the power to enforce its own safety code, which was far more extensive and detailed than any preceding regulations.[8]

One of the matters in which the new Committee was immediately involved was the reduction of overcrowding as a precaution against the loss of life in theatre fires. In the eighties and nineties seating capacities shrank by law. Drury Lane went down from 3,000 after the 1870 renovations to 2,500 in 1892, the Britannia from 3,923 to 3,450, the Standard from 3,400 to 2,800. These were large theatres, but the same thing also happened to smaller ones. The St James's, with 1,220 seats after the 1870 reconstruction, dropped to 1,000, and even the little Prince of Wales's was reduced from 814 in 1866 to 560 by the time it was closed as unsafe in 1882. A legal reduction of this kind, combined with the current tendency to build smaller theatres in the West End, meant that the days of the vast theatre auditorium in London were pretty much over. To the mid-Victorians, however, the highest seating capacity for a London theatre today, the Coliseum's 2,358, would have seemed only moderate.

Overcrowding was one aspect of safety; the larger issue, fire prevention, had by the 1880s led to a considerable literature of its own, notably *Prevention of Fire in Theatres* (1882) by Captain Shaw of the London Fire Brigade. Ever since the adoption of gas as a means of illuminating the stage in the first half of the nineteenth century, every theatre in Britain had become a potential death trap. Not only did gas leak from ill-fitting joints or perished tubing, but flaming out of unguarded or poorly guarded jets set fire to dancers, ignited scenery, curtains and borders, and generally constituted an

[8] These regulations, which were proclaimed in 1892, are printed in the 1892 Select Committee *Report*, pp. 400–405.

Plate 8 The audience of the Britannia Theatre at a benefit performance, 1901.
By courtesy of the Trustees of the Victoria and Albert Museum.

appalling risk in theatres with virtually no fire regulations. The hundreds of gas jets burning above and around the stage caused such high temperatures, sometimes over 100 degrees Fahrenheit on the gridiron, the highest point above the stage, that every material – wood, cloth, canvas, velvet, muslin, etc. – was tinder dry. For the benefit of the 1866 Select Committee, Shaw listed fifty fires that had broken out in London theatres in the last thirty-three years. Of these, six resulted in the total or almost total destruction of the theatre: Astley's (1841), the Garrick (1846), the Olympic (1849), the Pavilion (1856), Covent Garden (1856) and the Surrey (1865). In the provinces the situation was just as bad, with at least twenty-six theatres destroyed by fire between 1839 and 1880. The loss of the brand-new Theatre Royal, Exeter, in 1887, with over a hundred deaths, provoked a public outcry and a flurry of safety inventions. New safety curtains were installed, and experiments ranged from devices for extinguishing a fire quickly to fireproofing materials. Terry's Theatre, which opened several months after the Exeter fire, incorporated an asbestos safety curtain and an overhead stage sprinkler system (manual, not automatic). Calls were made to fireproof scenery, costumes and properties, to use iron instead of wood wherever possible, to redesign exit staircases, to install safety curtains that actually worked, and to use electricity instead of gas.

THE STAGE AND STAGE MACHINERY

Together with changes in auditorium design, seating arrangements and, tardily, safety practices, went changes in the relationship between stage and auditorium and the way in which the stage was used. The eighteenth-century stage was nearly uniform in design. A forestage projected beyond the proscenium arch, ending in a straight line or a slight curve. Directly on the audience side of the pro-scenium, where the front curtain hung, and on each side of it, stood a door, sometimes with a stage box or a window over it. Actors entered and exited through these doors, or between the wings on each side of the stage behind the proscenium arch. The back of the scenic area was closed off by shutters, their stage position dependent on the space and mechanical requirements for the next scene. Actors tended to come down front onto the forestage in order to catch the light from the footlights and the auditorium; the area behind the proscenium was poorly lit, and what light there was illuminated the scenery more than the actors. The front curtain was raised at the beginning of the play and usually remained up until the end of it; scene changes took place in full view of the audience.

During the various renovations and rebuildings of Drury Lane and Covent Garden at the end of the eighteenth and early in the nineteenth century, changes were made in the stage. The proscenium doors were taken away, put back at the request of the actors and taken away again. By 1837 they survived only in lesser London theatres and in the provinces. The forestage was further shortened, a process that had been going on since the end of the seventeenth century. In its place went the new orchestra stalls. Indeed, the stage was moving with architectural inevitability toward its final Victor-ian form: the picture-frame stage. The idea of the stage as a picture and the proscenium as its frame had been in the air for many years. George Saunders declared in 1790 that 'the scene is the picture, and the frontispiece, or in other words the frame, should contrast the picture, and thereby add to the illusion',[9] and Benjamin Wyatt said of his 1812 Drury Lane that the proscenium 'is to the Scene what the

---

[9] George Saunders, *A Treatise on Theatres* (London, 1790), p. 128.

frame of a Picture is to the Picture itself'.[10] Increasingly, as we shall see, the arts of painting and production came closer together. This development was concluded architecturally in 1880, when Bancroft put a moulded and gilded picture-frame, two feet wide, around the proscenium of the Haymarket, flush with the front of the stage. No longer could the actor come downstage into the auditorium in a close relationship with the pit in front of him and the stage boxes on either side of him. Fixed behind the proscenium, he was now part of a stage picture, integrated with scenic effect and lighting in a manner previously impossible. This time, the actors did not protest.

In fact, one of the striking features of the relationship between stage and audience in the Victorian period, especially after the introduction of the picture-frame stage, is the unanimous acceptance of the stage form. Nobody complained – as they certainly do today – about proscenium theatres, even large ones. Actors were happy working in them; audiences were happy seated in them. They did, of course, constitute the only form available. The picture-frame stage itself well suited the growing passivity and detachment of the Victorian middle-class audience. The attack on the proscenium theatre and the picture-frame stage, when it came, came almost entirely from theorists and the new breed of director and designer, not from actors or audience.[11]

The actual structure of the Victorian stage, as distinct from its architectural form, was inherited from the eighteenth century. What the audience saw was a rectangular proscenium opening; behind it was a working space larger than the auditorium itself. On both sides the stage extended into the wings to a distance more than equal to the width of the proscenium opening; that is, if the average fair-sized late Victorian provincial stage, designed to take the scenery of touring companies, had a proscenium opening 30' wide, then a minimum of 17' 6" on each side of that opening was needed for wing space and the accommodation of scenery and sub-stage machinery. Similarly, the height of the stage behind the opening was at least double that of the opening itself, say about 50'–60' for the standard 25'–30' proscenium height. The distance from the proscenium to the back wall of the stage, which was usually the back wall of the theatre and hidden from the audience by scenery, depended on the size of the lot the theatre was built on and could vary from 30' to 80'. The

[10] Benjamin Wyatt, *Observations on the Design for the Theatre Royal, Drury Lane* (London, 1813). Quoted in *The Development of the English Playhouse*, p. 167.

[11] William Poel, the founder of the Elizabethan Stage Society in 1894, had been an actor and was certainly opposed to the proscenium theatre. However, he used his platform stage only for antiquarian reconstructions of Shakespeare and other Elizabethan and Jacobean dramatists, not as a form suitable for other kinds of drama.

Plate 9   The gridiron, Tyne Theatre, Newcastle, showing drum and shaft
mechanism. By courtesy of the Museum of London.

area beneath the stage was excavated, ideally, to a depth of 30' for
the operation of the sub-stage machinery, but sometimes a high
water table made such a depth impossible.

At the very top of the backstage space, high above the stage, was
the gridiron. When the Victorian theatre began to use the space
above the stage more extensively than did the Georgian, employing
flying mechanisms for scenery as well as for special machines like
chariots and clouds descending from the heavens, the stage roof had
to be raised. Thus the modern fly-tower was born. The gridiron was
made of narrow wooden joists laid on beams, with sufficient space
between the joists to allow the passage of ropes attached to the scenes
or cloths, the borders of canvas that masked the above-stage impedi-
menta – the act drops, the front curtain, the gas battens – everything
that had to be raised, lowered and hung out of sight of the audience.
These ropes passed over pulleys, thence to a great drum over the
gridiron, and from there to cleats on the rail of a fly gallery between
the gridiron and the stage floor. Since until the very end of the
period all stage operations were managed manually and almost all
involved the lifting of heavy lumber and fabrics, counterweighting

Plate 10   The upper stage left fly gallery, Tyne Theatre, Newcastle, showing the flying lines. By courtesy of the Museum of London.

was extensively utilised to give the stage hands some mechanical advantage and to make these tasks humanly possible. Every theatre had at least one fly gallery attached to each side of the wall of the stage, running from the proscenium to the back wall. Many theatres had two on each side, and the largest three or four. They were accessible by stairs or ladders from the stage and staff could cross from right to left by a bridge at the back wall and by narrow catwalks farther downstage. The principal working gallery seems to have been the opposite prompt (o.p.) or stage right gallery; here a veritable jungle of ropes descended from the gridiron and were manipulated by the flymen at the stage manager's or prompter's signal, often with the aid of windlasses. The journalist George Augustus Sala left in 1855 a vivid impression of the fly galleries, describing his ascent to the carpenter's shop right under the roof of the theatre:

> We cross the darkened stage, and, ascending a very narrow staircase at the back thereof, mount into the lower range of 'flies.' A mixture this of the between-decks of a ship, a rope-walk, and the old wood-work of the

Chain-pier at Brighton. Here are windlasses, capstans, ropes, cables, chains, pulleys innumerable. Take care! or you will stumble across the species of winnowing-machine, used to imitate the noise of wind, and which is close to the large sheet of copper which makes the thunder. The tin cylinder, filled with peas, used for rain and hail, is down stairs; but you may see the wires, or 'travellers', used by 'flying fairies,' and the huge counterweights and lines which work the curtain and act-drop. Up then, again, by a ladder, into range of flies No. 2, where there are more pulleys, windlasses, and counterweights, with bridges crossing the stage, and lines working the borders, and gas-pipes, with coloured screens, called 'mediums,' which are used to throw a lurid light of moonlight on scenes of battles or conflagrations, where the employment of coloured fires is not desirable.[12]

Attached to the underside of the lowest fly gallery on each side were grooves into which the tops of the wings and shutters fitted for sliding into position for a new scene, or sliding off at the end of one just past. The top grooves were hinged to keep them out of the way when not in use and let down when a scene change occurred. The floor of the stage had several corresponding sets of grooves – most theatres had four sets – parallel to the proscenium. The advantage of this system, which in its essentials dated back to the Jacobean court masque and the Restoration theatre, was that scenery could be changed quickly: one set of wings and back shutters (the latter running right across the stage) withdrawn to reveal another in place behind it. Because the system was so standardised – matching sets of wings, shutters, and borders existed for palaces, streets, forests, cottages, prisons, country views, etc. – a large repertory could be mounted with relative ease, since, for example, a forest set could serve any play containing a forest scene. New scenes were painted for spectacles and for any occasion when the management particularly wished to impress; old ones were touched up by the scene-painter. This system served a theatre whose public knew perfectly well that they were watching a play and did not insist on the illusion of reality; scenery was a selective and aesthetic, almost suggestive representation of the interior and exterior world, not a replication of it.

To the Victorians, who were coming more and more to accept the doctrine of realism, or at least verisimilitude, in art, even in the theatre, the old methods seemed increasingly inadequate. They began to complain about matters that did not disturb the Georgians: the stiff geometry of the wings; the actors and stage staff visible in

[12] G. A. Sala, 'Getting Up a Pantomime', *Household Words*, vol. 20 (December 1851), pp. 289–96.

the wings from certain parts of the auditorium; the jerky progress of the shutters across the stage, each half pushed in its groove by a stage carpenter; the sharp dividing line between the shutters, clearly visible even when they were perfectly joined, which was often not the case; the inability of the flat, two-dimensional scenery to create a believable environment – in fact they were really complaining of the sheer *theatricality* of production technique. Gradually the groove system began to disappear, although it lasted in the provinces until the end of the century. It was replaced by flown scenery and free-standing scenes secured to the stage floor by braces or mounted on wheeled platforms. The new scenery was built out, three-dimensional, with, for example, rounded and solid-looking tree trunks instead of painted ones. Late Victorian theatres often used – as did Irving's Lyceum in the 1880s – a mixture of built-out scenery and the groove system, of painted sliding flats and three-dimensional solidity. The new scenery could be constructed of wood and canvas but was frequently made of moulded papier-mâché. For interior scenes, the box set with walls and a ceiling slowly replaced wings and shutters. Scene changes took longer and had now to be concealed from the audience by a front cloth which descended to hide the change going on behind. This procedure led to the necessity of the dramatist writing a 'carpenter's scene', which took place on the narrow strip between the front cloth and the edge of the stage, while carpenters banged and hammered away behind, getting ready a scene which would take up the whole depth of the stage. Intervals lengthened as both spectacle and the large-scale reproduction of the environment grew more popular and as more big scenes were written into new plays or deemed essential for revivals; additional stagehands had to be employed to work them. A prettily painted curtain called the act drop, frequently bearing a classical landscape, now fell at the end of each act, and the use of curtains of one kind or another to conceal changes became much more frequent.

The machinery beneath the stage, as vital to production and as traditional as the grooves, wings and shutters above it, was responsible for anything appearing from beneath the stage or sinking through it, including actors. The stage floor itself was largely made up of removable planking so constructed as to drop and slide off, when necessary, to right and left beneath the wings. This left openings for raising scenery or actors to stage level by three kinds of sub-stage devices: the bridge, the sloat and the trap.

Most decent-sized stages had four bridges, each one situated between a set of grooves and parallel to them; the narrow sloat cuts – there were usually eight – were located between the bridges. Like the

Plate 11   The mezzanine, Tyne Theatre, Newcastle, showing sloat and bridge winches. By courtesy of the Museum of London.

sloats and the traps, the bridges were operated from the first level down, the mezzanine, by ropes passing below to the last sub-stage level, the cellar, into which scenes could be lowered and which contained the drum and shaft used for raising each bridge. The ropes from the bridges were attached to these shafts by means of other ropes leading from the drums to windlasses in the mezzanine. The bridges themselves were heavy wooden platforms ranging approximately in size from 12' × 3' to 28' × 4' and although counterweighted rose slowly, noisily and jerkily to the stage floor. (It was no coincidence that the theatre orchestra always played vigorously and loudly during scene changes.) The sloat was a device for raising scenic flats such as a profile board ground row (rocks on the seashore, or a flowery meadowbank) through a narrow cut in the stage.

Trapwork was an important element of Victorian staging. Except for the upstage Corsican Trap, the traps were located downstage of the first set of grooves (nearest to the proscenium) and they were of several kinds. A Grave Trap, dead centre stage, was really a small

Plate 12   'Lifting a Fairy', 1893. *Strand Magazine.*

6′ × 3′ bridge. On either side of it, and slightly farther downstage, was a smaller trap, which could raise a single actor on a small platform slowly or quickly to stage level, according to the demands of the dramatic situation. These traps were popularly employed for the appearance and disappearance of ghosts in melodrama and demons and good fairies in pantomime. The smaller traps could be adapted for trick effects. Seemingly passing through the solid earth, a performer could arrive miraculously in the middle of a scene; this was achieved by speeding up the raising process and passing the sprite or demon through a circle of small hinged flaps, which fell back instantly after the passage of the actor's body, leaving no visible opening. Such an adaptation was called a Star Trap. Operated forcefully, it shot a performer dangerously high above the stage. (All traps were operated by stagehands hauling on ropes.) The Conquest management of the Grecian Theatre specialised in thrilling aerial pantomime combats involving the complex use of traps and overhead trapezes. A performer could disappear through a Vampire Trap as rapidly as he could appear through a Star Trap. A 'vamp' could either be placed in the stage floor or in a flat, and consisted of two hinged flaps; a performer stepping into it or diving through it simply vanished, for it was indistinguishable from the surrounding stage floor or painted flat. The Vampire was used chiefly in pantomime, but was also employed in melodrama. Indeed, it had been expressly developed for the sudden dissolution of the eponymous villain in Planché's *The Vampire* (1820), and was known in France as 'la trappe anglaise'. Another trap invented for a particular play was the Corsican Trap, devised for the mysterious appearance of the murdered Louis dei Franchi to his brother in *The Corsican Brothers*, the apparition rising gradually through the floor as he drifted from stage right to left. The actor stood on a platform which moved up an inclined plane, his body emerging through an opening lined with black bristles or brushes and fixed in strips of wood glued on canvas or 'scruto'. This revolved in a belt that seemed part of the stage, and travelled at the same speed as the rising platform containing the ghost. This trap had the honour for many years of disgorging, to the well-known Ghost Melody in the orchestra, the most famous and longest surviving ghost of the Victorian stage.

To the uninitiated the mezzanine must have seemed a veritable forest of traps, posts supporting the stage floor, sliders, tackle, sloats, and bridges, bustling with stage staff. The comparison with the 'tween-decks area of a ship was often used, and many stage carpenters had previous shipboard experience; they were perfectly at home in the theatre.

The staging methods described above were characteristically English; that is, although elements were shared in common with European countries there were marked differences, notably in the stage and sub-stage mechanisms. In Europe, for example, there were no fixed downstage positions for the traps and the chariot and pole method of changing scenery was in use. This comprised 'a framework under the stage floor, with an upright or "pole" passing through and above the floor. The "chariot" travels upon wheels running on a line of rails [on the mezzanine], and by this means the "pole" can be moved along the "slit" from one side of the stage to the other ... A "scene" can be fixed to the "pole", and can be easily moved, either on the stage, or on the "mezzanine" level, by pushing the frame along the rails.'[13] When he took over the management of the Lyceum in 1863, the French actor-manager Charles Fechter rebuilt the stage in the French manner, incorporating the chariot and pole system. However, after he left the Lyceum in 1867 the stage was reconstructed along the old lines. Even though a partial chariot and pole system was installed at the new English Opera House in 1891, the European method never really caught on in Britain.

This is not surprising. The English theatre was highly traditional and resisted change, especially in the area of technology. This fact was deplored by the more scientifically and technically minded toward the end of the nineteenth century, when the introduction and development of new stage machinery in continental theatres was in full swing. As we know, safety and protection against fire was one area badly in need of rethinking. New materials as well as new regulations were required, and the English attachment to wood as the all-purpose material for exit staircases, auditorium construction, the stage and machinery was much criticised by architects and technical journals. As early as 1840, R. M. Stephenson took out a patent for iron machinery to operate the scenery for a production at the Royalty Theatre in London, but it was too heavy to be worked manually, or even by a horse, and was abandoned after a few nights. The experiment of substituting iron for wood was not repeated for a long time. In 1861 the *Builder* condemned the old-fashioned machinery of the English stage compared to the German stage, especially 'the miserable contemptible mechanism' under the stage, and thought it peculiar 'that in England, where the application of machinery is more advanced than in any other country, the theatrical stages are perhaps the most ill-arranged and old-fashioned of any country' (20 April). In 1886 the *Engineer* deplored the failure of managers to install labour-saving hydraulic machinery for powering at least the front curtain and the act drop, and said of the Lyceum, 'It is curious to note the prejudice against iron existing amongst theatrical machinists; out of all the hoisting drums used at the theatre we found only two with iron barrels and gear: the old form of wooden wheel and axle prevails, and the same remark applies to ropes, which we were informed constantly have to be renewed, whereas if made of steel wire they would be far more durable' (2 April). In 1898 the *Electrician* concluded that the English

[13] E. O. Sachs and Ernest Woodrow, *Modern Opera Houses and Theatres* (London, 1896–98), vol. III Supplement, p. 15.

stage was much readier to recognise the advantage of electricity for lighting than for mechanical power, the theatre being far behind the general public in this respect, 'for it appears to possess no engineering tradition whatever. Not merely electrical power, but every form of mechanical power is practically unknown in stage-land ... The traditional methods to be found [on large modern stages] compare with modern engineering practice as much as a rope-hauling crowd of ancient Assyrians would compare with an electric motor' (30 December).

In fairness to the English stage, it must be pointed out that the thorough application in Europe of the principles of advanced engineering to stage construction and machinery dates only from the 1880s, and even then was only relevant to new constructions. Reformist zeal originated with engineers and architects, not with those who actually worked with the machinery. The stage engineer was a novel European occupation; the construction and operation of the English stage was mostly in the hands of stage carpenters holding to long-established practices. It was also obvious that the European preservation in state theatres of a genuine repertory that required almost nightly changes of dramatic fare necessitated a mechanical setup that would enable these changes to be made as efficiently and expeditiously as possible; there was no need for this in the commercial long-run system of the mid and late Victorian stage. From a business point of view, it was also far more difficult for the English actor-manager or investor to find capital out of his own pocket for expensive new machinery and the stage engineer; the theatres that went in for that sort of thing in Europe enjoyed public subsidy.

Nevertheless, in the last decade of the nineteenth century, some mechanical innovation did reach the English stage. Beerbohm Tree installed a flat instead of a raked stage in Her Majesty's in 1897, despite pooh-poohing from the profession. D'Oyle Carte's English Opera House had a wood and iron stage in addition to the partial chariot and pole system, and metal was used in the bridges and stage fittings. Five hydraulically powered bridges were built into the stage of the Lyric Theatre, London, at some point after it opened in 1888; Drury Lane installed two hydraulic bridges in 1897 and four electric bridges in 1899. In 1901 Covent Garden installed six electric bridges. These developments were lauded in the technical journals.

SCENE-PAINTING

The nature of Victorian stage production was as much painterly as mechanical and machinery was a means to a pictorial end. The art of the scene-painter was essential to the Victorian theatre in providing not only a pictorial representation of the world of a play, but also – depending upon the talent of the scenic artist and the quality of lighting – a beautiful impression of the natural world, if the scene were exterior. Early Victorian theatres had their resident scene-painters; the occupation could be dynastic, marked by dominant families like the Grieves and the Telbins. Later it became a common practice in London to contract scene-painting out to specialist studios that might be painting scenes for several theatres simultaneously. Whether in a theatre or not, a large painting studio was necessary. Before he moved to the studio the artist, in consultation with the manager, worked out the composition, colouring and lighting of his scenery on a scale model of the stage. A frame perhaps 40′ wide and 25′ high held the wood and canvas scene, and it could either be winched up and down through a cut in the floor which in a theatre led to the stage, or remain stationary while the artist raised and lowered the platform from which he was painting. In France scenes were laid flat on the floor and the painter walked over them with long-handled brushes. If in a theatre a separate studio was not available, the frame was fixed to the back wall of the stage and the rear gallery connecting the flies on each side used as a painting bridge. Frequently scenes were painted on cloths that were rolled when hung above the stage, a necessity in the days before fly towers when there was no adequate flying space. However rolled cloths took up more room and needed extra ropes and stagehands for their operation, and the constant rolling and unrolling led to serious wear and tear on paint and fabric.

One kind of scene that necessitated rolling and unrolling during the course of a performance, and was a notable pre-Victorian example of the romantic scene-painter's art, was the moving pano-rama or diorama – the words were virtually interchangeable in theatrical usage. The panorama unrolled as a single or double canvas from one side of the stage and was rolled up on the other; it was popular for depicting a journey or a change of natural setting, in Shakespeare as well as pantomime. Scenes could also be painted on 'gauzes' – linen or muslin – which when lit from the front looked like, for instance, the back wall of a room with door and windows, but when lit from behind (with the lights off or very low in front) revealed another scene entirely, perhaps the vision of a murder. An unpainted but dyed gauze could be kept down to provide misty, romantic effects, as Phelps did at Sadler's Wells for the middle three acts of *A Midsummer Night's Dream*.

In a large theatre the chief scene-painter did not do all the painting himself; the job was too big for one man. Other painters might take charge of some scenes in the same production. In a small provincial or touring company the single scene-painter might also be carpenter or stage manager, as well as coming on in small parts. In a London studio or major theatre a scenic artist would employ assistants for particular work on each scene, reserving the initial outlining with charcoal and ink and the difficult finishing bits for himself; naturally the designs were his. Fairly simple tasks, like soaking the canvas with size, priming it with whiting, drawing long straight lines, and 'laying in' masses of colour for the sky or foreground, were done by assistants. A colourman would grind and mix the colours which were purchased either as solid blocks or powder. Only a few colours came ready for use without grinding or mixing with water. The scene was then painted in distemper. Frederick Lloyds, who painted for Charles Kean, recommends thirty-one colours for the scene-painter, from plain white through venetian red and burnt sienna to blue verditer and drop black.[14] For greater effect, and especially for pantomimes, finished scenes were enriched with coloured foils and Dutch metal, an expensive high-glitter gilt leaf. The younger William Telbin, a principal scenic artist for Irving, believed that it was better to work from the back of the stage to the front, since presumably the nearer a scene to the audience the more subtle and detailed its finishing.

Because Victorian theatre production was dominated by a pictorial aesthetic, the scenic artist was an important figure; the closer production came to painting the more important he was. With the development of three-dimensional scenery this importance began to decrease, but for a long time built-out scenery co-existed with painted cloths and wings. Such a development marked the slow passage of the theatre from romanticism to realism, a development that can be studied to some extent in the work of the scene-painter. There is a practical reason for the primacy of the scene-painter in the Victorian theatre: for the first time his work was adequately lighted and perceived in far greater detail by the audience. The retreat of the actor behind the picture frame also drew much greater attention to the picture itself, now a bright and living scenic environment rather than a dim background.

LIGHTING AND SCENIC EFFECT

The traditionalism of Victorian stage technology did not extend to lighting; here there was little resistance to change. The theatre went

[14] F. Lloyds, *Practical Guide to Scene Painting and Painting in Distemper* (London, 1875), pp. 14–16.

from candles and oil lamps to electricity in two generations, an even faster progression than the society outside its doors, where electric lighting was pretty much confined to public buildings and wealthy homes until after the First World War. Before gaslight, theatres were lit by a combination of wax candles in the auditorium (in better theatres; others made do with cheaper and smellier tallow) distributed in sconces on the box fronts, and oil-burning lamps for the footlights and the wing lights. These last were arranged in 'ladders' placed behind each wing, vertical constructions of shelving with each shelf containing a lamp. The main function of wing lights was to illuminate the wing behind; the actors came down to the footlights and the auditorium lighting for most of their illumination. The Gas Light and Coke Company was formed in London in 1812, and gas lamps, much admired by the public, were placed on streets, squares, bridges and the fronts of public buildings, including theatres. In 1817 Drury Lane and the Lyceum installed gas lighting for the stage as well as the auditorium; other theatres followed suit. Some withstood innovation: the Haymarket did not introduce gas until 1843 and Sadler's Wells until 1853. In the provinces the conversion process was leisurely, just as it was from gas to electricity many years later.

In the auditorium gas illumination at first took the form of elaborate and beautiful chandeliers, festooned with drops of crystal. They looked most attractive but dazzled the occupants of the upper seats and obstructed their view of the stage. Gradually these chandeliers evolved into the 'sunburner' or 'sunlight' of the mid and late Victorian theatre, the gasburners concentrated together, the chandelier hanging closer to the ceiling, and the whole apparatus venting through flues above it to the outside air – almost the only means of ventilating the auditorium. Auditorium lighting was still left on during performance, although it might be lowered for special effects such as a ghostly vision or a moonlit scene. If anything, however, the level of auditorium light was brighter than it had been with candles, even though this level could now be easily regulated. In 1876 the critic Dutton Cook objected to the new sunburners, which 'shoot down fierce concentrated rays upon the audience ... Aching brows and distressed eyes, unavoidable under the existing system, are sufficient afflictions to warrant a demand for improvement.' Cook called for a compromise with managers: 'Let them make their stages as bright as they list if they will but leave the "auditorium" in twilight.'[15] Five years later Percy Fitzgerald qualified a similar argument: 'The body of the house should be kept dark while the

---

[15] Dutton Cook, *A Book of the Play* (London, 1876), vol. I, p. 168.

play is going on ... That almost Cimmerian gloom which certain theatres affect is an excess, as is also the bright gay glare which is found in French theatres. A theatre should be lit soberly enough to see faces and features and to read a play, but that utter darkness is unnatural, and in a measure destroys the illusion and intensifies the glare on stage.'[16] It is doubtful if the 'utter darkness' referred to meant that the house was completely blacked out during a performance, but certainly some theatres at least were headed in this direction. Irving made a practice of blacking out the Lyceum auditorium during scene changes, but there is no evidence that he did it during the stage action. Such a procedure was still socially unacceptable, and considered inappropriate for certain forms of drama. As late as the 1930s the actor-manager Seymour Hicks believed that for a comedy the house lights should be one-quarter up.

Stage gas lighting was arranged in several parts. At the front of the stage were the footlights. By the use of metal reflectors, the naked gas flame, which could be a foot high, was shielded from the audience, although the heat, glare and foulness of air caused by eighty or a hundred footlights were fearfully unpleasant for the actors. The shields themselves were a good eighteen inches high, and could obstruct the view of spectators in the front orchestra stalls. Many were the complaints about the height of the shields and the glare, and in the 1860s new systems were introduced whereby footlights could be partially sunk and the shields much lower. There were further complaints about the unnatural shadows cast upward upon the face of the actor, but nothing could really be done about this until it was eventually possible to do away with footlights and replace them by efficient lighting from the auditorium, a matter for the twentieth century.

The second main division of stage lighting, the wing lights, was a variation of the old ladder of oil lamps by the attachment of a vertical gas pipe to a wooden upright. The pipe was guarded, not very effectively, by a single wire cage, or the individual jets by wire globes. Because of a history of serious accidents when the dresses of dancers caught fire from contact with wing ladder jets extending almost to the floor, the Lord Chamberlain finally decreed in 1864 that such jets should be no less than four feet above the stage, that they had to be protected by a wire guard, and that wet blankets and buckets of water had to be kept in the wings at all times during a performance. The fire hazard from the footlights was even worse.

The Restoration and eighteenth-century theatre had used over-

---

[16] *The World behind the Scenes*, pp. 18–19.

head chandeliers to light the area behind the proscenium. Garrick got rid of these and introduced wing lights. Early in the Victorian period overhead stage lighting was reintroduced in the form of gas battens, which were lengths of gaspipe fastened to a heavy wooden (later metal) frame; sheet iron protected the wood from the flame. The battens could be anywhere between 25' and 70' long (as long as the proscenium was wide) and each contained scores of jets. They were hung by ropes from the gridiron, parallel to the proscenium, protected by a hoop-like wire guard, and concealed from the audience by the borders. Their number depended on the depth of the stage; four or five were standard in medium-sized theatres. It was their light that made the flies and the gridiron so hot and caused most of the fire risk during performance. The battens immeasurably increased the brightness and glare of the Victorian stage, as well as fully illuminating the upper scenery and making it finally possible for the actor to stay behind the proscenium arch and still be seen clearly.

The last category of gas stage lighting was portable. Varying short lengths of pipe were set up behind furniture, ground rows or other bits of scenery, or hung behind doors and windows in flats. Gas jets were also clustered at the top of a standard or bunch light, a vertical pipe set in a heavy iron base, which could be placed anywhere on the stage. The lengths, standards, wing lights and battens all had to be attached to the source of supply, and the means of connection was flexible hosepipe made of oiled leather or india-rubber attached to gas taps in the side or back walls of the stage; Irving had them set in the floor beside the wings. Whichever way it was done, there was no escaping the hundreds of feet of piping lying about the stage (out of sight of the audience, of course) and posing a hazard to the unwary. The gas supply to the stage and auditorium – there were thousands of jets in a fair-sized theatre – was regulated during performance at the gas plate or gas table on the prompt side by a gasman at the prompter's or stage manager's instructions. A gas plate was fixed to the wall where the mains supply came in.

Before the pilot light was invented around the middle of the century, the lighting of all gas instruments had to be done by hand, an especially cumbersome procedure in the case of the central chandelier or sunburner; in this case a lamplighter poked a long bamboo rod with an ignited sponge soaked in spirits at the end of it at the burners, while leaning out from the ventilating flue above, or actually standing on the chandelier – a perilous operation. Even after pilot lights were used for stage instruments, this primitive method prevailed in the auditorium. The pilot lights themselves had to be lit by hand, since there was no electric ignition. Before a performance the lamplighter went about his duties, lighting up both stage and auditorium; all lights were then turned as low as possible until the audience was admitted and the performance began.

The great advantage of gaslight over oil and candlelight was that it was much brighter and could be regulated. It could not, however, project a beam of light. When it was focussed, limelight could. After a demonstration of its brilliancy on a dark Irish night in 1825 it found its way into the theatre in 1837. By the fifties it was in regular use, and an indispensable part of stage lighting. Limelight was produced by the burning of lime, or calcium oxide, in an oxy-hydrogen flame. The operator controlled his lamp manually, adjusting the lines to the separate oxygen and hydrogen jets and turning the cylinder of lime in the flame by hand or by a rotating wheel outside the box containing the apparatus. The oxygen and hydrogen were stored in leather bags by the operator's feet; weights had to be laid on these bags so that the gas came out under pressure and sometimes the operator stood on the bags to obtain the desired pressure. Later in the century lines led to the instruments themselves from gas storage tanks, or from pressurised cylinders. Limelights were operated from the fly galleries – the lower gallery, if there were two on each side – and from perches behind either side of the proscenium opening; other positions backstage and in the wings were also possible.

The number of limes in use at one time in the big late Victorian spectacles – twenty-five were employed for the Brocken scene in the Lyceum *Faust* and twenty for the Drury Lane *Cinderella* in 1887 – necessitated additional appointments to the theatre's regular lime-light staff (eight under Irving), since there is no evidence that any satisfactory system was developed in which an operator could simultaneously handle more than one lime. Unlike gas, limelight could not be regulated from a central control. It could be focussed, however, as gas burners could not; the front of the lime box could be open for floodlighting or provided with a lens. Colour was also used. A relatively crude colouring process was utilised for footlights and battens, which consisted of placing changeable coloured glasses in front of the footlights and drawing different coloured cloths of silk or calico, sewn together in long strips, over the battens. Not more than three or four colours were possible in such systems. A limelight operator could slide small plates of painted glass into the end of his box, a tricky business when he had to maintain precise control of his beam at the same time. These coloured glasses and silks were known as mediums, and their range was severely limited. Red, amber and blue were the standard mediums. Irving, a specialist who was almost entirely responsible for the much-praised quality and subtlety of the

Lyceum lighting, used mediums of seven colours (red, two shades of amber, four shades of blue), although the Lyceum and other theatres may also have had a 'white frost' medium, which would have softened the unadulterated whiteness of the lime. Some years later the colour range had hardly changed. The limelight plot for Tree's *Henry VIII* in 1910 shows an extra shade of amber, but the whole production was lit – electrics as well as limes – only in white, amber and blue. Subtle lighting effects and area lighting were hardly possible, of course, in a theatre which kept its auditorium lights on; one of the reasons Irving's lighting was so artistic was his low level of house lighting.

Limelight was extremely bright, which is not surprising since it was originally considered as an illuminant for lighthouses. With the electric carbon-arc it was the first focussed light in the theatre and was used as a follow-spot. It was also a beautiful light in the effects it could achieve, being much employed in the depiction of sunrises, sunsets and any sort of romantic spectacle. Indeed, the number of scenes in plays incorporating these effects markedly increased after the lime became a standard feature of stage lighting. Spectacle effects of any kind would have been almost impossible without it, and the fairy scenes of pantomime were especially in its debt. Limelight with colour mediums also reflected well off glass, foil, metal and spangles sewn into costumes or into the set. 'But for this light', said one commentator, 'the most expensive adjuncts of such [spectacular] scenes would be lost to view. The concentrated rays of the lime-light penetrate and illumine where less potent light has little or no effect. Perhaps one of the most dazzlingly beautiful stage-effects that can be produced is a scene where jewelled armour is largely used, with various coloured lime-lights rays reflected upon it. Certainly for brilliance of spectacle we know of no effect more splendid.'[17]

Because it was also very bright and could be focussed, the electric carbon-arc was often confused with limelight, thus the strange term 'electric lime'. For example, in 1855 Charles Kean certainly used focussed light for the scene of Queen Katharine's dream in *Henry VIII*, and in several Shakespeare revivals thereafter. This may have been the first use of focussed light on the stage, but there is no evidence whether it was limelight or the electric carbon-arc. The latter produced its beam by a high voltage current jumping across a gap between two carbon electrodes, which became white-hot and discharged a light of great brilliance. The carbon-arc was hand-operated like the lime, and had to be connected to batteries on the

[17] 'Lime-light', *Stage*, 21 December 1883 in *Victorian Theatrical Trades*, ed. Michael R. Booth (London, 1981), p. 45.

premises, since theatres generated their own electricity until the arrival of a mains supply in the 1890s. The first use of the carbon-arc in an English theatre may have been in a pantomime in 1848. It was probably even brighter than limelight but its beam was not as steady, and limelight gradually ousted it in stage use.

The increasing brightness of stage lighting and the lack of any kind of lighting design – the position of lighting designer did not exist, all lighting being left to the heads of the gas and limelight departments, in consultation with the scenic artist, the stage manager and the manager – meant that unless special romantic effects were desired (and the stage was good at achieving them) actors and scenery were subjected to a general glare. Irving was exceptional as a manager in his use of stage lighting, and also exceptional in con- cerning himself so actively in its colour schemes and effects. Area lighting was hardly thought of, despite complaints like this early one in *Theatrical Observer* in 1826: 'The disposition of the lamps at present, is such that no shadow whatever can be presented to the audience, everything upon the stage and in the audience is a glare of undistinguished lights, painful to the eye ... A more concentrated light would be truly refreshing to the spectator' (15 September). The introduction of limelight and the dimming of at least some audi- toriums helped matters, but over forty years later 'there is no sunlight, no casting of shadows, which makes the whole richness of objects in average daily life ... On the stage the glare of gas is equable – coming from above, below, and from the sides; and such shadows as there are, are the coarse shadows of limelight.'[18] Such a difficulty could be partly remedied by painting shadows on the scene, but this did not reduce glare. The leading West End costume designer (although he was not called that) at the end of the century objected that 'in processions and big spectacles, the habit of reinforc- ing the fiery furnace of the footlights with enormous lime-boxes; and of supplementing these by others at the various entrances, is utterly destructive of light and shade; and drapery subjected to this searching glare loses all its beauty and meaning. Again, a partiality for coloured rays of light threatens to extinguish all colour in the dress, and is greatly to be deplored.'[19] Colour mixing in the modern sense was unknown.

Nevertheless, scenic beauty was notably achieved in the Victorian theatre and the use of light and the scene-painter's art were the only means of attaining it. The first scene of Boucicault's *The Shaughraun* (1875) is set outside a Connemara cottage: '*The ruins of Suil-a-more*

[18] Percy Fitzgerald, *Principles of Comedy and Dramatic Effect* (London, 1870), p. 30.
[19] C. Wilhelm, 'Art in the Ballet', *Magazine of Art* (1895), pp. 50–51.

Castle cover a bold headland in the distance. The Atlantic bounds the picture. Sunset.' In the foreground a girl churns a pail of milk. Any landscape watercolourist would have been pleased to paint this scene, or another one, the opening of A. C. Calmour's *Gilded Crime* (1883):

> The Dell, in Cumberland. A high bank at back of rock-work, covered with moss, ferns, and wild flowers. There is an opening in the centre, down which a narrow stream of water flows with a gurgle into a shallow pool, with a few water lilies upon it, centre. Through opening in rock-work, a distant pretty sunny landscape is seen, the trees forming a kind of arch on either side. Through foliage to R. is seen the top of an Elizabethan cottage ... tufts of grass in the foreground, and a portion of a fallen trunk covered with moss, R. C. Birds sing at intervals.

The combination of lighting and scenic art could also express something more powerful, such as the brooding Dartmoor scene in Watts Phillips's *Not Guilty* (1869):

> In extreme distances a vast extent of moor, wild and undulating, with huge boulder rocks on tors ... On the summit of this heap of rocks, stunted trees with other varieties of wild, coarse vegetation. Framed, so to speak, by this foreground, the quarries stretch out behind, full of caves and crevices, towering up or descending suddenly into deep fissures, old or neglected workings half-hidden by the hardy herbage which clings even to these rugged rocks. The prison is on a height: a gloomy range of buildings which, though distant, dominates by its very presence the savage scene. Convicts are grouped everywhere about at work, quarrying or wheeling off slate in red trucks, under the guard of wardens.

The Brocken scene in the Lyceum *Faust* utilised red limes playing upon massive rocks, in the background a bleak mountain landscape. Its climax was one of light as well as action:

> One minute a wild shrieking, singing crowd of misty shapes, moving hither and thither, clambering over the rocks and up the trees, dancing and turning; the next, after one last shriek, wilder, shriller than the rest, a silent, storm-beaten mountain top deserted but for one flaming form. Then, summoning them once more, he himself plunges into the midst of the reveling. Now the dreary light, that has been strangely glimmering, here glows through film and haze, there sweeps in a rolling vapour; now creeps like a thread, now leaps and plays, lighting up the great mountain and all the rugged shapes, and finally gushes forth, a shower of fiery rain, over the wild and howling crowd of witches, while the rocky ramparts on all their heights are set ablaze.[20]

Finally, the fairyland wonders of pantomime were lavishly revealed in the climactic transformation scene, a complex combination of changing scenery, lighting, music and groupings of performers that would take fifteen or twenty minutes to unfold:

[20] Joseph and Elizabeth Pennell, 'Pictorial Successes of Mr Irving's "Faust"', *Century Magazine*, vol. 35 (December 1887), p. 311.

All will recall in some elaborate transformation scene how quietly and gradually it is evolved. First the 'gauzes' lift slowly one behind the other – perhaps the most pleasing of all scenic effects – giving glimpses of 'the Realms of Bliss,' seen beyond in a tantalising fashion. Then is revealed a kind of half-glorified country, clouds and banks, evidently concealing much. Always a sort of pathetic and at the same time exultant strain rises, and is repeated as the changes go on. Now we hear the faint tinkle – signal to those aloft on 'bridges' to open more glories. Now some of the banks begin to part slowly, showing realms of light, with a few divine beings – fairies – rising slowly here and there. More breaks beyond and fairies rising, with a pyramid of these ladies beginning to mount slowly in the centre. Thus it goes on, the lights streaming on full, in every colour and from every quarter, in the richest effulgence. In some of the more daring efforts, the *'femmes suspendues'* seem to float in the air or rest on the frail support of sprays or branches of trees. While, finally, perhaps, at the back of all, the most glorious paradise of all will open, revealing the pure empyrean itself and some fair spirit aloft in a cloud among the stars, the apex of all. Then all motion ceases; the work is complete; the fumes of crimson, green, and blue fire begin to rise at the wings; the music bursts into a crash of exultation.[21]

The 'richest effulgence' of limelight in this description is complemented by the 'crimson, green, and blue fire'. Coloured fire was a valuable portable lighting device that originated early in the nineteenth century. Chemical powders of varying ingredients – strontium nitrate, sulphur, antimony, copper oxide, mercury sulphide, etc. – were mixed according to the colour desired, placed in iron boxes or pans concealed in the wings, attached to long shafts held by stagehands and ignited. They produced intensely bright, strongly coloured light for a short duration. Green and blue fire was traditional for the appearance of ghosts and spirits, red fire for villains and demons, and other colours such as white, yellow, purple and crimson for prettier and less supernatural effects. Coloured fires – the mixtures can still be purchased – were much used in melodrama and pantomime. They lasted the century, but were especially employed before the advent of limelight and its colour mediums.

The last step in the progress of Victorian lighting technology was, of course, electric light. The Savoy Theatre in London was the first to be lit entirely by electricity, in 1881, both on the stage and in the auditorium, although like other theatres that followed its example it had a complete backup system of gas lighting, a practice adhered to

[21] *The World behind the Scenes*, p. 89. The *femmes suspendues* were strapped individually to long 'irons' passing through the stage floor and securely anchored in the mezzanine. Alternatively, a whole group of them could be brought up on a bridge or on a French device, the *parallèle*, which provided pedestal stands of different heights. A combination of these methods could be used.

until the end of the century. In the 1880s several West End theatres were converted to electricity and new ones built with it, including the Adelphi, the Criterion, Terry's and the Court; provincial conversions were also undertaken. Since there were as yet few electricity supply companies, each theatre generated its own supply, with steam-engines and dynamo placed on ground next to the theatre, or sometimes, to the disapproval of safety experts, within it. Electric stage lighting, with the carbon-filament bulbs then in use, was whiter and colder than gas and better for revealing detail. It also virtually eliminated the appalling risk and the too often frightening reality of fire. Scene-painters had to make a sharp adjustment to it; there were complaints that the electric light revealed deficiencies in the scene that gas did not, and that it was too crude a medium for the traditional beauties of scenic art. The invention of dimmers, which inserted a resistance into the circuit so that lighting levels could be varied, allowed subtler gradations of light than gas was capable of. The new switchboard at Her Majesty's in 1897 had a dimmer scale of 0 to 10 (even the Savoy had six levels) as compared to the Off, ¼, ½, ¾ and Full of most gas-plate controls. The heat and foul atmosphere created by thousands of gas jets burning for several hours also disappeared and managers found that they had to begin heating their theatres in the winter. There did not seem, however, to be much of a reduction in the glare and excessive brightness so often objected to; it took the theatre some time to cope with the artistic possibilities of this new and flexible medium, whose demands and challenges eventually led to the new occupation of lighting designer. Electric light bulbs were at first very low powered, perhaps not more than twenty-five watts (it is hard to tell, because light output was given in candlepower until the watt was devised as a unit of measurement) and there were hundreds of them on the stage; 824 at the Savoy, 850 at the Adelphi. Theatres that had not installed electric light could contract for special purposes. For example, the Comedy in 1893 performed a farce, *To-day*, which reproduced in one scene the supper-room of the Savoy Hotel. Since the illumination in the hotel was electric, the Comedy management reproduced it by means of portable accumulation batteries, some built into the scene, which were removed and recharged twice a week.

In an 1898 editorial reviewing to its own satisfaction the accomplishments of electric light in the theatre, the *Electrician* professed amusement at the early 'ornamental or fantastic' manifestations of electricity upon the stage, including the carrying of storage batteries by the *corps de ballet* and the electric twinkling of fairy wands, these being 'amongst the many quaint uses to which electricity was first applied, at a time when the electric light as a main illuminant in the theatre was but little known and was at best a somewhat heroic experiment' (30 December). These quaint and ornamental uses were, however, highly popular; the late Victorians and Edwardians were fascinated by the application of electric light to an already long-established romantic stage fairyland, and from *Iolanthe* (1881) onward tiny electric lights powered by batteries sparkled in the hair, among the floral bouquets, and upon the costumes of female dancers and supers.

For these charming effects of lights on the person of the dancer, the common method was to place a storage battery weighing between a pound and a pound and a half in a small satchel fixed to the dress, from which ran two silk-covered wires to a lamp of about three or four watts in modern light measurement. However, Miss Navette in her Danse Electrique at the Alhambra (a big West End music hall) in 1893 did not carry storage batteries. The lamps on her dress, in the flowers she carried, and at the points of her parasol, were wired through her costume to metal plates in her shoes, and winked on when her feet came into contact with metal plates in the stage floor connected to a sub-stage battery. (A dancing deathtrap, we might think, but the voltage would have been very low, and Miss Navette seems to have got through her dance without injury.) For the same technical reasons a weird blue fire flowed from the sword of Faust as he clashed with Valentine in the Lyceum *Faust*; the right boot of each actor had a metal sole, with a connecting wire running from sword hilt to boot through the costume.

Special lighting effects had also been possible with gas (and for that matter, with oil), such as portable gaspipes carried by panto-mime fairies and simultaneously illuminated. Indeed, the Victorian stage revelled in special effects of all kinds. A magic lantern running on a truck behind the backcloth could project an image which grew larger as the lantern retreated from the cloth. This device was used as early as 1827 when Edward Fitzball persuaded the head carpenter at the Adelphi not to build an elaborate ship for his *The Flying Dutchman* but to adapt existing technology instead, far more cheaply. The lantern image became much brighter and more effective when limelight replaced oil, and two and even three lenses made the machine capable of cross-fades or 'dissolving views'. Lightning flashes were produced by igniting resin or lycopodium powder in flash-boxes attached to a bellows, or by cutting zig-zag transparencies in backcloths and illuminating them from behind, or by igniting magnesium powder in front of a reflector – these were only three ways of doing it; there were others. Realistically convincing flame and smoke could be simulated by a method that improved upon the red fire of an earlier period. Fitzgerald explains the effect:

> The ordinary limelight turned on to the full suffused the stage in a flood of light, while crimson glasses were used, which imparted a fierce glow of the same tint. Any vapour of the whitest kind moving in such a medium would at once give the notion of volumes of lurid smoke. Accordingly, a few braziers filled with a powder known as 'lycopodium' are placed at the wings, each fitted with a sort of forge bellows, each blast producing a sheet of flame and smoke. The lights in front being lowered, rows of little jets, duly screened, are made to follow the lines of the beams, rafters, &c., and thus make these edges stand out against the fierce blaze.[22]

Certain parts of the scenery – beams, rafters and so forth – could be pulled down from behind at the climactic moment, thus adding to the realism of the effect.

SOUND EFFECTS

The theatre was also capable of a wide variety of sound effects; this, of course, before sound recording. Evidently the first use of recorded sound on the English stage came in the offstage phonographic playing of a baby's cry in a farce, *The Judge*, at Terry's in 1890,[23] but using recorded sound never became general; almost all sound effects were produced traditionally. Thunder was done by rattling a sheet of iron or rolling cannon balls down a wooden trough. A good rumbling vibration was produced by striking a big wooden drum, with the skin stretched tightly over it, with leather-bound drum-sticks, or by beating on the drum with wooden balls held by hands in leather gloves. Wind was manufactured by a wind-machine: paddles projecting from a wooden drum (as in a paddle-steamer) were turned by a crank, the paddles rubbing against silk stretched tightly in a frame. The wind rose and fell and changed pitch as the crank handle was turned faster or more slowly. Rain was made by turning a handle attached to a big wooden box or cylinder containing dried peas; the handle turned wooden teeth in the box – or a smaller pea box with wooden skewers passing through it could simply be shaken by hand. These are only a few of the many sound effects produced in the wings or in the flies, and a large proportion of them had also been known in the eighteenth century. Collectively, however, they testify

[22] *Ibid.*, p. 53. The effect described was actually the work of a Parisian theatre, but the method was the same in England.

[23] See Jane W. Stedman, 'Enter a Phonograph', *Theatre Notebook*, vol. 30 (no. 1, 1976), pp. 3–5.

to the same sort of inventive fertility that characterised the work of
the sound effects man in the days of live radio drama, except that in
the theatre the sounds had to be distinctly audible at the back of large
auditoriums.

TECHNICAL REHEARSALS

When the separate technical elements of a production had been
perfected (or got together somehow – it depended on the theatre),
the last step before the dress rehearsal was a scenic rehearsal, or what
we would call a technical rehearsal, without actors unless they were
particularly needed. Here the manager would have his staff run
through the scene and lighting changes, observe the effect of the
lights on the painted scenery (probably for the first time), and test
any special effects. In a well-run theatre this scenic rehearsal would
be the culmination of a process of preparation which took place on
many nights after the play of the evening was over. Toward the end
of the process the principal scene-painter would also be present in
case there had to be any last-minute alterations to the scenes.
Augustus Harris's account of a final scenic rehearsal shows how all
the components of machinery, scene-painting, gas and limelight
came together:

> You sit with the scenic artists in the stalls or the circles – sometimes in one,
> sometimes in the other – to judge of the artistic effect, and to dispose the
> lighting of the various sets or pictures. The fly-men (that is, the carpenters
> up aloft), the cellar men (those below the stage), and the stage-carpenters
> have never yet worked together; and it appears almost marvellous,
> looking at the crowded cloths and borders, wings and ground-pieces,
> with the complicated ropes and pulleys above, and cuts and bridges in the
> stage, not to mention the traps and sliders, gas-battens and ladders, how a
> series of fifteen or sixteen scenes, besides the elaborate transformation
> scene, which, perhaps, demands the united skill of fifty or sixty men to
> work its marvels and develop its mysterious beauties, can even be worked
> with such systematic regularity and unerring correctness. A good master-
> carpenter is a general, and all his men depend on his lead in time of
> action. Then there are the gas-men, who have to raise or subdue the floats
> or footlights, the ground-rows, the wing-ladders, the battens or border-
> lights, and the bunch-lights or portable suns, which are required to give
> one effect to a brilliant tropical landscape or a bewilderingly luxurious
> palace. The limelights also have their special guardians. Each head of a
> department makes his special list of effects and changes, and notes the
> alterations or indications made at rehearsals.[24]

[24] 'The Hive of Pantomime', *Theatre* (January 1880), p. 15.

PICTORIALISM AND ARCHAEOLOGY

The kind of spectacle that Harris rehearsed with such care was a notable feature of the Victorian stage and, as we have seen, was not just confined to pantomime and melodrama but also included Shakespeare in its province. It had opponents: in fact the Victorian theatre was alive with critical controversy about the proper place of realism, archaeology, pictorialism and spectacle on the stage. The dominant trends of production were undoubtedly along these lines: the growing realism and social detail of Victorian painting, for instance, from the Pre-Raphaelites to W. P. Frith, influenced production methods that had been closer to painting than they had been before or have been since. Celebrated scene-painters like Clarkson Stanfield, David Roberts and David Cox went on to careers as famous easel artists and Academicians. Lawrence Alma-Tadema, Ford Madox Ford, and Edward Burne-Jones designed sets, costumes and properties for Irving and Tree. From about 1830 popular paintings were 'realised' on stage as act-ending tableaux through a combination of scenery, furniture, properties and actors frozen in action just as on a canvas. The word '*picture*' was the stage direction for such a tableau and for many a pictorial grouping.

Certainly the Victorians valued entertainment for its pictorial quality. The present time, said Charles Kean's biographer, 'is eminently pictorial'; scenic devices were needed to aid the imagination, not just words spoken from the stage.[25] 'All must be made palpable to sight', said another critic of the stage in the 1850s,[26] views unsurprising in an age that flocked to the exhibition of panoramas and dioramas, went to magic lantern lectures, visited the new art galleries, read illustrated magazines, bought cheap prints of popular paintings in their millions, looked through stereoscopes, was fascinated by the new art of photography and, by the end of the century, saw films. It was a pictorial culture, and the theatre was also pictorial.

Audiences, so it was argued, did not have the visual imagination of their ancestors; they were now too accustomed to pictures that told them everything. The stage, therefore, must communicate in the same way. Thus Shakespeare on stage was illustrated like a book, in a century when paintings and illustrated editions of Shakespeare were legion. For such audiences, said one writer, Shakespeare's verse 'requires for the full satisfaction of their thought the aid of bodily images to eke out what to them are but imperfect hints'. They 'are

---

[25] *The Life and Theatrical Times of Charles Kean*, vol. II, p. 63.
[26] William Bodham Donne, *Essays on the Drama* (London, 1858), p. 206.

best pleased when the eye is made interpreter to the sense'.[27] Thus on stage the Battle of Actium was fought, Richard and Bolingbroke entered London, and Henry V returned triumphant after victory. The fantasy world of Victorian pantomime was fully visualised, and melodrama presented splendid spectacles of British military victories and elegant social events. The visual image on the Victorian stage was neutral; it was never, as it is now, used to underline a theme or directorial point of view, or to reinforce or undercut the text, but for pictorial beauty, recreation of the contemporary and historical environment, archaeological display, or sheer spectacular effect.

Archaeology in the theatre was both pictorial and realistic, thus admirably suiting the cultural tendencies of the age. Greatly stimulated by discoveries at Nineveh in the 1840s and at Pompeii, Ephesus, Troy and Mycenae in the sixties and seventies, and also by the new scholarly and popular interest in the realities of the historical past, the theatre began to make its historical settings, costumes and properties as archaeologically correct as possible. This was a movement especially relevant to Shakespeare, but also to historical melodrama and revivals of Sheridan. Archaeological dogma was firmly expressed by E. W. Godwin, a leading figure in the Aesthetic movement and the father of Edward Gordon Craig. He declared that we go to the play 'to witness such a performance as will place us as nearly as possible as spectators of the original scene or of the thing represented, and this result is only possible where accuracy in every particular is assured'.[28] The archaeological method meant a great deal of research in churches, libraries, museums, art galleries and the actual locales of a historical play, and the time and expense could only be justified by a long run. When archaeology came together with spectacle on the stage, as it often did, in splendid processions, the market-places of ancient cities and sumptuous palace banquets, it satisfied public taste twice over.

REALISM

The historical realism of stage archaeology was part of a larger impetus toward realism. When Alfred Wigan at the Olympic in 1855 took the trouble to put red flock wallpaper in reduced size on a mirror facing the audience, thus reflecting the invisible 'fourth wall' of the room, it is not surprising that Godwin fussed with precisely reproducing sandals from Asia Minor for a drama set in Byzantine

[27] Charles Kenney, *Poets and Profits at Drury Lane Theatre* (London, 1875), p. 43.
[28] *Western Daily Press*, 11 October 1864. Quoted in John Stokes, *Resistible Theatres* (New York, 1972), p. 37.

Plate 13　Spectacle and archaeology: the Pyrrhic Dance in the banquet scene, *The Winter's Tale*, Princess's Theatre, 1856. By courtesy of the Trustees of the Victoria and Albert Museum.

times. The realistic principle was uncompromisingly stated by the architect and engineer E. O. Sachs at the end of the century: 'Actor and scene-painter alike must, above all, so labour that the audience shall forget that they are within the four walls of a theatre. But our stage methods prevent the realising of such an aim, and the impression of the audience that they are only witnessing a play is often far too palpable.'[29] Much of the technique of Victorian production and the withdrawal of the actors behind a fourth wall can be attributed to the increasing desire for realism. The difficulty was that the more pictorial the production in its picture frame and the more like beautiful art it became the less it resembled real life. This paradox was also reflected in critical comment. Critics complained, as we have seen, about the deficiencies of staging that broke the illusion – actors visible in the wings, stagehands dressed as footmen coming on to change the furniture, scenery ascending into the air, badly joined flats – yet they also complained that real furniture from department

[29] *Modern Opera Houses and Theatres*, vol. III Supplement, p. 6.

store showrooms looked unreal on stage. They criticised back shut-ters that moved and canvas borders that represented a ceiling or a sky for their lack of verisimilitude, yet praised well-painted scenery and furniture painted on scenery for its suggestiveness.

The paradox was of course insoluble. There was no way that the late Victorians could really pretend that a theatre was not a theatre and that they were not seeing a play, when the house lights stayed up and the graceful curve of the dress circle could be seen in all its gilded ornamentation with its impeccably and elegantly dressed patrons. And there was no way that a pictorial production style could be equated with realism. The only solution to the paradox was to eliminate it, to undermine the whole foundation and practice of Victorian stage production by abolishing painted scenery and romantic effects and all attempts at exact scenic recreation of the environment of a play. This was for the future and for the new race of director, scene designer and lighting designer. However, there were intimations enough: the revival of Greek drama in the 1880s on stages without prosceniums and very little or no scene-painting; William Poel's platform stage and tapestry curtains for his Eliza-bethan Stage Society revivals in the 1890s; Craig's experimental Purcell and Handel productions at the very end of Victoria's reign. The storm clouds were gathering over the settled Victorian ways of doing theatre. But until they broke – and the rain was a long time coming – all the arts of Victorian production, of stage machinery, lighting and scene-painting, served ends common and acceptable to audiences and theatre practitioners alike, ends that had their begin-nings in a wider society and culture outside the walls of the theatre.

4

The actor

Most of the complaints against late Victorian pictorial and spectacular production had been directed against the near obliteration of the individual actor by that method at its most extreme, by its emphasis on mass, colour and effects. Such complaints were not surprising, since except in a necessarily extravagant form like pantomime the actor had long been regarded as dominating the stage, more important than the text or the arts of production. It was an age of great star actors, each of whom had a considerable audience following and each of whom easily overshadowed his fellows.

Actors are not born as stars, however, and do not achieve stardom upon their first appearances. Even Edmund Kean, Macready and Irving, who towered over the theatre in their time, pursued long and often difficult stage apprenticeships before they qualified unreservedly in the public eye as stars. Kean had plodded his poverty-stricken way around the provincial theatre for ten years before he burst upon London as Shylock in 1814 and he had been on the stage since childhood. Macready, more fortunate in the fact that his father was a manager, had a smoother road through leading provincial theatres for six years but nevertheless took some time to establish himself in London as a star against the formidable competition of Kean. Irving took all of fifteen years in both London and the provinces before he achieved stardom in *The Bells* in 1871. Each of these actors reached the top, but the climb was steep and arduous.

GOING ON STAGE

The ways of getting on stage and getting ahead once on it were fairly clear at the beginning of the Victorian period. It helped if one were born into a theatrical family, as legions of Victorian actors were. Family dynasties such as the Terrys, the Comptons, the Farrens, and the Websters dominated the higher echelons of the acting profession. At the lowest level the family was the cement that held the strolling company together. At the outset of his career an actor's connections were invaluable: to be born into a theatrical family meant that as a child he could add to the family income. The presence of children in family-centred companies also meant an additional saving in that outsiders would not have to be hired for their roles. To bear a famous or even recognisable name ensured the novice without a family company to step into a position somewhere, not only because of the name itself but also because of family influence and family bonds: actors and actresses commonly married each other, and a large number of Victorian performers were interrelated.

Social, apart from family, origins were diverse, but evidence suggests that as the century wore on and acting became more acceptable as a field of employment the rising population of actors was matched by rising levels of class and education within the growing number of recruits to the profession. Testifying before the 1866 Select Committee, Horace Wigan, the manager of the Olympic, said 'Actors have risen in social importance. I think they are not as illiterate as they were, and that altogether their position is very much higher than it was' (1866 *Report*, p. 165). At the bottom of the theatrical hierarchy, in the strolling companies and the penny gaffs, educational attainments and social status were irrelevant, but by the end of the century, at least in the West End, the acting profession had a more middle and even upper middle-class composition compared to the predominantly lower middle- and working-class orientation of fifty years before. The number of actors was increasing rapidly, as the Census figures show. This was especially true in London, where wages in the West End had risen; a combination of better wages and the leisurely life of a West End actor in a long run attracted a different class of novice to the stage. From 1881 to 1891 the Census shows a national increase for actors of 61 per cent and for actresses 64 per cent; from 1891 to 1901 the increases are 67 per cent and 63.5 per cent respectively. Of course the general population was also increasing in these twenty years, but not as rapidly as this.

Because of their calling, their close mutual ties, and their peculiar hours of work, actors tended to be isolated from the community. This was especially true of the provincial actor. In this regard, Robert Courtneidge remembered the 1870s:

> The actor in the provinces formed one of a small tribe living practically
> apart from the rest of the world. Frowned on by the Church, viewed
> doubtfully and suspiciously by that large mass of opinion we call respect-
> able, he was not yet free from the prejudice that had always existed
> against his calling. If by some he was viewed more leniently, his private
> life and character were, in general, but lightly esteemed.[1]

In 1850 a neighbour of Samuel Phelps, by then the illustrious
manager of Sadler's Wells, threatened to remove his three children
from the school which Phelps's daughter attended because her father
was an actor. Moral prejudices against actors, and more particularly
against actresses, were stronger in the provinces than in London, and
only started to decline late in the century.

By the eighties and nineties the whole business of getting a job on
the professional stage had changed from the early and pre-Victorian
theatre. Although acting careers could be started in London, the
actor usually obtained an engagement in a small country company,
rose in the provinces to the position of a leading player with an
important stock company such as Bath, York, or Dublin, perhaps
made a summer engagement at the Haymarket in London and then
received a permanent position at Drury Lane or Covent Garden
which could last for many years, even for the remainder of his active
professional life. By 1837 the situation had become complicated by
the proliferation of minor theatres in the metropolis, the continual
financial difficulties of the two major theatres and the rapid decline
in the number of stock circuit companies in the country. After 1843
and the abolition of the monopoly privileges held by Drury Lane
and Covent Garden, any theatre could play the so-called legitimate
drama and acting talent was diffused over more theatres. This, it was
widely felt, led to a dilution of quality. The playwright Shirley
Brooks believed that the low state of the drama (as he put it) was
partly attributable 'to having an immense number of theatres in
which the audience are content with what they can get, namely one
good central figure, while the rest are stocks and puppets . . . There is
no single company now which is wholly composed of good actors'
(1866 *Report*, p. 159). Free trade in the drama, passionately advocated
for many years before 1843, did have its drawbacks.

If a novice were not a member of a theatrical family and thus
brought up to the stage, or helped by influence and connections, he
could follow one or more of several procedures. Writing to London
or country managers was a standard method, as was answering

---

[1] Robert Courtneidge, *I Was an Actor Once* (London, n.d.), p. 31.

advertisements in theatrical newspapers like the *Era* and the *Stage*. Since the latter was started in 1881, it was only in the last twenty years of the century that the actor could use both publications for advertising his availability and for replying to advertisements. Theatrical agents existed all through the Victorian period, but they were not highly regarded and, although they were pleased to take the money of novices, they did not exert themselves on their behalf. The dramatist H. J. Byron painted a vivid picture of the agent's premises in the fifties:

> Dingy and disreputable looking were the 'offices' when they were not actually in public-houses. The neighbourhood of Bow Street was the favourite locality for the 'agent,' and Bow Street itself twenty-five years ago was as remarkable for its 'professional' frequenters as for its odour of stale cabbages and its police-van. There the seedy 'utility man' rubbed shoulders with the loftiest 'leading gentleman', and the blue-chinned and deep-voiced representative of truculent bandits hob-nobbed with the side-splitting expositor of the broadest farce. Here the mighty provincial manager would haughtily interview the trembling applicant for some humble post, and condescendingly unbend in the presence of the equally magniloquent metropolitan 'star'. The whole 'mix-up' of the theatrical, vocal, equestrian, licensed-victualling and unlicensed liquoring was degrading and disgusting.[2]

Later in the century a common practice was for the beginner to offer a premium to a manager for the privilege of acting unpaid with his company for several months, with a modest wage guaranteed after that period. This practice was widespread and survived well into the twentieth century; Ralph Richardson began like this in Brighton in 1921. The problem was that bogus managers grew like weeds in this particular field: substantial premiums would be collected from several keen actors and actresses and a time appointed for rehearsals to begin – at which time the gathered company would find the doors closed, the office abandoned and the bogus manager absconded, shortly to surface under another name, in a new office, to carry out the same fraud all over again on a different group of unsuspecting performers. Many honourable managers took premiums, however, and many good touring companies accepted untried but presentable actors without a premium – if they were willing to act for nothing.

WORKLOAD

The early and traditional route for the novice, an engagement in a provincial company well below the first rank, meant the immediate

[2] 'Going on the Stage', *Theatre* (October 1879), pp. 130–31.

assumption of a back-breaking workload. A stock company was organised on true repertory principles, which meant that the evening's bill could be frequently changed, and because there might be two or three pieces on the bill a new actor was faced with a bewildering and exhausting variety of parts. The smaller and more makeshift a company the more doubling and trebling of roles in the same play, further increasing the workload. In his first engagement in a Yorkshire company in 1826, Phelps played six parts in *Macbeth*: a witch, Duncan, the First Murderer, Ross, an apparition, and a messenger.

This kind of workload was the beginner's responsibility until late in the nineteenth century. Going on stage in 1856 at Sunderland and then moving to two different Edinburgh theatres, Henry Irving played a total of 451 different roles in three years. In 1861 Squire Bancroft went on the stage at Cork, where he acted forty new parts in thirty-six nights, then thirty new leading parts (together with many familiar ones) in a six-week summer season at Devonport. In his first four years and four months as a country actor before he joined Marie Wilton at the Prince of Wales's, Bancroft played 346 different roles. In 1889 George Arliss joined the touring Irish Repertoire Company at Doncaster, to be met at the station by the stage manager and handed six long parts in Irish dramas and two farce parts, all to be played at Rotherham the following week. If a star visited a stock company for a week or two he brought his repertory with him, and the beginner was involved in heavy extra labour. In the early 1880s Jerome K. Jerome wrote to a friend from a country theatre about the two-week visit of a London star:

> His list consists of eighteen pieces -- eight 'legitimate,' five dramas, four comedies, and a farce; and we only had a week in which to prepare. There have been rehearsals at ten, and rehearsals at three, and rehearsals at eleven, after the performance was over. First, I took all the parts given me, and studied them straight off one after the other. Then I found I'd got them all jumbled up together in my head and the more I tried to remember what belonged to which, the more I forgot which belonged to what. At rehearsal I talked Shakespeare in the farce, and put most of the farce and a selection from all the five dramas into one of the comedies.[3]

The hours a novice had to put in to cope with this burden of work were excessive, even by contemporary factory hours. In 1827 Leman Rede estimated that an aspiring country actor in this situation 'will invariably have to study about *five hundred lines per diem* ... This will occupy the possessor of a good memory for six hours – his duties at

[3] Jerome K. Jerome, *On the Stage and Off* (London, n.d.), pp. 184–85.

the theatre embrace four hours in the morning for rehearsal, and about five at night; here are sixteen hours devoted to labour, to say nothing of the time required to study the character, after the mere attainment of the words.'[4] This estimate of sixteen hours for the working day was confirmed by other observers. As an actor developed in this system – if he survived – one of two things happened. If he remained near the bottom of the ladder, as so many did, he became familiar with an enormous number of parts and could draw on his experience, thus reducing his effort. If he climbed high in the ranks he appeared in fewer pieces and therefore played fewer parts.

For those familiar with modern theatre practice, a real act of historical imagination is required to understand *how* a Victorian actor could endure such initial drudgery and make anything of himself. Our disbelief that any good acting, let alone the star acting which distinguished the nineteenth-century stage could come out of such a system, is at first only reinforced by a knowledge of the rehearsal method then generally current. It would be useful to outline this process in order to understand how the Victorian actor prepared a part, and also to appreciate how a method of preparation and an attitude to acting differing so sharply from our own could produce the results it did.

REHEARSALS

The customary practice at the beginning of the Victorian period in established theatres dealing with a new play accepted by the management was for the author to read it to the acting company in the green room, the group being sometimes augmented by key officials like prompter, stage manager and head carpenter. This practice lasted the century: Pinero read *The Second Mrs Tanqueray* to Alexander's St James's company in 1893. There were exceptions: Macready's prompter at Drury Lane read Browning's *A Blot in the Scutcheon* to the actors (very badly, to the actors' amusement and Browning's annoyance); Phelps read Tom Taylor's *The Fool's Revenge* to the Sadler's Wells company and Irving would read Lyceum plays to his actors, playing all the parts with energy. After the reading, roles would be assigned and rehearsals commenced. A play already in the company's repertory was not read, for the actors (unless they were new) had already played the parts.

The first job of the actor, if he were performing at any level above that of a strolling company or portable theatre, was to get hold of

[4] Leman Rede, *The Road to the Stage* (London, 1827), p. 8.

the printed words of the part and memorise them. A simple matter today, but not so in the nineteenth century. Unless a beginner possessed his own library of cheap acting editions – these were printed mostly for amateurs – he took his turn at the company script and copied his part from it, with cues. This could mean sitting up half the night scribbling hurriedly while another actor waited for the script. Thus for a play new to him the actor had until rehearsals began no idea of the plot or how his character related to other characters. Later in the century touring companies provided type-written parts, but this was no help to a complete understanding of the text. Jerome gives his first part '*in extenso*' as he received it from the management, complete with cues and stage directions:

> **Joe Junks**
> *Act I, scene 1*
>
> ——————— comes home.
> It's a rough night.
> ——————— if he does.
> Ay. Ay.
> ——————— stand back.
> (*Together*) 'Tis he!
> *Fall down as scene closes in.*
> Act IV, scene 2
> *On with rioters.*[5]

Such a practice lasted well into the twentieth century, and an experienced actor would over the years accumulate a very large number of tattered and greasy parts. Irving, who took the trouble to have his acting versions privately printed and distributed to his casts, was an extraordinary exception to the general custom.

When the Victorian stock company played a large repertory and when the actor was almost solely responsible for the interpretation of his part, there was neither time nor necessity for an extended rehearsal period. Even new plays produced by major companies were given only a few rehearsals. On 10 February 1842, Macready began to mark the text of Gerald Griffin's tragedy *Gisippus* for performance at Drury Lane; it was done for the first time on the 23rd. After the reading of *A Blot in the Scutcheon* on 28 January 1843, to the Drury Lane actors, Macready, who began reading the play only three days before, records four rehearsals (there may have been more) before the first performance on 11 February. At lesser theatres the rehearsals of a new piece would

---

[5] *On the Stage and Off*, p. 49. I suspect that Jerome actually made this excerpt up, but there is no doubt that a beginner would be given small parts in this fashion, as well as much longer ones.

not take as long. Mr Fogg, the melodrama author of Albert Smith's novel *The Fortunes of the Scattergood Family*, first published in 1845, receives a promise from the management of 'a transpontine theatre' that his play would be brought out three days after it was accepted, 'quite a sufficient space of time to get up the most elaborate minor theatre drama ever written, including scenes, dresses, incidental music, and lastly, being of least consequence, the words of the author'.[6] Only pieces of a complicated technical nature – spectacles or pantomimes – might receive a relatively long rehearsal period by the standards of the day and that might be a matter of nine or ten rehearsals.

Like opera stars today with their music, actors were expected to come to the first rehearsal knowing most of their lines. Rehearsals did not deal in textual interpretation or character exploration; that was the actor's business. Often they were merely a matter of running quickly through the lines and arranging exits, entrances and stage business. Pieces already in the repertory did not require rehearsal at all, although one would be called for a new actor or a visiting star. However, the star might not attend the rehearsal, but call members of the company to his hotel room for their scenes with him. When Barry Sullivan was on tour his stage manager, according to Robert Courtneidge, would rehearse in his place, with care. Many of the leading actor-managers had a reputation for thorough and careful rehearsals, even in the limited time available, among them Macready, Charles Kean and – under the long-run system when much more time was available – Irving. In his earlier days as a touring star, Kean 'would steadily go through his own scenes word for word (although he must have acted the parts hundreds of times), slowly and deliberately dwelling upon each sentence, just as he would at night'.[7]

Macready, Kean and Irving, however, were at the zenith of theatrical quality. There was also a nadir. Under a system such as this, a great deal of careless and sloppy work was done. Sometimes it did not show: for instance, when Charles Dillon starred as Louis XI at Manchester in the 1870s, one of the company asked him in rehearsal, '"Where would you like me to be in this scene, Mr. Dillon?" "Wherever you like, laddie, I shall find you at night," was the careless response, and Dillon, tugging at his imperial, mumbled through his lines, not troubling to do more. I stood at the wings that night and watched this unrehearsed scene. It was a masterpiece that positively electrified me.'[8] Accounts of slipshod and perfunctory rehearsals abound; that all performances at this level were not equally slipshod and perfunctory, but frequently excellent, was a

[6] Albert Smith, *The Fortunes of the Scattergood Family* (London, 1853), pp. 36–37.
[7] *Mr and Mrs Bancroft On and Off the Stage*, vol. I, p. 240.
[8] *I Was an Actor Once*, pp. 55–56.

credit to the system and to the experienced actor who knew exactly
what he was about, rehearsal or no. Nevertheless, these deficiencies
were keenly felt by the beginner, for whose benefit the company
reluctantly went through the motions of a rehearsal. Jerome describes
such a rehearsal of a melodrama, probably about 1880 at Astley's:

> The speeches, with the exception of the very short ones, were not given at
> full length. The last two or three words, forming the cues, were clearly
> spoken, but the rest was, as a rule, mumbled through, skipped altogether,
> or else represented by a droning 'er,er,er' interspersed with occasional
> disjointed phrases. A scene of any length, between only two or three of
> the characters, – and there are many such – was cut out entirely, and gone
> through apart by the people concerned. Thus, while the main rehearsal
> was proceeding in the centre of the stage, a minor one was generally
> going on at the same time in some quiet corner – two men fighting a duel
> with walking sticks; a father denouncing his son, and turning him out of
> doors; or some dashing young gallant, in a big check ulster, making love
> to some sweet young damsel, whose little boy, aged seven, was sitting on
> her lap.[9]

One reason why the actor was free to develop his own part in his
own way was that there was no 'director' or 'producer' in the
Victorian theatre. His office was discharged in rehearsal by one or
more members of the stage hierarchy: the leading actor, the manager
or actor-manager, the stage manager and the prompter. The direction of a play was known as 'stage management' and sometimes given
into the hands of the stage-manager, who in small companies might
also be an actor. The conscientious manager, like Macready, Kean or
Irving, served as director in all but name, superintending every
aspect of rehearsal from understanding and speaking the text to stage
movement, scene changes and lighting. A manager like Augustus
Harris drilled his company exhaustively in pantomime rehearsals.
From the 1860s dramatists took increasing responsibility for the
production of their plays. Dion Boucicault was known as a hard
taskmaster in rehearsal; the Bancrofts seem to have turned over the
rehearsal of Tom Robertson's comedies to Robertson himself,
although he knew his business: he had previously been an actor,
scene-painter, prompter and stage-manager. W. S. Gilbert had sole
authority over the direction of rehearsals for the Savoy operas and in
the 1890s Pinero had the reputation of a martinet for insisting that
actors obey every movement, gesture, inflection, stress and pause he
gave them. In many respects, then, Victorian plays *were* 'directed' in
the modern sense. Where their practice differed from our own,
however, is that whoever was in charge of rehearsals did not help the

[9] *On the Stage and Off*, pp. 52–53.

Plate 14   A melodrama rehearsal, *c.* 1880. Jerome, *On the Stage and Off*.

actor to develop a character or work with him toward a particular
interpretation of a role or a text. The Victorian theatre did not
possess such a thing as a governing idea of a play in the mind of one
person, who sought by collaboration or imposition to bring it out
prominently in performance.

The central position of the actor in the Victorian theatre was as
true of the fourth-rate company as the first; indeed, in the former the
actor would have been left completely to his own devices, whereas in
the latter he might receive some advice and practical assistance from
the manager or stage-manager. The actor's company experience
could in fact vary widely. As the provincial stock company declined
and the touring company flourished, and as long runs increased in
the West End, going on stage became more difficult for the actor
who really wanted to learn his job. A beginner could apply to several
kinds of companies. If he were lucky or knew somebody in London
management, looked well on the stage and was of the right social
class with the right manners, he could obtain walk-on parts in the
West End. This was pleasant and certainly not taxing, but there was
little to be learned about acting from saying the same few lines, night

after night, in a play that might run for months. When George Arliss reached the West End in 1899, he found that his hard knocks in the provinces for the past ten years had given him a great advantage over actors who had stayed in the West End and played not more than twenty parts in this time.

TOURING COMPANY EMPLOYMENT

A berth with a touring company was an obvious choice for the beginner. There was more than one kind of touring company, as we know. The ones with the best pay scales and the most financial security – the bogus embezzling manager who made off with the takings and abandoned his unpaid and penniless company in some remote country town was a commonplace of the Victorian theatre – were those with a respectable classical, romantic or modern reper- tory, or those run by established managements touring West End hits. It was hard to find a position with a good touring company, easier to get a job in two other sorts of touring company, the fit-up and the portable theatre.

Almost nothing is known of the actor's experience at probably the lowest level of all, the urban penny gaff, except that remuneration was pitiful and actors frequently half-starved. Starvation is not one of the occupational hazards of the modern stage. In the Victorian period it was a very real threat.

The tour of the West End hit was common throughout the provinces in the 1880s and 1890s and the number of such companies steadily increased. For the actor, however, the benefits were doubt- ful, not in the area of wages, which were adequate, but from the point of view of experience and the actor's art. Procedures were strictly laid down. It was the practice of managements to rehearse in London while the West End show to which they had the touring rights was still running. The casts they engaged to play in the provinces were required to become so familiar with the acting mannerisms and stage business of the original cast that they could replicate them on tour. Leopold Wagner says of the productions the Gatti brothers sent on tour that they were rehearsed by their own stage manager at their own theatre, the Adelphi:

> The *artistes* they have engaged for the tour are expected to give a faithful imitation of the original exponents of the drama, down to the minutest detail. Night after night, as long as the rehearsals are in progress, will their 'specially-selected London company' be found seated in various parts of the house carefully watching the play, and taking in all the 'points' that win applause from the pit and gallery. A new reading of a part will not be

tolerated. The least attempt at originality might endanger an enthusiastic performer's engagement.[10]

Other managements did the same. This practice directly affected casting, for the touring management tended to select actors for their physical and vocal resemblance to members of the original cast rather than for individual acting abilities. The parrot factor was enhanced by a rigid stage traditionalism still strong in many quarters. Weedon Grossmith recalls that when he took his first London stage role in the 1880s at the Gaiety in an antiquated Charles Mathews piece entitled *Woodcock's Little Game* he was 'asked by the producer to do the same business that Charles Mathews did, and when making my exit at the end of the first act, the stage manager said, "Now, Mr Grossmith, throw the tails of your frock coat over the back of your head." "Why?" I asked. "Because Mathews did it," he replied.'[11]

The fit-up company took everything with it, including a pro-scenium, calling at small towns and villages which no regular company visited, playing in halls, assembly rooms and corn exchanges. At the top end of the fit-up scale, D'Oyly Carte sent Gilbert and Sullivan operas around to small towns with prettily painted scenes, but the average fit-up had no such pretensions to elegance. At least a fit-up played a repertoire of pieces, allowing the young actor every chance of learning his business; there was, however, the old problem of getting time alone with the company's only script and the familiar grinding labour of memorising a part in a few hours.

In companies at the portable and strolling level there were usually no scripts at all. The actors, provided with all sorts of stock senti-ments and emotional responses to every conceivable melodramatic situation, improvised their lines at rehearsals around the basic plot. By the time one or two performances had occurred, speeches were fairly well set.[12] These companies were constructed around a family nucleus – the manager, his wife, one or two children, a sister, a brother – and probably the main reason for the absence of a script was that the family could not read or write; at this level of theatre educational qualifications were neither required nor necessary. A portable theatre was a booth or tent ranging in comfort and appoint-ments from the miserably makeshift to the relatively sumptuous.

[10] *How to Get on the Stage*, p. 61.

[11] Weedon Grossmith, *From Studio to Stage* (London, 1913), p. 167.

[12] Shakespeare must have been treated differently. Did the actors improvise their own words around Shakespeare's plots, or did they learn it orally from older members of the company? Or was there, in his case, a script? The best portable companies, such as Wild's and Thorne's and Douglas's, some of which played regular seasons of full-length plays in towns, no doubt used scripts as a general policy.

When portable theatres were set up at big fairs, the actors were expected to parade outside the booth in costume before each show; there were two or three shows of an evening and perhaps half a dozen on Saturday. The portable repertory at the fairs consisted almost entirely of cut-down melodramas, Shakespeare, farce and pantomime. Engagements were easy to find: in the eighties and nineties one simply answered an advertisement in the *Stage*.

Experience at the portable and strolling level was readily available to the neophyte, but the demise of the stock company as a training ground severely limited his learning experience. Many deplored this loss and severely berated the modish young West End or touring actor whose good looks, polished manners, dress and middle-class social skills were his sole qualification for the stage. The stock company, they said, gave an actor a rigorous on-the-job training in which he developed breadth and emotional power and was able to use his wide experience of roles already played to prepare new ones. Others argued that the stock company rarely rose above respectable mediocrity, having too much work to do and too little time to do it in. They claimed that the audience and the dramatist were much better served by the careful casting, the longer rehearsal period and the more finished production given to the long-running or touring play. The debate between the two opposed camps was heated and extended well into the twentieth century. The provision of adequate training was also much discussed. The amateur dramatic society, which boomed in the 1880s and 1890s, was thought by some to be the best way of supplying the professional stage, but decried by others. Attempts had been made in the late Victorian period to start drama schools, but although none survived they pointed the way to the training of the future. The Royal Academy of Dramatic Art was founded by Beerbohm Tree in 1904,[13] and the Central School of Speech and Drama followed in 1906.

THE WEST END ACTOR

The social style and poise of the new West End actor might have been criticised by traditionalists, but it was part of the upward social mobility of the class-conscious West End stage and West End management. Professional organisation is another sign of social and professional respectability, and with the formation of the Actors'

---

[13] Tree himself, a graduate of the amateur theatre, had been criticised for not being vocally and physically equipped for Shakespeare. 'There can be no doubt that a year or two with a good stock company in his early days would have imparted a breadth and finish to his later work' (Joe Graham, *An Old Stock Actor's Memories* [London, 1930], p. 210).

Association in 1891 the theatre took its first steps toward unioni-
sation. The gradual lessening of religious and moral hostility toward
the theatre also made the actor more socially acceptable and the
knighthoods awarded to Irving in 1895 and Bancroft in 1897 were
official recognition, not only of their own merit and contribution to
the theatre, but also of the whole social process that had brought the
West End actor and actor-manager to the place he occupied in public
esteem at the end of the century. Not surprisingly, Irving and
Bancroft were the first two presidents of the Actors' Association.
The *Theatre* summed up the position to its own satisfaction in 1897:

> It is not only that our leading players dine with royalty, and entertain the
> most exclusive people; it is not only that heads of the calling are on terms
> of familiarity with 'the best'; it is that, for the first time in the history of
> histrionics in this country, acting is regarded – not merely here and there,
> but more or less generally – as a profession to be adopted as one adopts
> Medicine, Law, or the Church, the Army, the Navy, or the Civil Service.
>
> (February 1897, p. 65)

There is some truth in this, but really the only actors to have
benefited substantially from this social process were West End actors
in good companies and actors at or near the top of their profession.
The great mass of provincial actors struggled on as before, unrecognised and unrewarded in social or financial terms.

ACTRESSES

Throughout this chapter the word 'actor' has been used generically;
actresses had the same opportunities – except that there were fewer
parts for them – and faced the same problems as their male counterparts. Nevertheless, one must, briefly at least, consider Victorian
actresses apart from actors, since their sex and some of the specific
stage positions they filled (because of their sex) made them liable to
circumstances in which actors were not placed. The Victorian stage
provided economic opportunities for women not available elsewhere, especially in the period before they began in large numbers to
enter vocations previously reserved for men, such as office work and
the retail trades. An actress did not compete with an actor for the
same job, so was no threat to him economically. Her pay scales were
the same as an actor's, except in specialised areas like the chorus. A
woman could thus receive the theatrical wage appropriate to her
ability without depressing the wage scale for men; in fact the actress
at the top of her profession would not only be paid more than most
other male colleagues but might also employ them in the capacity of

manager. Female managers in the Victorian period were relatively few in number, but several, such as Madame Vestris, Marie Wilton, Ada Swanborough, Lily Langtry and Sarah Thorne (at Margate) ran their companies with distinction.

However, there were difficulties of a purely sexual nature. No matter how moral and hard-working the majority of actresses might be – and they went through exactly the same drudgery at the lower levels as actors – the public associated the life of an actress with a life of immoral and degenerate ease. The public and exhibitionist nature of their art, the suspect institution in which they were employed, the gaudy skimpiness of their burlesque and pantomime costumes, the element of deceit essential to acting a role, the morally tarnished characters they sometimes had to undertake – these and other factors largely convinced a Victorian public that treasured quite different moral and domestic ideals for women that actresses were unfit for family society; worse, that they were no better than prostitutes – indeed, for some they *were* prostitutes. These attitudes, no matter how unjustified, even extended to the families of young women who wished to go on the stage. Unless they had theatrical parents, they could face extreme and uncomprehending parental hostility if they made their wishes known or tried to join a company. Many women started their stage careers in secret, under assumed names, rather than endure disgrace and family ostracism. Such hostility was much greater from middle-class than working-class parents; many working-class families looked upon acting simply as a job paying better wages than most jobs available to their daughters, like domestic service, the mill or the needle. Middle-class prejudices died hard, even though near the end of the century numbers of educated middle-class women were looking for and finding stage work, aided in their quest by the theatre's need for such actresses to play their character counterparts in the middle-class drawing-room drama so popular in the West End and on tour. The upward social mobility of the actress is an interesting phenomenon of the Victorian stage.

In addition to being far more the victims of moral prejudice than actors, actresses also coped with a variety of occupational hazards which their male colleagues did not experience. Sympathetic moralists both inside and outside the theatre were continually warning of the dangers of sexual temptation for the unprotected young actress away from home for the first time and ignorant of the snares and pitfalls of stage life. However, sexual harassment and exploitation were apparently more of a danger for the poorly paid, struggling working-class actress, dancer or chorister than the middle-class recruit attempting utility roles as the first step on the ladder.

The nature of the work was also more hazardous in certain specialised roles. Until fairly late in the century and the introduction of new safety measures, a dancer could suffer terrible burns or even death by her costume catching fire from the naked flame of a footlight or wing-light. The transformation scene of a pantomime, in which numbers of coryphées (or ballet girls) were strapped aloft in irons to populate pantomime's Aquatic Abode of the Denizens of the Deep or the Crimson Bower of Christmas Berries, exposed them to excessive heat and the noxious fumes of the special lighting that made the transformation scene at its best a thing of wondrous beauty. Tom Robertson vividly described their fifteen or twenty minutes of suffering: 'The poor pale girl is swung up to terrific heights, imprisoned in and upon iron wires, dazzled by rows of hot flaring gas and choked by the smoke of coloured fires.'[14] John Doran, visiting backstage during a Drury Lane pantomime, commented optimistically that there was no danger of the girls being roasted alive, provided they were released in time from the irons. Nevertheless, 'seldom a night passes without one or two of them fainting; and I remember, on once assisting several of them to alight, as they neared the ground and they were screened from the public gaze, that their hands were cold and clammy, like clay.'[15]

COSTUME AND MAKEUP

Another problem for actresses, economic rather than physical, was costume. For much of the Victorian period most companies expected actors and actresses to find their own costumes and accessories. There was no costume designer or any person responsible for (or even really interested in) colour harmonies or costume quality on stage, except perhaps in the case of deliberately archaeological productions. All through the century a good wardrobe was a great advantage for a performer of either sex; in first-rate companies parts had to be dressed well – at the actor's expense – and he could be out of a job if his wardrobe was inadequate. On the lower levels a good wardrobe alone might secure him a position. As late as the 1890s aspirants were advised that 'when "writing in" for an engagement, the inclusion of the all-important sentence, "Good wardrobe on and off the stage," has great weight with a manager ... A bad actor is often tolerated in an inferior company if he brings with him a goodly assortment of serviceable properties, for to dress a part well

[14] 'Theatrical Types: No. XI – The Corps de Ballet', *Illustrated Times*, 16 July 1864.
[15] John Doran, *In and About Drury Lane* (London, 1881), vol. I, p. 17.

reflects credit on the management.'[16] Toward the end of the century first-class managements provided costumes for their performers, both in the West End and on tour. In other managements this might be done for actors but not actresses, and the former would still have to find boots, shoes, tights, hosiery, swords, ruffs, etc. It was also common for both actors and actresses to find their own wigs and modern costumes, no matter how amply their wants were supplied in period pieces. Thus in the matter of costume, actresses were on the whole economically disadvantaged in comparison to actors, for the greater extent of a female wardrobe, even if reduced to basic essentials, imposed a heavy financial burden upon those earning the low wages which poorer companies paid. In such companies actresses could be reduced to the same expedient as actors, one of whom, playing at Portsmouth in the 1870s, recalled 'a dress coat being handed from one to another in the wings several times during a performance ... A white tie was easily made from a strip of notepaper, and even a shirt front could be managed from highly glazed notepaper.'[17] During his own struggles at Barnsley Robert Courtneidge remembered the inventiveness of a fellow actor, a real artist of costume and makeup:

> If he wanted a wig, he would manufacture it out of an old stocking, stitching whatever shade and mass of crape hair he required upon this foundation. Paper, white and brown, served him for many purposes. If he had to wear a dress-suit, a sheet of white cardboard made him a shirt-front, cuffs, and a collar. On these were painted studs, and to the collar was attached a paper tie. Pins, needles, and thread transformed his own seedy black coat and vest into a fashionable appearance, and if a silk hat was wanted he would make the top with brown paper, blacked and varnished. This he slipped over his weather-beaten bowler, which was carefully touched-up around the rims to match. For a sporting character, Reg walked on stage in improvised gaiters of brown paper, glued on to a piece of calico, a paper vest backed with the same cheap material, on which he had stamped a spotted pattern, with a cardboard collar, a stock, and a flower in his buttonhole made of coloured paper. If spats were needed, he covered the tops of his boots with a thick white paste. His ingenuity was endless, affording us constant amusement, but from the front he was the best-dressed man in the company.[18]

About the only article the professional actor is now required to supply is makeup, and he uses the greasepaints introduced around 1877 by Leichner. These became widespread in the 1880s, and by the

[16] Leopold Wagner, *How to Get on the Stage*, pp. 88–89.
[17] Russel Crauford, *Ramblings of an Old Mummer* (London, 1909), pp. 25–26.
[18] *I Was an Actor Once*, pp. 90–91.

end of the century Leichner had put on the market twenty-two numbered sticks of different colours and tints. The old pre-greasepaint dry makeup was based on the use of powders, powders in combination with grease, and preparations like cochineal, whitening, and white and red lead – some of them dangerous to health. Certain colours and mixtures were conventionally used for age and for stock characters, such as Youth, Death, Frenchmen, Jews, Americans, Indians, Mulattoes, Scots and Sailors; others represented the actor's lines of business, like Heavy Man and Low Comedy. A Samuel French makeup guide published before the introduction of greasepaints recommends the use of Ruddy Rouge for sunburnt faces, 'most essential for low comedy, country, or seamen's faces'.[19] French also sold a complete pre-greasepaint makeup box, which would have been mainly purchased by amateurs. It contained, according to the advertisement, 'everything necessary for making up the face': Rouge, Pearl Powder, Whiting, Mongolian, Ruddy Rouge, Powdered Antimony, Joining Paste, Violet Powder, Chrome Blue, Burnt Cork, Pencils, Spirit Gum, Indian Ink, Burnt Umber, Puff, Camel Hair Brushes, Hare's Foot, Wool, Crape Hair, Cold Cream, Paint Saucer, Miniature Puffs, Scissors and Looking Glasses. Later, similar boxes could be bought equipped with greasepaints, although Wagner advises that half a dozen of the lowest numbers would serve the young actor, for ordinary purposes, for a long time. In addition, 'a black and brown lining pencil; a cake of lip-salve; some yellow chrome as a groundwork for old men's faces; cotton-wool roughed over for pimples, Bardolph noses, or bloated cheeks; and powdered blue for giving the chin an unshaven appearance, or producing hollow cheeks, should be procured'.[20] As the century progressed, the technique of makeup as well as its constituents changed, as stage lighting became stronger and went from candles and oil through gas and limelight to electricity. What passed

---

[19] Quoted in *The World behind the Scenes*, p. 124. Several handbooks on theatrical makeup were published in the last quarter of the nineteenth century. Also listed by Samuel French are a wide variety of wigs, beards and whiskers. The professional actor, however, always made his own beards, moustaches and whiskers, and travelled, as did the actress, with a basic selection of wigs.

[20] *How to Get on the Stage*, p. 156. Even without their regular makeup ingredients, actors could be extraordinarily ingenious. One old actor at the Lyric, Hammersmith, in the 1890s, resorted to substitutes when denied access to makeup: 'Whereupon he disappeared, only to be heard vigorously scraping the wall beneath the stage with his jack knife. He skilfully blended a mixture of brick dust and spittle into a fine paste, and, once this satisfied his judgment, he applied it all over his neck and face. On returning to the dressing-room, he made up his eyes with the black deposit from the gas-mantle. He dusted off with Fuller's earth, a commodity he carried in his snuff-box. After the performance, the veteran actor removed his elaborate disguise with the aid of butcher's lard, an effective substitute for cold cream' (John M. East, *'Neath the Mask* [London, 1967], p. 99.)

for nature under gas was washed out by electricity. The size of the auditorium also influenced making up: the larger the theatre the broader the method.

WAGES

The income actors received improved as time went on, but only for the upper and middle echelon of West End performers. The rest of the profession struggled on as best they could, on barely adequate or quite inadequate wages, especially given the fact that for much of the period, as we have seen, the provision of wigs, costumes, footwear and accessories was partly or wholly the responsibility of the player, and had to be bought out of a purse already depleted by the expenses of travel (which some managements did not pay) and accommodation while touring. Furthermore, actors were not paid when they were sick or otherwise unable to perform. Kean's Princess's Theatre was a glowing exception to this rule, but rare was the individual manager whose generosity exceeded his desire for economy. Neither were they paid for rehearsals. Later in the nineteenth century some companies gave half-pay for rehearsal, and individual stars might negotiate satisfactory rehearsal terms. Nor was there any assistance or compensation for the actor left stranded by the absconding manager. Necessary reforms in these areas had to wait until the founding of the Actors' Association and more particularly of Equity, which absorbed the Actors' Association, in 1929.

A traditional method of supplementing the actor's income, the benefit performance, died out in the Victorian theatre, although it never really helped the subordinate actor. Under this system an actor would pay, unless he could command his own terms or were exceptionally favoured by management, the fixed nightly expenses of the house and keep the rest of the box office himself – often a risky business from the actor's point of view. The benefit lasted a long time. Ellen Terry took annual benefits at the Lyceum until 1895, and some West End managers awarded themselves benefits, Irving among them. At a different level of company organisation the provincial performer might still have to push the sale of his 'bespeak' tickets from door to door and from shop to shop, fawning obsequiously upon the better families and more prosperous tradesmen. Many actors and commentators considered the bespeak demeaning, but it survived at least into the 1890s.

Actual wages varied widely between London and the provinces and between leading actors and the rest. E. W. Elton, an actor at the Surrey, told the 1832 Select Committee that the highest wage he knew 'in a provincial theatre of the very first class is three guineas a week', out of which came the cost of costumes and travelling, 'yet it is expected a man receiving that salary shall be able to embody the first characters of Shakespeare' (1832 *Report*, p. 235). Provincial salaries did not get much better than this, and were often a deal worse. The level of touring salaries depended on the standard of the company, good for first-class tours out of the West End, low for lesser companies. Wagner noted that 25–30s. a week for a small part, £2 to £3 for 'a line of business', and a maximum of £5 for a lead 'may be said to strike an average of an actor's salary on tour' (p. 153). A beginner in a decent stock or touring company might receive a guinea a week, a wage that hardly changed for a century. One cannot assume, however, that wages were always *paid*. It was not only the bogus manager who was a threat to poorly remunerated actors. Many a provincial and London manager (especially outside the West End) trod a fine line between staying solvent and going bankrupt, and many either fell behind in paying wages or simply could not pay them. Actors in many companies had to pester their managers continually and resort to the most desperate expedients to obtain any part of what they were owed. In portable theatres and strolling companies actors practised the ancient Commonwealth system, of sharing, dividing box-office receipts after each performance; there was no weekly wage. Working in a sharing company presented two problems. Firstly, receipts might be so pitiful that they would literally constitute starvation wages. Secondly, in any established sharing company management got the best pickings. As Wagner explains, 'the manager takes one share *as* manager, two as proprietor, one as actor, one for the use of his scenes and properties, and one for wear and tear ... Thus, with the claims of his wife and children, he captures, perhaps, twelve shares out of the regulation twenty; so that when the necessary deductions for rent, gas, and orchestra have been made, there remains little enough for outside supporters' (p. 113).

In London wages in suburban and non-West End theatres were much the same as in the provinces, in some cases even less. It was in the West End that the actor had his best chance at a decent or even comfortable living wage. Even here, however, wages for minor actors, choristers and the corps de ballet were anything but handsome, varying in the case of the chorus and general ballet between 10s. and 40s. a week in the eighties and nineties, with male choristers averaging better than female. Supers, who usually had other jobs in the day, often in the same theatre, were by this time earning 1s.6d. to

2s.6d. a performance. Utility actors might get 25s. or 30s. a week, walk-ons a guinea. In 1899 Wagner says that 'from £2 to £5 a week might be set down as the average salary of a subordinate actor in a West End theatre, according to the part he is cast for' (p. 154). Such wages had changed little over a generation. Polly Eccles, the sister of Esther in Robertson's *Caste* (1867) is dancing in the ballet for 18s. a week, while Esther in Act I has received a good offer to dance Columbine in a pantomime at Manchester for £4 a week, 'dresses to be found'. By the 1860s many actors were playing in dramatic sketches at the music halls because the pay was better than in theatres.

Only the leading actors at the top West End theatres in the last twenty or thirty years of the nineteenth century substantially and sometimes dazzlingly increased their incomes. In 1871 Madge Robertson was receiving the highest weekly wage in Buckstone's first-class comedy company at the Haymarket, £12, while her husband W. H. Kendal and W. H. Chippendale earned £11. These were then high West End wages. The Bancrofts, who paid wages no higher than this at the Prince of Wales's in the 1860s, were proud of raising them considerably at the Haymarket in the 1880s. John Hare played Sam Gerridge in *Caste* for £5 in 1867; in 1889 Wyndham offered him £100 to play the same part at the Criterion. The first-rate West End actor could now make £50 or £60 a week, stars much more. In pantomime Augustus Harris was in the nineties paying a Principal Boy £60 to £100, a Clown £30 to £40, and a top dancer £30 to £50. Music hall stars in pantomime and in their own territory received even higher wages. Yet these, it must be repeated, were sums earned by only a relative handful in the profession. The rest of them did not participate in the new affluence of the West End manager or the growing prosperity of late Victorian England and the majority drudged on as before, scarcely known and poorly paid.

The Victorian actor's employment opportunities, his job and working conditions and his remuneration are relatively easy to describe, since there is scattered here and there a great deal of information, most of it factual and objective in content. To describe Victorian acting – or any acting of the past – is a harder task, since acting comes fully into life only in the theatre and not on the printed page; it is also viewed by subjective observers who record appreciation or condemnation rather than facts. From our own point of view it is also difficult to get close to Victorian acting because of the traditional nature of many aspects of its practice. In today's theatre we do not set much store by traditions of acting, but the Victorians did, practising as well as respecting them.

PICTORIALISATION AND ELEVATION

Although acting was changing by 1837, the early Victorian actor inherited concepts and styles of performance handed down for generations. The eighteenth century believed that the major passions – joy, grief, anger, fear, jealousy, etc. – expressed themselves in a universal language of gesture, movement and facial expression. By the very assumption of these outward forms, it was argued, the actor would then feel the appropriate passion. The business of the actor was to pictorialise these passions in order to make them accessible and understandable to the audience; such pictorialisation was also a visual way of treating text and character. The increasingly pictorial nature of nineteenth-century stage production was a fitting context for the actor to continue with these techniques, especially if he were to survive as an individual the increasing stage emphasis on light, colour and mass. The idea that beauty was a principal aim of the actor was also inherited from the eighteenth century and held all through the Victorian period, being firmly expressed at the end of it by no less an actor than Irving. Thus the body and voice of the actor were to be consciously beautiful, a doctrine which also accorded well with the considered beauty of scene painting and the stage picture. The actor also made a picture of himself, a work of art in his own right, even a statue, since eighteenth-century acting manuals advised the player to study ancient statuary for graceful attitudes and forceful expressions of the passions. Pictorial and marmoreal vocabulary recurred in the everyday terminology of the critic, as when Thomas De Quincey, praising Helen Faucet's Antigone in 1845, exclaimed, 'What a revelation of beauty! forth stepped, walking in brightness, the most faultless of Grecian marbles ... What perfection of Athenian sculpture! the noble figure, the lovely arms, the fluent drapery! What an unveiling of the ideal statuesque!'[21] Likewise, Ellen Terry's Portia was 'a dream of beautiful pictures' to the painter Graham Robertson, and Clement Scott thought she could have stepped out of a modern canvas.

Finally, the inherited concept of tragedy as larger than life, and therefore tragic acting as necessarily larger than behaviour in daily living or in any other kind of acting is a very old one. In voice, gesture, attitude, facial expression and general deportment the tragic actor conceived of his art as ideal, an intelligible and powerful universalisation of the profounder depths of human experience and suffering. These notions began to break down in the nineteenth

---

[21] 'The Antigone of Sophocles', *The Works of Thomas De Quincey*, 2nd edn (Edinburgh, 1863), vol. XIII, p. 225.

century under the pressure of a drama concerned above all with contemporary domestic life and reflecting a growing interest in social and psychological realism, but from beginning to end the tragic actor was a special breed and his art a special art. The 'style in passion' of Charles Kemble, still acting in the early Victorian years, 'was uniformly lofty. There was variety indeed ... but it was a variety confined within the limits of what may be called heroic delivery, seldom or never a marked transition from it to colloquial realism.'[22] In full flow, the great tragic actor at the top of his form powerfully affected audiences, as witness numerous testimonies to the performances of Garrick, John Philip Kemble, Mrs Siddons, Edmund Kean and others. Prince Pückler-Muskau's account of Kean's Othello as he strangled Desdemona is one example (and this was in 1828, when Kean had much declined):

> The blood froze in one's veins, and even the boisterous and turbulent English public was for a time speechless, motionless – as if struck by lightning. Nay, I must acknowledge that sometimes during the tragedy, Othello's long torment ... was so painful, and the terror of what I knew was to follow grew upon me so involuntarily, that I turned away my face from a scene too horrible to contemplate.[23]

Such power was deployed in modern tragedy as well as Shakespeare, and the actor of melodrama also partook of it to the fullest extent of his own art, which was stamped with his own authority and force.

VOCAL DELIVERY AND MUSIC

One of the most praised attributes of Kean's acting was the musicality of his voice. His son Charles was criticised by George Henry Lewes for lacking it and praised by Ellen Terry for having it. To commend an actor for the music of his delivery was a commonplace of dramatic reviewing and it is clear that at least until Irving the ability to make a beautiful sound was a necessary accomplishment for the serious actor. In the late seventeenth century the declamatory music of heroic tragedy in the Restoration theatre was likened to recitative, and the association between music and the actor's voice was still very close in the nineteenth. Writing of the fine tragic actress Eliza O'Neill, who left the stage in 1819, one commentator remembered her 'deeply sonorous voice'. When Juliet is about to take the potion 'her words come forth like the tones of a low toned Eolian harp, rising and falling in their musical melancholy, till as it

---

[22] Westland Marston, *Our Recent Actors* (London, 1888), vol. I, p. 131. And Kemble was principally a comedian.

[23] *A Regency Visitor*, pp. 304–5.

Mr. C. KEAN, as

RICHARD III.

Plate 15   Charles Kean as Richard III, Drury Lane, 1838. Twopence coloured print. By courtesy of the University of Bristol Theatre Collection.

were the whole force of the blast swept the lyre into a shriek of horror. The action and the attitudes, so accompanied by the full music of her declaration, were enough to raise the spirit of the Poet from his quiet in Hades.'[24]

As an approach to vocal delivery in the theatre, the musical structuring of a speech lasted well into the twentieth century. When Fanny Kemble reappeared on the English stage in 1847, John Coleman recalled her thirty-line speech in Sheridan Knowles's *The Hunchback* in which the heroine pleads with her guardian to break off a match with a man she does not love: 'As it proceeded her voice gained strength, changing from the flute to the bell – from the bell to the clarion. Then upon a rising *sostenuto* of concentrated agony and defiance, she smote and stabbed Walter with that awful "Do it! Nor leave the task to me!"'[25] Such musical structuring can be easily detected in old recordings of Victorian and Edwardian actors, notably Ellen Terry, whose cadenced, musical pitch, intensified vibrato in moments of emotion, and sweetness and melody of voice are very marked even on the recordings she made in 1911 when she was in her sixties. At times her voice is declamatory, and this aspect of the voice also survived the century, being much in evidence in recordings. Robert Courtneidge remarked it as a fault of the old stock company actors that they had 'a tendency to be declamatory, to feel a sensuous delight in the sound of their own voices as they rolled out the glorious periods of Shakespeare and the older blank verse dramatists'.[26]

Victorian actors were not only accustomed to the music of their own voices but also to that of an orchestra, often a sizeable one. This orchestra was not used merely for overture and entr'acte music, but covered scene changes as well, cued entrances, sounded character motifs, took actors off stage, reinforced mood and often played *with*, or at least *under*, an actor's voice, as existing promptbooks with music cues demonstrate. Melodrama was especially dependent upon musical accompaniment, which was frequently almost continuous. The effect of this accompaniment on the actor's voice must have been considerable: he would need to dominate it, of course, but also to listen to it, to *use* it, to feed off it musically and emotionally, to incorporate its suggestive power into his own voice and his own performance generally.

[24] George Wightwick, *Theatricals, 45 Years Ago* (Portishead, 1862), pp. 4–5.
[25] 'Fanny Kemble', *Theatre* (March 1893), p. 143.
[26] *I Was an Actor Once*, p. 243.

ACTING SPACE

The need for authority over the space of large auditoriums as well as over the music was a significant requirement of Victorian acting. Ellen Terry remembered how, when she was in the Princess's company in the 1850s, Mrs Kean would sit in the gallery until she could hear every word spoken by the child actress on the stage. In the *Illustrated Times* in 1864, Tom Robertson noted of tragedians that 'the habit of addressing distant galleries gives a fearful distinctness to their utterance. They are terribly impartial to each letter of every word they utter ... The constant use of the voice renders its tones deep, rich, and mellow' (30 January). In our own age, when few actors express a fondness for performing in large theatres, it is interesting to read the testimony of the leading actors of the day to the 1832 Select Committee; they were almost unanimous in arguing for acting in a large theatre rather than a small one. Charles Kemble believed that if the audience crowded upon an actor in a small theatre his mind was distracted and his power lessened. Edmund Kean thought that 'the larger the stage the better the actor' (1832 *Report*, p. 87). T. P. Cooke, the definitive sailor hero of nautical melodrama, said that serious acting should be looked at from a distance rather than close up, and Macready, referring to the stage of the Haymarket (smaller than that of Drury Lane or Covent Garden) declared that in Shakespeare, 'when a great number have occupied the stage, I have felt the want of space, and too great proximity of the performers to me' (p. 132). Earlier actors, however, had been alarmed by the vast spaces of the new Drury Lane and Covent Garden, and complained. It was then felt that such large theatres led to a coarser and too strongly physical acting style (given the difficulties in hearing), but by the 1830s the actors seem to have adjusted.

Macready's view conveys a notable feature of early Victorian acting, the necessity of stage space between the star and other members of the company, unless the business of the scene dictated a passing proximity – a custom confirmed by contemporary prints. A stock company actor did not get too close to a star unless asked; the magic circle around the star was not to be violated with impunity by a lesser actor. There was also a custom that the star spoke more slowly than any other actor on stage, in order, one supposes, to assert status and to distinguish himself from the mass in large-cast spectacle plays.

THE POINT

Other traditional aspects of early Victorian acting included the 'point', a moment of intense physical or emotional action which was momentarily frozen in a powerful attitude or tableau – a kind of individualising of the group 'picture' that frequently concluded an act, but much older. The point was identical in nature and function to the Japanese 'mie', which can still be seen in kabuki. Edmund Kean's acting was full of point-making, and audiences anticipated traditional points with relish. A good description of a point is Coleman's: when Fanny Kemble finished the speech from *The Hunchback* mentioned above, 'she strode down to the right hand corner, returned to the centre, and then came to anchor, her right hand clutched on the back of the great oaken chair, her left thrown out toward Walter, her blazing eyes fixed on him in an attitude of denunciation and defiance.'[27] Points were usually taken dead centre, as far downstage as possible, and directed at the audience as much as at another actor. Before the growing demands of realism and the concept of the 'fourth wall', Victorian acting was strongly presentational, and the practice of facing front and addressing the audience rather than a fellow actor survived for a long time. Even in the 1890s one critic could compare Febvre of the Comédie Française to William Farren (then in his sixties), who 'constantly comes down to the footlights to make his points, and throughout his work acts deliberately at the audience'.[28] Actors did find, however, the new orchestra stalls audience much less demonstrative than the lively pit the stalls replaced; the old points did not go down so well with this more moneyed and more passive clientele, which forced an adjustment in acting style and the relationship of the actor to the audience. In any case, the retreat of the actor behind the proscenium made it much harder to relate intimately to the audience; previously, coming down to the footlights would bring him well out into the auditorium, with spectators on three sides.

THE STOCK COMPANY AND LINES OF BUSINESS

The customary acting practices of an older theatre tradition were maintained by the survival of the stock company, at least until the mid-Victorian period. A stock company facilitated the performance of a large repertory by a division into 'lines of business', a method by

[27] 'Fanny Kemble', p. 143.
[28] Edward F. Spence, 'The Acting of the Comédie Française', *Theatre* (August, 1893), p. 75. William Farren's father, who left the stage in 1855, did exactly the same thing.

which actors were able to cope with a great number of parts through specialising in certain stock character types repeated from play to play. If, for instance, a melodramatic actor found his company niche in the playing of villains, he would be that company's performer of all the principal villains in its repertory. One villain would not be identical to another, and would exhibit different characteristics of dress, class and social conduct, as well as genre – Gothic, nautical, domestic – but the *essential* villain remained the same, with the same basic character traits and patterns of behaviour carried over from melodrama to melodrama. Thus the actor of villainy, confronted with a part in a new melodrama, would bring his experience of the stereotype to the performance of this part, absorbing what variations there were from the previous roles of his villainous career. Other actors in the company would likewise deal with melodramatic characters such as the hero, heroine, comic man and good old man, since these all fell within recognised and distinct lines of business. The acting of melodrama, indeed, although undoubtedly more externalised, stylised and stereotyped than that of tragedy, was – at least for the portrayal of the serious emotions – close to tragic acting. Both kinds could be encompassed by the same stock company. Macready moved with ease from playing melodramatic villains to leading parts in tragedy, and many of his contemporaries performed with equal facility in both styles.

In Victorian theatrical terminology, the actor of villains was a 'heavy man', a reference to the nature of his part rather than his bulk. A full-size first-class stock company in a major theatre ought to possess, according to Dion Boucicault:

> A leading man, leading juvenile man, heavy man, first old man, first low comedian, walking gentleman, second old man and utility, second low comedian and character actor, second walking gentleman and utility, leading woman, leading juvenile woman, heavy woman, first old woman, first chambermaid, walking lady, second old woman and utility, second chambermaid and character actress, second walking lady and utility walking lady.[29]

It can be seen that every male line of business had its female equivalent. Boucicault's list adds up to eighteen, despite the omission of light comedian, an essential and popular comic stock character. No provincial stock company could afford this number; thus the doubling and trebling of parts necessary to play the classical repertory. It is not difficult to look at, say, *Hamlet*, from the point of view of stock company casting. The distribution of some of the characters

[29] Quoted in Dutton Cook, *Hours with the Players* (London, 1883), p. 243.

is obvious: Hamlet – leading man; Claudius – heavy man; Laertes – juvenile lead; Polonius – first old man; Gravediggers – first and second low comedians, Horatio – walking gentleman;[30] Ophelia – female juvenile lead or ingénue, to use the French term in common English use; Gertrude – leading lady, perhaps, but since it is not really a leading part, possibly heavy woman. Smaller parts, such as Osric, Rosencrantz, and Guildenstern would be played by utility actors, and in most companies some of these parts would be doubled and others cut. The same company would also play comedy, which similarly was easily divisible into lines of business.

When a touring star visited the provincial stock company, it was customary for each actor to take one step down in the hierarchy of parts. This might mean a brief sojourn outside one's line of business, but the system was flexible enough to accommodate necessary variations. A leading actor, for example, did not have a line of business, but simply played all the leading parts of whatever character description, although he might specialise in tragedy and play little or no comedy. If there were casting problems, some actors were versatile enough to cross lines of business. The responsibility of the 'character' actor was to play parts that did not fit into the usual categories, such as drunkards, comic villains, village idiots and a whole range of special characters with particular and marked peculiarities.

Since lines of business preserved character stereotyping, in spite of the variety possible within each line, they served to maintain traditions and customs of performance, as well as a standard set of characters for the dramatist to write for, that might otherwise have disappeared much sooner from the stage. They resisted change, or at least made it much slower. In the area of comedy, for example, the careful distinction between the low comedian and the light comedian lasted for almost the whole of the nineteenth century. The two lines of business were never confused, and the actors who specialised in them were entirely different in style.

The low comedian, the direct descendant of the Elizabethan clown, was fundamentally a farce actor, but also necessary for comedy and melodrama, in which he played the part of comic man. He often took the roles of countrymen, servants, street sellers, nouveau-riche landowners and working-class eccentrics, the low comedian being commonly a considerable social cut below the light comedian. He was either energetically ludicrous or phlegmatically droll and the helpless victim of chance and misunderstanding. The

[30] A walking gentleman or lady was a friend or confidante of the hero or heroine and acted as a 'feed' to the principal performer.

low comedian made an immediate impact upon the audience. J. B. Buckstone's voice offstage would set the audience roaring, and his face was irresistibly funny. Edward Wright, Buckstone's contemporary and the star low comedian of the Adelphi in the 1840s, would reduce the audience to paroxysms of laughter at a stroke. According to one spectator, Wright would

> ... without uttering a word across the footlights, give the audience a confidential wink and send them into convulsions ... Never have I heard such laughter as that which he evoked, never have I seen people so completely collapsed and exhausted by the mere effect of their mirth. In some of Wright's scenes in *The Green Bushes* I have fallen helpless, spineless, across the front of the box, almost sick with laughter.[31]

J. L. Toole, the last of the great low comedians (he left the stage in 1895) had a similar effect.

The light comedian played the dashing gentleman lover. Tom Robertson's satirical description of him in the *Illustrated Times* could have applied equally, except for details of costume, to the light comedian of fifty years before:

> Conceive a boisterous, blatant fellow, in a green coat and brass buttons, buckskin breeches and boots; or in a blue frock, white waistcoat, and straw-coloured continuations, always talking at the top of his voice, slapping you heavily upon the back, laughing for five minutes consecutively, jumping over the chairs and tables, haranguing a mob from your drawing-room window, going down upon his knees to your daughter or your wife or both, kissing your servant-maid, borrowing your loose cash, and introducing a sheriff's officer to your family as an old college friend.   (19 March 1864)

An actor like Charles Mathews, the *nonpareil* of modern comedy in the early and mid-Victorian period, would be much more stylish and restrained in a gentlemanly fashion than Robertson suggests, but of the general run of light comedians, many of whom modelled themselves upon Mathews but did not possess half his talent, the description is probably close to the truth. Although always the stage dandy, Mathews was careful to separate himself from the race of light comedians, and never considered his acting as belonging to a particular line of business. When Macready wrote to Henry Compton in 1841 about a light comedian who had applied for a position at Drury Lane, he asked, 'Is he vivacious on the stage? Is he bustling? Is he light, elastic, and nimble in his movements? Has he a

---

[31] *Edmund Yates: His Recollections and Experiences* (London, 1884), vol. i, pp. 197–98. *The Green Bushes* (1845) is a melodrama by Buckstone, in which Wright played the travelling showman Grinnidge.

hearty and ready laugh? Has he humour? Does he make his effects with care and judgment? Does he give evidence of genius, or seem likely to do so? Or is he merely even, level, unoffending, and thus far agreeable?'[32]

Out of the early Victorian light comedian and closely allied to him came the mid-Victorian eccentric comedian, whose mannerisms of dress and behaviour were extreme and who was best exemplified by E. A. Sothern's Lord Dundreary in Tom Taylor's *Our American Cousin* (1858), a creation of languorous personal foppishness combined with inspired idiocy of speech, walk and stage business. His style, compounded of passive vapidity and gross absurdity, illustrated George Henry Lewes's complaint that in general the English actor knew of no medium 'between the extreme of apathy and the extreme of exaggeration. His passion runs into rant, his drollery into grotesqueness; he forces his voice, takes the stage, saws the air, and dresses hyperbolically.'[33]

With the disappearance of the stock company repertory and its replacement by the metropolitan long run and the touring play, the old lines of business began to break down. However, it took many years for the styles that marked these lines to die away: the lofty declamatory grandeur of the leading man in tragedy, the demonic physicality and high emotional intensity of the heavy man in melodrama, the manic energy of the light comedian. Even as late as 1931 the late Victorian and Edwardian actor Seymour Hicks could still advise what he still called the light comedian that his was a difficult 'line of business,' since he needed 'excessive speed at times and always bell-like distinctness of speech. Your manner must be ever alert, your twinkle perpetual, and your gaiety a thing to be envied.'[34] English acting was slow to change, especially in Shakespeare and the older drama, and Victorian traditions of performance, themselves descended from the eighteenth century, did not suddenly vanish from the stage upon the death of Queen Victoria.

MELODRAMATIC ACTING

Despite the long persistence of these traditions, however, acting had in fact been changing for many years. One of the most obvious changes was the disappearance, noticed by many critics, of the older style of melodramatic acting that characterised the early Gothic,

[32] *Memoir of Henry Compton*, ed. Charles and Edward Compton (London, 1879), pp. 98–99.
[33] George Henry Lewes, *On Actors and the Art of Acting* (London, 1875), p. 241.
[34] Seymour Hicks, *Acting* (London, 1931), pp. 67–68. The fifth chapter contains advice on the playing of several traditional lines of business.

nautical and domestic melodrama. A vivid description of such a style is provided by Westland Marston, who as a boy visited Sadler's Wells in 1834 and saw George Almar in a villain's role:

> I was curious enough, even on the first night of attending a theatre, to ask myself why Mr. Almar made such incessant use of his arms. Now they were antithetically extended, the one skyward, the other earthward, like the sails of a windmill; now they were folded sternly across his bosom; now raised in denunciation; now clasped in entreaty, and considerately maintained in their positions long enough to impress the entire audience at leisure with the effect intended.[35]

Forty years later such acting was not seen, at least in the West End, where melodrama still flourished but was becoming gentrified, in acting style as well as content. However, one must always be careful in generalising to make geographical distinctions: the more emphatic kinds of melodramatic acting survived outside the West End and the major provincial centres, especially in the East End, on the Surrey side of the Thames, and in the lesser touring companies. Melodrama was changing its nature as society changed and, while a villain remained a villain and a hero a hero, the new kind of villain and hero were socially distinct from their predecessors and subtler in characterisation. The older acting styles would have been inappropriate for their portrayal, and the changing and more middle-class West End audience would have found them merely amusing, as even middle-class tastes in acting were not the same as they were a generation ago.

TRANSVESTISM AND DURATION

One of the most interesting, if perhaps relatively minor, changes in acting was that a member of the audience in the late Victorian period was less likely to see a woman playing a man's part – with the notable exception of pantomime, in which the Principal Boy was always a shapely female in tights. Transvestism had by no means disappeared by the end of the century, but it was a standard feature of the early and mid-Victorian stage. Priscilla Horton was Macready's Ariel; Elizabeth Poole played the Fool in Charles Kean's *Lear*; the American Charlotte Cushman's Romeo was a popular role in her repertoire, and Marie Wilton played a long succession of boys' parts in burlesques. There were at least half-a-dozen female Hamlets. These are only a few examples of the cross-sexual nature of Victorian casting. Men also played women's parts, but only in pantomime and

[35] *Our Recent Actors*, vol. I, p. 7.

burlesque, whereas women undertook serious male roles. It is doubtful if this aspect of Victorian acting is explicable only in terms of the
exigencies of casting and the popularity of certain actresses. Wider
social and psychological factors must be relevant, and the subject is
well worth closer investigation.

The long engagement of an actor with a part was an important
aspect of that actor's appeal; this was as true of the pre-Victorian
theatre as the Victorian. Like James O'Neill in *The Count of Monte
Cristo* or Geneviève Ward in *Forget Me Not*, the touring star could be
so completely identified with a particular role that he or she would
play it hundreds or thousands of times all over the world. Within the
stock company system such single-mindedness was quite impracti-
cal, but actors nevertheless kept many roles in their repertoires for
the whole course of their acting careers. Macready first played
Macbeth at Covent Garden in 1820; in 1851 his very last performance was in the same character. For over thirty years he played the
part and was still making discoveries about the character and the
acting of it at the end of his career. By the time Irving came to play
Hamlet at the Lyceum under the Bateman management in 1874, he
had appeared in the play at eight different theatres, seven of them
provincial (Osric at the Princess's in 1859 was his only previous
London *Hamlet*), and had acted eight different characters: the Priest,
Osric, Guildenstern, Horatio, the Ghost, Claudius, Laertes (at four
theatres) and Hamlet (at three). On two occasions – in Manchester in
1861 and Birmingham in 1865 – he had played Laertes with two star
Hamlets, the American Edwin Booth and Fechter respectively. His
experience, and Macready's, was simply impossible under the
long-run system; only in his own touring company could a star
repeat a part as often as he wished and as often as commercial
imperatives allowed. Today we are lucky to see a star attempt a great
classical part more than once or twice during his career.

REALISM, REFINEMENT AND THE DOMESTIC

The general response of drama to social change, to the increasing
materialisation and urbanisation of Victorian life, and the growing
population of *dramatis personae* by middle-class characters living in
middle-class urban settings, was to attempt – at least in comedy and
the serious drama – to match the increasing verisimilitude of stage
setting with an increasing verisimilitude of characterisation and
social behaviour on stage. When at the end of the nineteenth century
this verisimilitude presented the drawing-rooms of Mayfair on
stage, it was no longer possible for the actor to behave as if he were in

a bandit's hideout or an East End pub. Thus, as we have seen, an entirely new race of young actors and actresses, themselves of the right social class and with the right manners, had to be found to inhabit these drawing-rooms. In other words, the drama was becoming more 'realistic', at any rate in the sense of replicating the social surface of life and the behaviour of ordinary people in situations of stress or comic entanglement. Near the end of the century the plays of Ibsen, liked or disliked, were a powerful impulse toward the seriously realistic presentation of middle-class family life and the detail of social environment, but much earlier than that the influence of the French stage had modified the melodramatic and comic extremism of English drama and therefore of characterisation and acting. It had also gradually led to a new tightness and credibility of plot structure, often the weakest part of English playwriting.

The supposed refinement of French social behaviour as well as French plays was adapted wholesale to the English stage. The 'gentlemanly melodrama' of the 1850s, especially manifested in a play like *The Corsican Brothers*, showed itself not only in its version of Parisian high society but also in the restrained and socially proper acting of Charles Kean in the double role of the dei Franchi twins. A French actor whose charm, gracefulness and natural manners impressed London audiences of the 1850s was Charles Fechter, and his Hamlet of 1861 was, despite its flaws, the realisation of a thoroughly modern prince, a nineteenth-century gentleman with taste and breeding. The new kind of French social polish in English acting was perfectly represented by Alfred Wigan, an actor with a classical education who had formerly been a schoolteacher and was later to manage the Olympic and the St James's. It was Wigan who played the prototype of the fashionable, silky, top-hatted and fur-coated villain on the English stage, Château-Renaud in *The Corsican Brothers* in 1852. Westland Marston thought that with his stage characteristics of 'extreme refinement, delicate perception, and truth to nature, combined with deep, though quiet feeling' he was 'peculiarly fitted for the representation of various types of Frenchmen' (II, 252). Wigan's acting in English middle-class characters showed the same quiet restraint; the *Times* said of the hen-pecked hero of *Still Waters Run Deep*, 'The acting of Mr Wigan as *John Mildmay* exactly corresponds to Mr Tom Taylor's dialogue, in which everything like common-place exaggeration is shunned, and the language is made to approximate as much as possible to that of real life . . . Seldom do we see acting so rigidly truthful' (16 May 1855).

'Real life' in Victorian painting, the theatre and the novel, was progressively associated with the portrayal of the home, the virtues of domestic life, and the family under strain. At the beginning of the Victorian period Richard Hengist Horne deplored the tendency of the theatre to 'shadow forth the smaller peculiarities of an actual and every-day life domesticity',[36] but soon it was much more than a tendency and much too dominating and ubiquitous to resist. The themes of home and family became prominent in the drama and acting also reflected the same concerns, especially the nineteenth-century artistic obsession with the father–daughter relationship, which strongly colours melodrama as well as affecting other kinds of plays. The best example of an actor outstanding in depicting the tenderness of domestic love was Macready. In his performance of the title role in Sheridan Knowles's tragedy *Virginius* (1820), Macready – who has to kill his daughter to save her from the evil decemvir Appius – made audiences weep because of his overwhelming feeling for Virginia; the role of Virginius stayed in his repertoire for thirty years. Reviewing his King John in the *Tatler*, Leigh Hunt said that Macready was best 'where he approaches domestic passion, and has to give way to soft or overwhelming emotions', but faulted him in his delineation of what Hunt called the 'ideal' (29 November 1830). Macready himself was the father of a large family whom he adored, and for whom he endured the drudgery of acting; he held all the familial ideals of his time. He had three daughters, one of whom died at the age of three while Macready was rehearsing Bulwer's *Money*. Large families and the deaths of children – Macready outlived all six children by his first wife – were inescapable domestic realities for the Victorians; it is not surprising that actors were imbued with the domestic spirit in performance.

APPROACHES TO ACTING

The increasing refinement of middle-class social behaviour, the influence of French drama and French acting, and the growing social and domestic realism of dramatic text, setting and character do not entirely explain the changes that came over Victorian acting. The pre-Victorian actor could approach a part in several ways. There was the old and continuing controversy, crystallised by Diderot in *Paradoxe sur le comédien* (not published until 1830), about whether an actor should feel the emotions he portrays or simulate them by outward forms, that is, whether his intellect or his emotions should control his acting. The argument between factions pro and con lasted right through the nineteenth century, and no leading actor would have been unaware of it. Whatever the actor's choice, the

[36] R. H. Horne, *A New Spirit of the Age* (London, 1844), vol. II, p. 99.

result was visualised in the language of gesture, attitude and facial expression already referred to. Feeling and technique were one thing, approach to character another. An actor could take either a situational or holistic view of his character. In other words, he could play his part from situation to situation, playing each significant dramatic moment for what it was and extracting the maximum passion and effect from it, plotting his course through the play from emotional climax to emotional climax, saving himself in between and making a 'point', if appropriate, at each climax. This is what Edmund Kean did. The other approach was to view the character as dramatically unified and attempt to show this unity, the governing 'idea' of the character, on stage. John Philip Kemble was an actor of this type, sometimes accused of being too intellectual in performance. Certainly by the early nineteenth century the notion that character was the vital element of a play was common among both actors and critics; the meaning of a play could be found in the life and experience of the principal character or characters. The object of the literary or theatrical critic, such as Coleridge and William Hazlitt, was to analyse a character and show the springs of motivation that lead to action and behaviour. The object of the actor was to explain this motivation on stage through carefully selected emotional responses to the events of a play, responses in harmony with a total interpretation of the character.

Such an approach was focussed principally on Shakespeare, but it affected the stage characterisations of many non-Shakespearean leading roles in the Romantic period. Indeed, the importance attached to individual character was thoroughly Romantic. The poet created the agonised Romantic hero; the critic wrote about him; the actor played him. Romantic individualism in performance was psychologically based, as were critical studies of motivation in Shakespeare. According to Marston, Macready combined psychological perception with a coherent and unified view of character:

> Of the qualities to which Macready owed his eminence, the highest and most remarkable were his psychological insight and his artistic power of translating his emotions into strikingly appropriate – often absolutely symbolic – forms of expression. If it be granted that one or two tragedians have, in some parts, excelled him in the sudden revelation of passion, it is yet probable that he has never been excelled, if equalled, in the complete and harmonious development of character. In all his great impersonations was shown the same faculty of grasping the central idea of his part, and of making all the lights thrown upon details correspond with that idea.[37]

[37] *Our Recent Actors*, vol. 1, p. 99.

Plate 16   Macready as Henry V, 1830. *The Dramatic Magazine*.

Plate 17   The heroic actor: Lewis Waller as Henry V, Lyceum Theatre, 1900.
By courtesy of the University of Bristol Theatre Collection.

PSYCHOLOGY

The Victorian theatre, affected as it was by so many major social and cultural developments, could hardly have been isolated from the findings of modern psychologists, many of which were popularised in the press and available in cheap library editions. Psychology had for some time been moving away from the metaphysical and spiritual and concentrating on scientific facts; in the nineteenth century it became physiological, neurological, experimental and analytic. The work of Gustav Fechner, Rudolph Lotze, Johannes Müller, and Wilhelm Wundt in Germany was complemented in Britain by that of Charles Bell, James Mill, Alexander Bain, Charles Darwin and Herbert Spencer. The polymath George Henry Lewes was not only playwright, dramatic critic of the *Leader* and author of one of the best Victorian studies of acting, *On Actors and the Art of Acting* (1875), but also Professor of Physiology in the University of London and author of a series of volumes under the general title *Problems of Life and the Mind.* The third of these, published in 1879, was *The Study of Psychology: Its Object, Scope, and Method.* In it he insisted that the social activities of man were capable of psychological study, thus heralding a new development in the field, which in Britain had for the past generation been largely concerned with the examination of abnormal and pathological states. All this, of course, before Freud, and, some of it, at least, grist for the actor's mill.

The interest in abnormal states of mind among nineteenth-century psychologists and literary critics is relevant to the extensive contemporary debate over *Hamlet.* Writers sought psychological explanations for Hamlet's alleged delay in killing Claudius: he was too weak and melancholy to take positive action; he was too much of a thinker to live in the real world and be decisive; he was mad; he was not mad, but sensitive to the point of hysteria. If Macready's psychological insight assisted him in presenting emotions truthfully and strikingly on stage, Irving's Hamlet in 1874 was a Victorian benchmark for psychological analysis on the actor's part and the meticulous construction of a psychologically complex but credible character within the bounds of the doctrine, which Irving did not question, that the meaning of the play could be found in the meaning of the central character. Irving substantially domesticated *Hamlet* by the usual Victorian excision of Fortinbras and Shakespeare's ending, as well as reducing almost to extinction the sense of a festering Danish body politic existing outside Hamlet's personal relationships

Plate 18   Caricature of Irving as Mathias in *The Bells*. Watercolour by F. D. Marshall. By courtesy of the University of Bristol Theatre Collection.

with Ophelia and Gertrude.[38] He rejected the traditional points, developed new business and exhibited a 'natural', unconventional and contemporary Hamlet. In this he followed the also unconventional Fechter, who, all critics agreed, was thoroughly modern in the part. Fechter delivered the text colloquially, behaved as a well-bred man of the time who might have been seen strolling in the fashionable areas of London or Paris, and devised business 'expositive of a purpose to be "natural" and to illustrate the behaviour of every-day life'.[39] Irving did not go so far, although he stressed the ordinary, human qualities of a noble but tormented prince. The classic gestures and attitudes had gone. He revived *Hamlet* at his own Lyceum in 1878 and again in 1881 and 1885. It was one of the great performances of the late Victorian stage, in which a psychological and domestic modernity triumphed over theatrical tradition.

No one suggested to Irving how he might play Hamlet, or directed any Victorian star toward a particular interpretation of a part that would suit another conception than the actor's. Real changes in theatre practice came when the actor was no longer supreme, no longer entirely responsible for interpretation. Experiments in set and costume design and lighting led eventually to the creation of the part of Designer in all these areas; the new figure of the Producer or Director worked in collaboration with the Designer to make thematic statements about a play simply by the adoption of a specific lighting or set design. Sometimes this design is so prominent that it tells the audience exactly what to think, never mind the text or the actors.

For better or worse, the Victorian stage was a neutral space; it did not make statements about content because all it tried to do, sometimes with archaeological punctiliousness, was reproduce by illusionistic means the complete physical environment of a play, whether historical or contemporary. Production could be on a very large scale and effects elaborate, but this served only the cause of spectacle, which existed for its own pictorial sake. Lighting lit the actor and the scenery; it could be romantic and atmospheric but did not underline a theme or symbol arbitrarily selected by the director. The actor interpreted character and not the play; that was up to the audience. The combination of a longer rehearsal period allowed for by the long run and the psychological complexity of new dramatic characterisation meant that the actor needed to, and had more time

---

[38] A homely domestic touch that was thoroughly Victorian, but objected to by some critics as undignified, was giving the Ghost a dressing-gown for his appearance in the Closet Scene.

[39] William Winter, *Shakespeare on Stage: First Series* (New York, 1911), p. 404.

to, explore a part in collaboration with his colleagues and the director. Ibsen, Strindberg and Chekhov, for example, could not be effectively produced after half a dozen rehearsals and even leading actors found themselves requiring assistance with interpretation. It did not take long for the director, who also assumed sole authority for the visual quality of a production, to interpret on his own account and to persuade (or require) the actors to acquiesce in his interpretation. The Victorian actor was finally being modernised: his old independent life was ending, and the new world of director's theatre was being born.

5

Dramatists and the drama

If the acting practices of the Victorian theatre are remote from modern experience and require an act of historical understanding on our own part, the same is true of the drama which these actors performed. While a handful of Victorian plays prove popular on the stage today and others are occasionally rediscovered and revived, their success does not bring nearer to our own comprehension the thousands of forgotten pieces that entertained the audiences of Victoria's reign. In order to appreciate them, we need to know of the conventions they honoured as well as of the conditions in which they were written and the social and cultural life to which they gave expression.

As the playwright is important in an assessment of the drama itself, it might be best to begin with his own professional position. In this case, 'his' reflects sexual statistics as well as being a useful generic possessive. In Allardyce Nicoll's lists of authors and plays in volumes IV (1800–1850) and V (1850–1900). of *A History of English Drama 1660–1900*, 427 authors of plays either printed or produced, or both – some of these are printed dramatic poems or monologues – are clearly identified as women, out of a total of 3,486. The percentage of women dramatists in the second half of the century is greater than in the first, and they are mostly clustered in the 1880s and 1890s. In the first half of the century, the majority of female playwrights listed produced work between 1800 and 1825, and the incidence of plays printed but not acted is higher. Two other factors must be taken into account. There is an overlap of names between volumes IV and V since, obviously, some authors were active in both periods. The real totals, therefore, will be somewhat smaller, but set against this is the fact that there are more women authors than Nicoll's totals suggest, since many dramatists are identified only by surname or surname and initials, since there are hordes of plays by 'unknown authors' and numbers of pseudonyms, and since many plays and authors never got into Nicoll's lists at all.

INCOME AND COPYRIGHT

At the end of the eighteenth century and early in the nineteenth, when the theatre was still prosperous and both Covent Garden and Drury Lane were enlarged to accommodate more spectators, a dramatist with an established reputation could do well for himself financially. The copyright of a successful play published, often handsomely, in a 3s. or 5s. octavo edition, would fetch between £100 and £200. In the theatre a new system was introduced in the 1790s of paying an author writing for the patent houses £33 6s. 8d. for each of the first nine nights of a mainpiece and £100 each on the twentieth and fortieth nights – a total of £500 if a play lasted that long. An afterpiece fetched much less, usually a lump sum of about £100. The minor theatres of the 1820s and 1830s paid more modestly, between £50 and £70 to a leading dramatist such as Douglas Jerrold or J. B. Buckstone. Thus a prolific dramatist could, in these financial circumstances, earn a reasonable if not princely income, and some writers did very well out of hit comedies: in 1803 George Colman made £1,200 from *John Bull*, and in 1807 Thomas Morton received £1,000 for *Town and Country*, both performed at Covent Garden, then the preëminent company for comedy.

As we have seen, the end of the Napoleonic War in 1815 brought economic hardship to the theatre as it did to the nation, and payments to dramatists dwindled in size as bankruptcies among managers increaed. These payments were substantially reduced by a different and ungenerous method of remuneration widely introduced in the 1840s, a flat payment of £50 or £100 an act in the West End and far less outside it. No payments were made for revivals, and it did not matter how long a play ran. A manager could make a small fortune from a smash hit and his playwrights receive a relative pittance. Tom Taylor, the author of *The Ticket-of-Leave Man*, which had a record long run of 407 performances at the Olympic in the sixties and remained one of the most popular melodramas of the century, was paid £200 for the play. His hit comedy of the same decade, *Our American Cousin*, ran a year and profited the manager of the Haymarket, Buckstone, £20,000. Taylor received £150. In the sixties the Bancrofts began paying Tom Robertson a fixed sum for every performance of his comedies at the Prince of Wales's, from £1 a night for *Society* in 1865 to £5 a night for *M.P.* in 1870. Thus for much of the Victorian period it was almost impossible for a dramatist, no matter how successful, to live comfortably only by writing plays. Robertson was exceptionally prosperous for a playwright of the sixties, and only a generous and honourable manager like Macready would insist that Bulwer accept £600 for *Richelieu* in 1839. Sheridan Knowles, with Bulwer the most eminent dramatist of the 1830s, also received £600 for *Love* at Covent Garden. As an actor, Charles Kean offered Knowles £1,000 for a play that never materialised, and when he became a manager in the 1850s was noted for his generosity to authors. When this generosity is translated in figures, we see that in the first three years of his Princess's management Kean paid out £3,685 for nineteen original plays, or an average of £194 a play (including afterpieces), and £1,135 for eleven adaptations or translations from the French, or £103 a play. Kean's 'house' dramatist at the Princess's for several years was Boucicault, and this was another way a playwright could ensure himself a regular if modest income. He had to work hard for his £3 or £5 a week: in 1845, for instance, George Dibdin Pitt wrote seventeen melodramas and a pantomime for the Britannia, and acted as well.

Thus, like Jerrold, Taylor, Robertson and W. S. Gilbert, dramatists had to work at other trades like journalism to earn a sufficient income. Even the highest earnings of Victorian dramatists pale beside the sums paid to successful novelists. At the same time as the income of dramatists was declining in the early Victorian years, that of novelists and journalists was rising. In 1840 Chapman and Hall gave Dickens £3,000 for a six-month copyright on *Barnaby Rudge*. While Knowles, the most celebrated dramatist of the 1820s and 1830s, made a total of £4,600 from writing for the stage, Trollope listed his earnings from his novels as £61,000. Dickens, who profited handsomely from journalism himself, could as an editor offer £1,000 for a short story in *All the Year Round* in the sixties. The financial incentive to write fiction or other kinds of journalistic material rather than plays was compelling, especially since a publisher or magazine editor might well treat the author better than a theatre manager treated him, at least in that his work would not be subject to inordinate delays in production or ruthless rewriting. Because fees for plays were so low, the pressure on dramatists to write quickly or to adapt French – or sometimes German – plays rather than create original work was considerable; quantity rather than quality was necessary to maintain any sort of income level.

Neither was the dramatist helped financially by the copyright situation. The copyright value of a published play had fallen off to almost nothing by the beginning of the Victorian period. The market for well-printed plays had virtually vanished; what was published appeared in cheap and nasty acting editions designed largely for stage use by amateurs. The publishers of these editions paid authors only a few pounds for a copyright and then collected the performance fees for each play on their lists. Before 1833 there was no copyright in performance: if a play were printed it could be freely acted, and an author received nothing from provincial performances of a London success, published or unpublished. The Dramatic Copyright Act of 1833 gave an author sole property of an unpublished work and exclusive rights of representation. The Dramatic Authors' Society was founded to protect the interests of dramatists, collect their provincial fees and struggle to close loopholes in the law, the chief one being that the Act of 1833 was interpreted to mean that a publisher who held a copyright could still collect the performance fees rather than the author; it was no wonder that playwrights were reluctant to see their work printed. The Society took time to be effective and efficient, and even then some popular playwrights, like Boucicault, refused to join and made their own lucrative financial agreements. The Secretary of the Society in the sixties, J. Stirling Coyne, explained to the Select Committee how it operated:

> A dramatic author receives from the manager of a London theatre a certain sum for the right of acting a piece in London, either for a limited number of years, or for the entire copyright, and that piece belongs to the manager in London during the term of the arrangement, whatever that may be, but the copyright belongs to the author in the provinces. The author gives, through the secretary, permission to the managers of theatres in the provinces to play all the pieces on the list of the Dramatic Authors' Society for a certain sum per year or per month, according to the duration of the season. He sells the London right, and the London manager reserves the piece for his own theatre, generally for a term of three years, and then it reverts to the author, but the provincial right is in all cases reserved by the author himself ... The Society receives the sum agreed upon in bulk, and it is distributed among the authors *pro rata* according to the number of pieces that each author may have had acted during the year at that [provincial] theatre.   (1866 *Report*, p. 209)

The financial and legal position of playwrights improved in the 1860s. Firstly, led by Boucicault and then by F. C. Burnand, dramatists began to demand sharing arrangements with managers instead of the usual payment by act. Boucicault himself profited to the extent of thousands of pounds when he made such arrangements with Webster of the Adelphi for *The Colleen Bawn* in 1860 and *The Octoroon* in 1861. Secondly, the system of payment by act or payment per night was gradually replaced by a royalty system. As opposed to Taylor's £200 for *The Ticket-of-Leave Man*, for example, Henry Arthur Jones made over the years £18,000 from his melodrama *The Silver King*, and Pinero over £30,000 from *The Second Mrs Tanqueray*. Edmund Yates, whose father was manager of the Adelphi and accustomed to giving Buckstone £70 for the London rights to a three-act play, reflected upon the changed situation in the 1880s:

> Now I have been furnished by a worthy friend of mine, a writer of melodrama of the present day ... with a return of the fees which he has received for one piece alone, which at the time of writing are within 150*l.* of a total of *ten thousand pounds*, and which are still rolling in at the rate of 100*l.* a week! In this return, America, really unknown in the early days as a money-producer for the English dramatist, figures for 800*l.* more than London; the provinces, valued by Buckstone at a 10*l.* note, yield nearly 3000*l.*; while Australia, at that time chiefly known as a receptacle for convicts, yields more than double the amount originally paid by my father for the whole acting copyright.[1]

The sums received by Jones and Pinero probably included royalites from publication, and with the passage of much more effective copyright legislation the popular dramatist was assured of a substantial income from the reading public. The Berne Convention of 1886 prevented the widespread pilfering of French and German drama and gave English dramatists more incentive to do original work; more important was a new American copyright law of 1891 that put a stop to transatlantic piracy; it was only then that leading dramatists saw their plays through the press as a matter of course, now writing lengthy stage directions for the reader rather than the stage manager. An example is from Shaw's *The Philanderer*: '*The library remains unoccupied for ten minutes.*'

CENSORSHIP AND AUDIENCE TASTE

Victorian playwrights were subject to legal as well as financial constraints. In their case the law took the form of the Examiner of Plays, an official who exercised power of censorship on behalf of the Lord Chamberlain, whom we have encountered in another capacity as a licenser of theatres. He also, through his Examiner, licensed the drama. Early in the reign of Victoria, the Theatre

[1] *Edmund Yates: His Recollections and Experiences* (London, 1884), vol. I, p. 34.

Regulation Act of 1843 superseded the Licensing Act of 1737, abolishing the monopolies and privileges of Drury Lane and Covent Garden and giving all theatres the freedom to play any kind of drama, but also tightening censorship. Now all theatres in Great Britain, including those previously licensed by local magistrates, had to submit to the Lord Chamberlain any piece performed 'for hire', and he had absolute authority to forbid performance of the whole or any part of a play. This legal right lasted until 1968.

In practice, the Examiner of Plays exercised the Lord Chamberlain's authority in matters of religion and politics. The free expression of sexual problems and the overt employment of sexual humour were by no means aspects of the Victorian novel and public taste, conservative in these matters, also ensured their absence on the stage. Here the Examiner followed public taste from a safe distance, rather than suppressing an urgent and collective creative desire. The playwright Shirley Brooks did not believe that censorship of the drama on moral matters was necessary: 'I believe that the British public are tolerably fastidious, as far as questions of public indecency go, and I think you might leave the matter to them.' This was just as true, he said of East End and transpontine audiences (1866 *Report*, p. 158). There was, in fact, a considerable degree of unanimity among witnesses testifying to the 1832 and 1866 Select Committees and among other sources that a working-class audience was much less tolerant of any suggestion of sexual impropriety than a West End audience.

English dramatists would certainly, if allowed, have given some expression to religious and political subject matter, especially since religious and political controversies in the Victorian period were frequently intense and attracted public attention. In these areas the Examiner of Plays had to be vigilant, and many a passage containing an alleged or actual political or religious allusion was struck out of an otherwise acceptable script. Some scripts were rejected entirely. The dramatist James Kenney believed that 'the real ground to be depended on for the necessity of a licenser, is with reference to the political allusions which may act upon the feeling or passions of an audience' (p. 230). The legal exclusion of politics and religion from the stage was a restriction that contributed to the feeling among many contemporaries that the drama was trivial and isolated from the mainstream of English life. The Lord Chamberlain, however, was hardly challenged on this exclusion until the 1890s. Victorian managers and dramatists found it on the whole advantageous to have the boundaries of their subject matter clearly and safely laid out for them; in the same way Hollywood subscribed for many years, with

little protest, to the restrictions of the Hays Office on the acceptabi-
lity of material for the screen.

When we turn from the position of the dramatist to the content
of what he wrote, we see that 1837 did not, chronologically speaking, represent a new departure. If anything, the start of the Victorian years indicated development and change rather than a beginning. The principal forms of pre-Victorian theatre – poetic tragedy,
verse and prose comedy, farce, melodrama, pantomime and
extravaganza – continued into the 1840s, but significant changes
were taking place. The legitimate tragedy, an inheritance of the
Elizabethans and the Romantic poets who imitated them, was at its
last gasp. The rapid evolution of nineteenth-century British society,
the growth of industries and great cities, the social turbulence of
revolution abroad, war and depression, the explosion of population,
new technology and new transport systems – all this, as we have
noted, changed the theatre and its audience, which was no longer
satisfied with refinement and literature on stage and the leisurely
exploration of character and mental action that distinguishes the
drama written by the Romantics and their followers. Much of the
eighteenth-century repertory was jettisoned in the nineteenth,
leaving Shakespeare and a few tragedies, comedies, farces and
musical pieces. Times had changed, the public had changed and
tastes had changed.

Yet some writers were doubtful about the dramatic value of the
new society. Richard Hengist Horne, who deplored the realistic,
domestic and quotidian character of the new theatre and was a firm
adherent of the ideal in drama, doubted 'whether the circumstances
of modern society and civilization are eventful enough to give new
incidents to the Drama'.[2] J. W. Cole even thought that modern life
was too monotonous to afford subjects for comic drama: 'There are
few salient eccentricities in modern manners to afford subject for
illustration or caricature ... Now, we are all alike; ever in a hurry,
on the one high road of utilitarianism, thinking, travelling, and
sleeping at railway speed.'[3] Horne did admit to the demise of the
five-act legitimate play, 'which includes philosophical exposition of
human character and philosophical and rhetorical documentation
upon it. But the most legitimate, because the genuine offspring of
the age, is that Drama which catches the manners as they rise and
embodies the characteristics of the time.'[4]

[2] *A New Spirit of the Age* (London, 1844), vol. II, p. 123.
[3] *The Life and Theatrical Times of Charles Kean*, vol. II, p. 336.
[4] *A New Spirit of the Age*, vol. II, p. 90.

TRAGEDY

The authors of other plays, however, persisted in ignoring their own age and composing verse tragedies and comedies in imitation of the Elizabethans. Even Jerrold, who wrote a lively prose tragedy, *Thomas à Becket*, for the Surrey in 1829 and was a leading melodramatist, felt it necessary to give his actors a contorted pseudo-Elizabethan speech to utter.[5] By the 1830s and the waning of the Romantic adoration of the Elizabethan drama such plays became less frequent, but they were still written, and in much the same tradition, characterised by a sort of dramatic bloodlessness, leisurely philosophical introspection, static and descriptive passages of verse, a noble hero, seemingly without flaw, and an idealised heroine overflowing with goodness and innocence. (Here at least is a sign of the Victorian times: the flawless heroine and the too noble hero often appear in Victorian melodrama, and their very perfection can be dramatically enervating.) What is missing is the colour and agony of some of the Romantic tragedies, such as Coleridge's *Remorse* (1813) and Byron's *Marino Faliero* (1821), despite their other weaknesses. The early Victorian tragic authors were obsessed with historical fact, an over-indulgence in which hopelessly clogs Browning's *Strafford* (1837) and James White's *The Earl of Gowrie* (1852) to the point of obscurity. Even Bulwer, who believed he was writing an important historical play in *Richelieu* (1839), peppered the first edition with historical footnotes, restored the acting version to its original length (it had been sensibly cut by Macready for the stage), and commented in the Preface that many of the passages omitted in representation are essential for the reader, those which 'contain either the subtler strokes of character or the more poetical embellishments of description ... To judge the author's conception of Richelieu fairly, and to estimate how far it is consistent with historical portraiture, the play must be *read*.'

Bulwer at least had the expert assistance of Macready in making *Richelieu* not only stageworthy but also successful, and other verse plays were similarly rescued by leading actors, like Thomas Noon Talfourd's lifeless neo-classical *Ion* (1836) – by Macready and later Ellen Tree – but the point is that, far from 'declining', as many critics alleged, because of its separation from literature, much nineteenth-century drama suffered from its conscious striving to be literary

---

[5] A classic example is given in this play of the acting of the passions (in this case Anger) when the hero's friend comments on the former's reaction to the news of the evil monk's scheme to seduce the heroine: 'I see the big veins twist like young snakes within your brow – your fingers clutch the air – and your feet grind into the earth. 'Tis well: your extreme love is writ in your disordered frame!'

rather than theatrical. George Henry Lewes saw this when he wrote in the *Leader* that he wished many dramatists had never known the Elizabethan drama:

> Who are the successful dramatists of our day? Precisely those who do *not* imitate the Elizabethan form! ... We do wish that the dramatist should not be an archaeologist, that he should not strive to revive defunct forms, but produce a nineteenth-century drama: something that will appeal to a wider audience than that of a few critics and black-letter students.
>
> (3 August, 1850)

However, the old-fashioned poetic tragedy was still written after 1850, although it appeared infrequently. Tom Taylor essayed the genre with *Joan of Arc* (1871), Tennyson with *Queen Mary* (1876) and *Becket* (1893), which Irving successfully adapted for the stage. Other dramatists attempted blank verse tragedies in contemporary settings, with indifferent or disastrous results. The two main early Victorian examples of this attempt are Westland Marston's *The Patrician's Daughter* (1842) and Browning's *A Blot in the Scutcheon* (1843), both given by Macready at Drury Lane. Although Marston declared in his Preface to the published play that it was a tragedy 'indebted for its incident, and passion, to the habits and spirit of the age', *The Patrician's Daughter* is only Victorian in its portrayal of class enmity and centres its plot on a misunderstanding between a radical politician and the daughter of a cabinet minister. Despite the political vocation of these two characters the play is not about politics at all and perhaps, given the Examiner of Plays, could not be. *A Blot in the Scutcheon* is written in the compressed and jagged verse characteristic of Browning and weighted down with 'Action in Character rather than Character in Action', as Browning put it in the Preface to *Strafford*. Like *Strafford*, it failed.

KNOWLES

The admired Sheridan Knowles never again achieved the tragic success of *Virginius*, but his poetic tragedies and comedies, like *Virginius*, are interestingly marked by the powerful father–daughter and father–son relationships that were a feature of so many Victorian melodramas. *The Rose of Arragon* (1842), in which the Keans took the leading roles, betrays many of the faults of the pseudo-Elizabethan: excessively long speeches, tortured syntax and vocabulary and a turgid plot. Set in medieval Spain, it concerns the marriage of the peasant girl Olivia to the Prince of Arragon and the troubles, treacheries and revolts that ensue. The most prominent relationship is that between Olivia's brother Alasco and his father. A better play and more simply written, though not a tragedy, is *The Daughter* (1836), in which Knowles uses the then popular melodramatic character of the wrecker. Robert is almost persuaded by his daughter Marian to give up his grisly occupation of robbing dead bodies thrown up by the sea, but goes out one last time in a storm to obtain the spoils from one last wreck. He is framed for murdering an unconscious castaway for his gold by a villainous brother wrecker who desires Marian, then convicted in court on his daughter's evidence, and freed only as a part of the villain's design, which is eventually frustrated. The chief interest is the extended agony of several scenes between father and daughter, in which anger, fear, horror and remorse are at war with their intense love for each other.

Knowles did not begin writing comedies until the 1830s, and they suffer badly with a mixture of pseudo-Elizabethan blank verse (though on occasion he could write it passably well) and a fearfully crabbed imitation of Shakespearean prose. Of his three comedies, *The Love-Chase* (1837) is the most stylish and witty, with good characters for actors to play and three love plots under careful control. The maid Lydia, like Virginia in *Virginius*, is another of Knowles's ideal young women, a type that populated Victorian comedy and melodrama for many years.

The Love-Chase, *The Daughter*, *The Rose of Arragon*, *The Patrician's Daughter*, *Ion* and others are all 'legitimate' plays, all first performed at the leading London theatres, and most of them placed on the stage by the principal actors of the day. They represented a high-minded effort to attract and entertain audiences with traditional material of the old school. Despite some temporary successes created by these actors, it was an effort doomed to failure. The educated middle-class audience with literary tastes at whom these plays were aimed was not sufficient in number to make them profitable at the box office and they were, ultimately – despite their long survival – out of tune with the theatrical spirit of the time and out of favour with the new audiences who were not to be found in the pit and boxes of Drury Lane and Covent Garden.

MELODRAMA

The serious drama that *did* satisfy the taste of the time, whether of the pit and box audience of the patent theatres, the new theatres of the East End and the Surrey side of the Thames, or the touring portable theatres and the provincial Theatres Royal, was melodrama. Melodrama contains every possible ingredient of popular appeal: strong emotion, both pathetic and potentially tragic, low comedy, romantic colouring, remarkable events in an exciting and suspenseful plot, physical sensations, sharply delineated stock characters, domestic sentiment, domestic settings and domestic life, love, joy, suffering, morality, the reward of virtue and the punishment of vice. In these respects the Victorian theatre was indeed close to literature, for the Victorian novel possesses the same characteristics with the same appeal. Above all, even if melodramas were located, as they often were, in the historical past or in a foreign country, they had a sense of immediate contemporaneity, of appeal to the domestic, emotional and imaginative life of their audience. For working-class audiences they offered characters and settings from urban working-class life and perhaps for some an escape from the mean streets and long hours of labour, a refuge, however brief, in romantic fantasy. The endurance of melodrama in popular favour is striking, since it remained a dominant form of theatrical entertainment for a hundred years, and is the nineteenth century's unique contribution to the English drama.

The main outlines of the development of melodrama are surely familiar; by the beginning of the Victorian period the pattern was set. The earliest English melodrama – Thomas Holcroft's *A Tale of Mystery* (1802) at Covent Garden was evidently the first piece to be called a melodrama, or 'melodrame' – was Gothic in nature and influenced by the English Gothic novel of the late eighteenth century, the German *Sturm und Drang* drama and Parisian melodrama of the post-Revolutionary period. Well before *A Tale of Mystery*, plays were appearing in the London minor theatres on the Surrey side that were melodramas in all but name, as well as lurid Gothic dramas like Matthew Gregory Lewis's *The Castle Spectre* (1797) at the patent theatres. Because the Licensing Act of 1737 forbade stage speech at theatres not holding a licence to perform the legitimate drama, the early minor theatres playing melodrama resorted to a combination of musical accompaniment and dumbshow to convey plot and meaning. These features of melodrama remained enshrined in the genre long after such restrictions had been removed. Of all nineteenth-century dramatic forms melodrama is the most indebted to music for mood, entrance and exit cues and leitmotifs to accompany its stock characters. The interpretation of emotion by means of gesture, bodily attitude and facial expression, long essential to tragic acting, became extended and habitual in melodrama, at first by legal necessity and then by custom. As late as 1870 an East End drama by Colin Hazlewood, *Taking the Veil*, has '*music descriptive of warbling birds,*' '*music cautious,*' '*music to realize picture,*' '*plaintive music continued piano*' and many more music cues in the printed stage directions. (The majority of such cues do not appear in printed melodrama texts.) In B. F. Rayner's *The Dumb Man of Manchester* (1837), the dumb boy Tom '*by a series of picturesque representations, relates that at the age of ten years he was tending sheep on the mountain; while asleep one escapes; he follows it, and falls into a deep ravine; catching a branch as he fell, he hung by the hands until he was released, and that the fright deprived him of the faculty of speech*'. The dumb character of melodrama survived comfortably at least into the 1840s.

The content of the Gothic melodrama was as highly Romantic as its settings, and included awful tyrants dwelling in gloomy castle fastnesses, robber bands lurking in forests and caves, heroes unjustly languishing in dark dungeons, fearful heroines fleeing villainy, humble cottagers, loyal comic servants, frightful spectres, much thunder and lightning, desperate combats and the triumph of virtue. The Gothic form is splendidly exemplified by such plays as Isaac Pocock's *The Miller and His Men* (1813), Samuel Arnold's *The Woodman's Hut* (1814) and William Dimond's *The Broken Sword* (1816) – all, incidentally, first performed at Drury Lane and Covent Garden. The taste for melodrama was ubiquitous and classless; it was by no means a kind of theatre appealing only to the lower classes of society.

During the 1820s a different sort of melodrama, the nautical, began to share the stage with the Gothic. Nautical drama had its roots in patriotic entertainments about Britain's naval victories in the war with France that were staged in the water tank on the stage of Sadler's Wells in the first two decades of the century, but before that the heroic sailor was a feature of Surrey side dramas. The war with France created the military and nautical melodrama that glorified British soldiers and sailors and Britain itself.[6] Such a melodrama kept the stage for the whole century and its actual historical battles were fought with equal zest in the circus ring at Astley's (later Sanger's), and upon the stages of Drury Lane and the Standard, to name only three late Victorian locations. The nautical sub-genre is a good instance of melodrama's immediate response to contemporary events, as was the rush of Crimean War melodramas in the 1850s and Boer War plays at the end of the century. Nautical melodrama also

---

[6] A jingoistic patriotism, thoroughly reflective of popular feeling, is rampant in many melodramas, especially those with scenes in foreign countries. Entirely typical is the speech of the English hero to an audience of Mexicans in Henry Leslie's *The Sin and the Sorrow* (1866): 'The Englishman set you to work, *created* this village, and *made* the port. There is the school the Englishman built – there the chapel he founded, that you might worship heaven in your own form. Why, you and such as you should bless the Englishman's energy and the Englishman's wealth, which to fertile fields converts your barren lands and transforms a useless body to a prosperous people.'

embraced wreckers and pirates as characters and frequently showed storms and shipwrecks as well as engagements at sea. The hero of nautical melodrama, much influenced in his nature and development by the sea songs of Charles Dibdin the Elder, from whose sailor figures – Tom Bowling, Ben the Boatswain, Ben Block, etc. – and song titles many of the heroes' names are taken, spoke in a curious nautical metaphor, was devoted to his country and his captain, brave in conflict against villainy and the enemy and true to his sweetheart on shore. Edward Fitzball's *The Red Rover* (1829), Jerrold's *Black-Eyed Susan* (1829), and J. T. Haines's *My Poll and My Partner Joe* (1835) – another Dibdin song title – are excellent specimens of the nautical, but as in the case of the Gothic and domestic, dozens of good examples might be selected.

The sailor-hero of melodrama also has a domestic existence: a loved one in a cottage living with her old mother, a villainous squire with amatory designs upon the heroine, a landlord ruthlessly bent on eviction for non-payment of rent, a village that was his childhood home. Indeed, the principal categories of melodrama overlapped with each other to a considerable extent. *The Miller and His Men*, for instance, possesses a strong element of the domestic, as does *Black-Eyed Susan*, and in two other nautical plays, Fitzball's *The Inchcape Bell* (1828) and Buckstone's *The Dream at Sea* (1835), the Gothic and nautical are skilfully mixed. Buckstone's *Luke the Labourer* (1826), a domestic rural melodrama, contains a valiant sailor who saves the heroine from villainy. Domestic melodrama with a native setting, first introduced in the 1820s, prevailed over the other kinds by the 1840s and dominated the stage thereafter. It too suited the taste of audiences, dealing, however indirectly, with social problems like drink, gambling, crime, poverty, homelessness, strikes and the slave trade. This melodrama became increasingly urban in content and far more socially comprehensive then earlier drama in that, for the first time in the history of English drama, it treated lower-class characters and working-class life seriously and with compassion – as in John Walker's powerful *The Factory Lad* (1832) – as well as, again for the first time, presenting as detailed a visual image as stage art would allow of the metropolitan environment. The acrimony of melo-dramatic class conflict is socially interesting as well as dramatically strong, as is melodrama's muted note of protest against social oppression and legal injustice. Such features are especially prominent in domestic melodrama.

By 1837 all the necessary and familiar elements of melodrama were in place, including the basic character stereotypes of hero, heroine, villain, comic man, comic woman, good old man and good old woman, the high-flown rhetoric and the physical thrills of fire, explosion, shipwreck and earthquake. The domestic form may have dominated, but the old-style Gothic and nautical melodrama long survived outside the West End; again, one has to be careful to make geographical distinctions. What followed during the reign of Victoria was a movement in the direction of greater social and domestic realism (matching a similar movement in production style), a toning down of the rhetoric and ornateness of dialogue and a less extravagant treatment of character. There were, however, so many exceptions, some of them geographical, in all three of these areas that it is impossible to make categorical statements. West End melodrama virtually ceased to have a social conscience as it became more middle-class; the social status of its characters and settings also rose to reflect the increasingly middle-class character of its audiences.

In terms of production technique as well as content, melodrama became more sensational – thus the mid-Victorian term 'sensation drama' – especially at those theatres with large and well-equipped stages. The physical was elaborated and natural catastrophes were multiplied. A horse race, an avalanche, a train wreck became the whole point of the act or the play. These spectacles were staged as realistically as possible, but a quieter and everyday realism was also the vogue. Critical discussion of this point covered familiar ground. In 1871 Thomas Purnell, the drama critic of the *Athenaeum*, declared, 'An audience no longer enjoys the representation of what is beyond its reach. The present and the near now best satisfies it. Every man judges what is laid before him by his own experience. Resemblance to what he is acquainted with is the measure of excellence. Truth to current existence is the criterion of merit he applies to a drama.'[7] Thus the care taken to replicate the squares and public buildings of London, the bank interior (*The Ticket-of-Leave Man*), the hansom cab crossing Waterloo Bridge (Andrew Halliday's *The Great City*, 1867), the exterior of Victoria Station and the underground of the new Metropolitan Railway (Boucicault's *After Dark*, 1868).

The Victorian 'drama' of some artistic pretensions, such as Bulwer's *The Lady of Lyons* (1838) or *Richelieu*, both written in verse, represented an evolution of the old poetic tragedy and a compromise with melodrama. The tragic was domesticated; evil failed to destroy good, which emerged not only triumphant but also materially rewarded. In this way only did the 'legitimate' survive the Act of 1843 and come to terms with its age. Every Victorian play bearing the name of 'drama' is a melodrama of one kind or another, in four

[7] Thomas Purnell, *Dramatists of the Present Day* (London, 1871), pp. 80–81.

acts, perhaps, instead of two or three. For the serious playwright who wished to remain in touch with his audience and their taste, 'drama' and comedy, which was often strongly melodramatic, were the only forms available.

The enormous and enduring appeal of melodrama depended upon a content that in its social and mental life closely related to the daily existence and imaginative needs of its audience and this content manifested itself in the endless repetition of basic, even archetypal situations and character relationships. Familiarity was an essential aspect of melodramatic appeal, the same sort of familiarity and character stereotyping that is so important in the pre-Sam Peckinpah Western film and remains significant in any television situation comedy or soap opera series. It is impossible in short space to document all aspects of this appeal, but a few examples of content and technique may be given.

The father–daughter relationship of the stage, already powerful in X the pre-Victorian legitimate tragedy and comedy, as well as in the earlier melodrama, is a standard feature of Victorian theatre, an idealistic dramatisation of the family bond deemed so important in Victorian domestic life. Innumerable plays depict a father doting on his beloved daughter, falling out with her through some misunderstanding or action on her part that does not meet with parental favour, and being tearfully reconciled with her at the end; the reconciliation being emotionally protracted and sometimes including a ritualistic blessing. Such a play is H. T. Craven's *Milky White* (1864), a variation of his previously successful *The Chimney Corner* (1861), which showed the chandler Peter Probity alternating between bouts of despair at the apparent loss of several thousand pounds and outbursts of parental love. In *Milky White* the irascible and deaf old dairyman, White, adores his daughter Anne while happily engaging in litigation with all his neighbours. He is cured of his deafness and, misunderstanding what she says, concludes she hates him and drives her from the house; then takes miserably to his bed. Of course the misunderstanding is cleared up before the final curtain. One verse of a song, 'Early Love', written especially for the play, is sung by Anne:

> Whom did I love as time flew on,
> And she [Anne's mother] was lost – for ever gone?
> Whose doting lip was ever near
> To kiss away my orphan tear?
> Whose fond affection taught me then,
> With ardour fresh, to love again?
> No stranger lur'd my heart; but rather,
> I clung alone to thee – my father!

Possibly more interesting than the frequent depiction of a loving father–daughter relationship is the attempt by some melodramatists to go right against the grain and, using all the conventional emotional associations of such a bond, show an 'unnatural' father–daughter relationship. In *Seven Sins* (1874), by George Conquest and Paul Meritt, performed in the East End, the heroine, Faith, who has already spent years in a 'Female Convict Prison' because she confessed to her father's crime – the murder of *his* father for a wallet of £250 – is upon her release drugged by the same father (who in the meantime has killed her mother), rushed unconscious by special train to a lonely, derelict house in Essex and subjected to a murderous assault with a knife in order to ensure her silence. The usual audience feeling when a heroine is in danger – apprehension, suspense, and fear – must have been considerably heightened by the shocking relationship between this villain and this heroine.[8] Similarly, if less violently, George Dibdin Pitt in *Simon Lee* (1841) and *The Beggar's Petition* (1841) portrayed unnatural parent-child relations. In the former, the rich and miserly Hatherleigh turns his daughter Grace out of doors for marrying a farmer, Simon Lee, whom he dislikes, and then persecutes Lee relentlessly for poaching even though the couple live in poverty. In the latter, a daughter runs off with a wealthy young man and becomes contemptuously indifferent to the plight of her destitute and starving parents.

The daughter in such cases is the heroine, and of all characters in melodrama – despite an unusual play like *The Beggar's Petition* – she suffers the most, particularly in temperance melodrama with a drunken husband who beats her and, as in Jerrold's *Fifteen Years of a Drunkard's Life* (1828) and T. P. Taylor's *The Bottle* (1847), kills her. At the least he will spend the meagre household money on drink, leaving her and the children starving. The indigent mother crossing the stage with a hungry child in a snowstorm is a quintessential scene of melodramatic pathos. The four-year-old Bertie of A. C. Calmour's *Gilded Crime* (1884), wandering the streets of London with his mother, begs her for food:

> BERTIE.   (*As he passes barrow, stretching out his arms to bread.*) There's bread, mother, oh give Bertie some. Do – I'm so hungry, so hungry, mother.
>
> ELLEN.   Oh what shall I do? What shall I do? They won't give me relief at the workhouse till night, and he may be dead by then.
>
> BERTIE.   (*Stretching out his arms toward bread.*) Mother, bread!

[8] *Seven Sins, or Passion's Paradise* is an interestingly allegorical melodrama, quite apart from its exciting action and highly physical climax. Each of the seven deadly sins is personified by one of the principal *dramatis personae*. The sin is listed in the text after the character's name, and he – for they are all male – behaves accordingly.

> ELLEN. God forgive me. I can't see his agony. I can't see my child
> starving. Oh, forgive me. *(Takes loaf and tears it to pieces.)* There, my
> love, my darling, you shall not die, there's bread for you. *(Gives piece,*
> *child snatches it, and begins ravenously to eat it.)* Oh, oh, oh, it's piteous to
> see him hungry.

Pathos is a major part of melodrama's appeal, and the heroine
carries its burden. A standard pathetic scene is set in prison, where
the heroine (sometimes her child as well) comes to bid a last farewell
to the hero, who is to die on the morrow, unjustly sentenced – as it
often happens – for the villain's crimes. Perhaps the most famous of
these scenes is the beautifully written farewell between William and
Susan in *Black-Eyed Susan*. There is also such a scene in *Simon Lee*,
and another in Hazlewood's *Waiting for the Verdict* (1859) between
the hero and his family – wife, two children, and father – which
concludes thus:

> MARTHA. No, no, not yet; I have a thousand things to say. *(Music – leads*
> CHILDREN *to door.)* Oh, Jasper, my husband, I cannot part with thee; I
> cannot! Oh, Jasper, husband, hus – *(Faints in the arms of* HYLTON. JASPER
> *sinks on seat –* CHILD *runs to him, he looks at it, buries his face in hands, and*
> *sobs bitterly as the scene closes. Tableau.)*

Jasper is saved at the very last moment from the scaffold by the
real murderer's dying confession. The suspensefully delayed and
almost miraculous deliverance of the innocent is a common finale. A
last-minute reprieve arrives for Simon Lee, but not before his
agonised wife has taken poison. William of *Black-Eyed Susan* is
luckier, with the intervention of his captain rescuing him from a
shipboard execution. Supernatural intercession is often effective in
Gothic melodrama. In W. E. Suter's *The Accusing Spirit* (1860), a late
Gothic survival in the East End, the ghost of the man he has
murdered appears to the villain Eric as he is about to pronounce
sentence upon an innocent man: '*Music tremuloso, piano. The wall at*
L. C. becomes transparent and discovers the SHADE *of* RODOLPHE, *pale and*
bleeding, one hand pointing to the wound on his breast, and the other
extending toward ERIC *as if forbidding him to proceed.*' An admirable
example of a timely reprieve can be found in H. P. Grattan's *The*
White Boys (1836), when the hero O'Brien (admittedly guilty but
acting from the noblest of motives), on the point of execution for
desertion from the British army and for leading the Irish rebels, is
graciously permitted to give his firing squad the order to shoot:

> *(Music.* O'BRIEN *throws off his coat, kneels, and prays – all the* PEASANTS *kneel,*
> *the women weeping.* O'BRIEN *faces the* SOLDIERS *– bares his breast to them.)*
> O'BRIEN Ready! (SOLDIERS *come to the action.)* Present! (SOLDIERS *do so. As*

Plate 19   The reprieve: *Hands Across the Sea*, 1888. Touring poster.

> O'BRIEN *is about to give the word, 'Fire', a wild scream is heard without, and*
> NORAH, *her face ashey pale, her hair streaming behind her, dashes through the*
> *crowd of* PEASANTS, *with a convulsive effort, exclaims,* 'Edward! Edward!
> Pardon! Pardon!' *and falls senseless at* O'BRIEN's *feet, letting the paper fall*
> *on the stage.*)

A good melodramatist was a master of climax, and Grattan was not content to leave matters here. The reprieve Norah carries is a blank piece of paper, which the villain has substituted for the real pardon. The execution is about to resume when the hero's friend rushes on stage, strikes down the villain, takes the pardon from him, and presents it to the commanding officer.

The return from the dead, another vital example of melodramatic technique, is allied to the last-minute reprieve. Melodrama is full of apparently murdered characters who reappear in time to foil villainy. In Hazlewood's *Lady Audley's Secret* (1863) no fewer than three victims of her murderous propensities come back seemingly from the dead, one from being hit over the head with an iron bar and thrown down a well, the other two from a burning inn.

The strong curtain ending an act or the play is absolutely essential to melodramatic technique. This climax, which occurs in every melodrama, can be emotional or physical, or a combination of both.

Dumb show, scenic effect, violent physical activity, and a compound of intense emotions given full visual expression are vital elements in an often extended and virtually or entirely wordless scene that inevitably concludes in a tableau. At the end of *Taking the Veil* the headquarters of the Inquisition is attacked by French soldiers, among them the hero Horace in search of his imprisoned Christine:

> *Music and shouts kept on. Noise of conflict.* FRENCH SOLDIERS *discovered* R. *and* L. *They fire at Inquisition.* GENERAL VICTOR *discovered leading the attack. Enter* HORACE, R., *with hatchet. He goes up to doors of Inquisition, breaks them open, and enters. He is followed by* WILHELM *with sword, also* CORPORAL, *who enter* L. PAPAL SOLDIERS *enter from Inquisition, led by* CAPTAIN DARMFELDT. *He is attacked by* GENERAL VICTOR *and killed.* FRENCH SOLDIERS *enter* R. *and run into building with lighted torches. The Inquisition is seen in flames. Conflict between* FRENCH *and* PAPAL TROOPS. MARTHA, NUNS, *and* SISTER AGATHA *enter from Inquisition screaming and running off* R. *and* L. *Crash. The Inquisition breaks and falls.* HORACE *bears on* CHRISTINE *from the ruins, followed by* WILHELM *and* CORPORAL. *Loud shouts.* WILHELM *joins the hands of* CHRISTINE *and* HORACE. GENERAL VICTOR *is seen on steps at back waving French flag. Shouts. Explosions. Tableau of victory for the French. The Marseillaise played forte as the Curtain falls.*

As exciting emotionally as the conclusion of *Taking the Veil* is physically is an act ending in Suter's *The Robbers of the Pyrenees* (1862), in which the father curses his murderous son Raoul in front of Raoul's wife Henriette and guests gathered for a christening:

> DE BREVENNES. (*Wildly*). Wretch! Be thou accursed! (*Choking, he falls back into the arms of two of the* GUESTS. HENRIETTE, *screaming, gets free and staggering towards* DE BREVENNES *falls senseless at his feet.* RAOUL, *shuddering, dashes his hands to his head despairingly, and rushes up* C., *sees the body, and recoils trembling to* R. GUESTS *in attitudes of horror. Music.*)

No less effective, but softly pathetic rather than intensely anguished, is the ending of T. A. Palmer's *East Lynne* (1874), a version of Mrs Henry Wood's famous novel, when Isabel, who had fled her home with a seducing villain but returned, disguised and humbled, as a governess to her children, reveals her identity and dies:

> *Music trem. to curtain. 'Then you'll remember me.'*
> ISABEL.   Be kind and loving to Lucy and little Archie, do not let their mother's sin be visited on them!
> CARLYLE.   Never, never, they are dear to me as you once were!
> ISABEL.   Aye, as I once was, and as I might – alas – I might have been, even now. Ah, is this death? 'Tis hard to part! Farewell, dear Archibald, my husband once and loved now in death, as I never loved before! Farewell, until eternity! Think of me sometimes, keep one

little corner of your heart for me – your poor – erring – lost Isabel.
(Dies. Slow curtain.)

The meaning of *East Lynne* is contained in the emotional life and suffering of Lady Isabel. The suffering heroine is a melodramatic archetype, necessary to the functioning of the whole genre. So, for that matter, is the archetype of the hero or villain, for melodrama is above all the drama of the struggle of the individual soul, the Romantic concentration of all significance and purpose in the odyssey of one man or one woman. While it is true that melodrama deals powerfully in social problems – the effect of the introduction of steam-powered cotton looms, the harshness of parish poor relief, the destructive force of alcohol, and so on – the dramatic and emotional value of such issues is personalised in the figure of hero or heroine, or both. The strike in G. F. Taylor's *The Factory Strike* (1836) is precipitated solely by the villainous strikeleader, an act of personal malice rather than a collective action necessary in a confrontation with an employer who has lowered wages in order to compete with business rivals who have introduced machinery. Apart from the hero's comment, 'Oh, little did he, who first contemplated doing manual labour by machinery think of the misery it would excite', there is no treatment of the social aspects of the economic situation. The attack upon poor relief in both this play and *The Factory Lad* is made by one character, and the problem seems to have no existence beyond him. While the starving Simon Lee is legally prevented from shooting game, it is not the game laws but Hatherleigh's personal enmity that sends him to jail under sentence of death, and Hatherleigh's evil in turn is individual rather than social. In the background, admittedly, is Hatherleigh's social role as a member of the property-owning, game-law enforcing classes, as in the background of every seducing squire or peer is his membership of the landed or aristocratic classes. The act of villainy and its consequences, however, are always individual in nature; evil is created in the psyche of the villain rather than his social being.

It is the villain who thinks, decides, makes new plans when the old ones go wrong, the villain who acts while the hero and heroine react. The villain is the active principle of melodrama, the hero and heroine, while often extremely vigorous in their exertions, are essentially passive in that this energy is usually a defensive response to a situation created by the villain's wiles. The criminal acts of melodrama committed by the villain and his henchmen embrace a multitudinous assortment of felonies, including theft, perjury, forgery, coining, fraud, embezzlement, suppression of evidence, blackmail, assault, kidnapping, poaching, destruction of property, attempted rape, attempted infanticide, smuggling, piracy, arson, treason and murder in many varieties: stabbing, shooting, bludgeoning, strangulation, suffocation, poisoning, burning, drowning and defenestration, among others.

The world the villain inhabits eventually overcomes him; he is not quite clever or criminally skilled enough for it, but it is environmentally well suited to his criminality. In the interestingly environmental and poverty-stricken settings provided in melodrama for the urban working class and vagrant sections of society, the villain can be found in the rabbit warren of St Giles in London or in other crime-infested slums. Melodrama also matches the dark deeds of evildoers with a hostile and disturbed nature. Romantic melodrama of the pre-Victorian period specialised scenically in mountainous landscapes, moors, forests, ruins and the architecture of remote castles and gloomy dungeons. Sometimes a rural landscape will be bathed in sunshine, a sign of peace and tranquillity of short duration given the plots of melodrama and the endless struggle between good and evil. More typical of the physical landscape of melodrama are darkness and tempest imposed upon wild or forbidding scenery. The concluding scene of H. M. Milner's *The Gambler's Fate* (1827) is set in '*A Ravine, running between a tremendous range of rocky precipices*' and illuminated by '*the moon struggling through a stormy sky − the storm rages terrifically − thunder, lightning, and rain.*' Such a setting and such atmospheric effects are absolutely appropriate to the context of this short scene, in which a bolt of lightning strikes a hollow oak tree, revealing the corpse of the hero's uncle, foully murdered by one of the two assassins − one of them is his father − now approaching through storm and night; this *coup de théâtre* is quickly followed by the reunion of the hero with his distraught mother and the death of both assassins. Such a scene is not merely romantically decorative, but reveals the emotional and thematic states of melodrama − a mental and spiritual landscape expressive of the heart of melodramatic darkness.

In such a landscape the villain is truly at war with nature as well as virtue. The rolling thunder, the bolts of lightning and the raging storm are melodramatically indicative, not only of a disturbance in the elements symbolising the upheaval of civil and natural order − melodramatists knew their *Lear* and *Macbeth* − but also of a potential for natural cataclysm that can usefully vanquish the villain. Such a cataclysm disposes of the characters' fates in a manner befitting their moral conduct; thus the effect of natural catastrophe upon human beings is not merely a matter of chance, as it would seem to be upon superficial examination, but operates as a sentient agent of divine order and justice.

The occurrence of forest fires, avalanches, floods, earthquakes and volcanic eruptions in melodrama is too common to be remarked. In Edward Fitzball's *The Earthquake* (1829), the evil Robber of the Black Mountains is about to put the hero and heroine to death when the timely and eponymous earthquake intervenes, burying the Robber and his followers but leaving the hero and heroine untouched. Seventy years later, in Cecil Raleigh's *Hearts are Trumps* at Drury Lane, an Alpine avalanche sweeps the villain to his death without so much as bouncing a snowball off the hero.

MIDDLE-CLASS PREJUDICE

Crime and villainy are ubiquitous in melodrama. Almost all melodramas depend upon criminal activity, or at the very least on powerful criminal intent, for their very existence. Violent crime was supposed by the governing classes to be a characteristic of lower-class behaviour, and the Victorian middle-class fear of the potential for disturbance and even anarchy in the lower orders comes out strongly in the continued attribution of criminality to melodrama's working-class audiences. It is not merely a matter of a generalised class prejudice, but also a conscious attempt to blacken and control the amusements of the people already familiar in the legislation abolishing the London fairs and sporting events like cock-fighting and prize-fighting. There is a paradox here: on one hand many middle-class commentators praised melodrama for arousing a love of virtue and a detestation of vice in the unlettered audience; on the other they declared that the audience itself was inherently criminal. 'Come with me,' said George Augustus Sala of the Victoria in 1859, 'and sit on the coarse deal benches in the coarsely and tawdrily decorated theatre' and listen to the 'sorrily-dressed' actors 'tearing their passion to tatters':

> But in what description of pieces? In dramas, I declare and maintain, in which, for all the jargon, silliness, and buffoonery, the immutable principles of right and justice are asserted; in which virtue, in the end, is always triumphant, and vice is punished; in which cowardice and falsehood are hissed, and bravery and integrity vehemently applauded; in which, were we to sift away the bad grammar, and the extravagant action, we should find the dictates of the purest and highest morality.[9]

[9] G. A. Sala, *Twice Round the Clock* (London, 1859), p. 271.

One must go to the West End for immorally suggestive dialogue and plots, Sala insisted, an argument echoed in the 1890s by the Examiner of Plays, E. F. S. Piggott, in his testimony to the Select Committee:

> I have always found this, that the equivocal, the risky, the immoral and the indecent plays are intended for West End audiences, certainly not for the East End. The farther east you go the more moral your audience is; you may get a gallery full of roughs in which every other boy is a pickpocket, and yet their collective sympathy is in favour of self-sacrifice; collectively they have a horror of vice and a ferocious love of virtue. A boy might pick your pocket as you left the theatre, but have his reserve of fine sentiment in his heart. *(1892 Report,* p. 332)

Piggott seems to have been unaware of a paradox, or perhaps he thought it no paradox. T. W. Erle, the author of a valuable account of melodrama and acting practices at London working-class theatres around 1860, was more severe. The Victoria, he pronounced, 'is largely graced by the presence of embryo and mature convicts, and gentlemen on tickets-of-leave during their transient intervals of sojourn in the bosom of Lambeth Society.'[10] In *Adelbert the Deserter* at the Royal Effingham in Whitechapel, a speech against capital punishment is 'warmly applauded by the house, the matter being one of individual interest to a large portion of the audience, seeing that every execution at the Old Bailey diminishes the R. E. audience by one'.[11] One can doubt, to say the least, the statistical accuracy of Erle's observations, and note the tone of amused contempt in which they are made. The problem – a serious one for historians of Victorian theatre – is that almost all the accounts we have of urban working-class theatres come from middle-class journalists, novelists and proto-sociologists. Even the best of them, like Dickens (as witness *Nicholas Nickleby* and the company of Vincent Crummles), treat popular theatre as material for comedy, moral disapproval or both.

CLASS HATRED

The class basis for this view of working-class audiences is obvious. Just as obvious is the class structure and class bitterness of melodrama itself, a noteworthy aspect of its character demonstrated in a variety of social and personal relationships: peer and cottager, squire and

---

[10] T. W. Erle, *Letters from a Theatrical Scene-Painter* (London, 1880), p. 101.
[11] *Ibid.,* p. 16. Erle even advised his readers, if they wished to venture into the 'partially-explored districts of Whitechapel', to resign themselves to the loss of their pocket watches and to take disinfectant with them (pp. 19–20).

peasant, landlord and tenant, seducer and victim, master and man. In play after play it is the character with class status, wealth and privilege who is the criminal, and the representative of the underclass who is oppressed and criminalised. It is the rich landowner or profligate earl who attempts the seduction of the heroine, never the farmer's son or the factory hand who tries the virtue of the squire's daughter or master's wife. It is the vicious baronet who in *Gilded Crime* suffocates the starving heroine's little child and then strikes down the heroine's mother with a '*thick, gold headed cane*'. 'I'll put the workman's head under my heel and crush it with as little remorse as I would you', the evil seducer and factory foreman tells the dissident hand in Arthur Moss's *The Workman's Foe*, a music-hall sketch written as late as 1900. A sense of class injustice and class hatred permeates melodrama, to a considerable extent shaping the character and status of the villain and the nature of his crime.

BUSINESS CRIME

Often, however, melodramatic crime is kept within the middle-class family, so to speak, and there is no particular class antagonism. This is especially true of business crime. In accordance with the growth of commerce and financial institutions in the City of London, mid-Victorian drama extended its subject matter to business life. The offices of City bankers were put on stage, as in Boucicault's adaptation for London of his *The Poor of New York* (1857) as *The Streets of London* (1864), which deals with the effect upon one family of the financial panics of 1837 and 1857, and contains a spectacular fire and Trafalgar Square in the snow as well as the office of the villainous Bloodgood. Taylor's *Settling Day*, with its replication of real City business premises, is similar to 'MR GIBSON's *Bill-broking office in Nicholas Lane, City*' in *The Ticket-of-Leave Man*; in both cases care has been taken to make the stage office authentic in its details. The humiliation of business failure and the loss of fortune and the consequence of a very reduced standard of living or even abject poverty for the family involved, is a prominent theme in this kind of drama, as it is in the Victorian novel. It also occurs in Victorian comedy. Henry Arthur Jones, who never thought highly of the commercial spirit, deplored the 'steady, persistent glorification of money-making and industrious respectable business life' and complained that 'Victorian drama reeks of the spirit of successful tradesmen and is relative to the age of Clapham Junction.'[12]

---

[12] Henry Arthur Jones, 'The Theatre and the Mob', *Nineteenth Century*, vol. 14 (September 1883), p. 450.

Since business themes were popular, business crime was therefore a popular sub-section of melodramatic villainy from the railway swindles and speculations of the 1840s until the end of the century. In the actual business world such crime was a middle-class matter, and so it was in the drama. Captain Hawksley of Tom Taylor's *Still Waters Run Deep* (1855), which has an entirely middle-class cast of characters except for a servant, is a forger of bills of exchange and a swindler in fraudulent joint-stock companies, as well as being a blackmailer with evil designs upon the heroine. Her quiet husband, Mildmay, seemingly timid and henpecked, not only exposes Hawksley's schemes and has him arrested, but is also his physical superior, stopping a blow, forcing him into a chair, and telling him, 'Take care. If we come to that game, remember it's town versus country; a hale Lancashire lad against a battered London roué; fresh air and exercise to smoke and speculation.' *Still Waters Run Deep* is also, interestingly, concerned with the rightful place of the husband in the Victorian home and the morally imperative necessity of the subordination of the womenfolk of a household to his will – a notable theme in Victorian comedy.

The protean nature of the imaginative and skilled criminal, especially the one who comfortably located himself in a middle-class environment and practised business swindles but could also turn his hand to other sorts of crime, is emphasised in T. W. Moncrieff's *The Scamps of London* (1843), when the villain contemptuously asks the hero, 'Who is it you'd denounce? Devereux, Fox Skinner – fool! Both are assumed names. Then I have fifty callings – the well-dressed gambler, the swell mob's chief, the humble hawker, and needy beggar. Easily could I appear in any one of these characters.' The chief villain of the *Ticket-of-Leave Man*, Dalton, is just such a person as Devereux. He too forges bills and passes, when he wishes to, '*dressed as a respectable elderly commercial man.*' In another manifestation, attired as a jobber and general dealer, he plants counterfeit banknotes. Dalton is also a safecracker, burglar and pickpocket; the detective of the play says that 'he has as many outsides as he has aliases. You may identify him for a felon today and pull your hat off to him for a parson tomorrow.' Thus the occurrence of business themes in the drama meant that the hero of business must be partnered with a villain of business and ensured the stage existence and proliferation of the fraud, swindler, embezzler, bill forger and speculator, a character type that can function at the heart of a prosperous middle-class world or lead a more marginal life on its fringes.

Clearly, the nature of criminality in melodrama was changing as the decades passed. Both the villain and his criminal activity were becoming more sophisticated and his class status was rising. This is especially true of the domestic melodramas of city life. The villain of this kind of play had completely altered his occupation, his life style, his clothes and his methods – though not his fundamental character and motivation – from the bandit, tyrant, smuggler and pirate of the old Gothic and nautical melodrama. There is more to the villain, however, than his fraudulent business dealings or his extensive criminal activity. And here one enters the realm of speculation about the reasons audiences went loyally to melodramas over a hundred years, aside from the obvious ones like action, thrills, spectacle, low comedy, poetic justice and, possibly, escape from a difficult and unrewarding life. Conventionally, nineteenth-century audiences hissed villainy and applauded virtue and the utterance of virtuous sentiments. But there is evidence of the opposite audience reaction to the stage presentation of unshakeable virtue, not only in a late Victorian middle class increasingly cynical about melodrama, but also a generation earlier from the galleries of largely working-class and lower middle-class urban theatres heavily populated by equally cynical juveniles. The stage villain often played directly to these galleries, hurling moral defiance at them and receiving in return white-hot execrations bursting from a thousand throats. This is ambivalent. The execration was almost a mark of respect, and actors who played villains to local working-class audiences year after year were much admired in the community. For in a century – and this is pure conjecture – in which a series of harsh criminal laws were only slowly being dismantled, and in which for a large segment of society economic betterment and an escape from a bleak environment seemed impossible dreams, there *was* something to admire in the villain. Sexually threatening, often a master thief, forger, gambler or assassin, ruthlessly exploiting others whether he was aristocrat, squire, factory owner or urban criminal, he *did* things, and did them in style. He failed, of course, but he failed gloriously and the failures were sometimes the fault of coincidence or natural catastrophe rather than weakness of planning or execution. One wonders, in fact, if he would have failed so frequently had not the Examiner of Plays kept a careful eye upon the morality of the drama. From the point of view of the middle class, which enjoyed melodrama just as much as their social inferiors, could the villain and the extensive criminality of melodrama in some manner incarnate the threat of the 'predatory classes' (as they were called), safely exorcised on the stage through the triumph of virtue? The problem with this idea is that much melodramatic crime is a middle-class product. Even here, though, there may have been a secret and vicarious satisfaction in the overt, though temporary stage violation of domestic ideals and of the accepted mores of social and familial behaviour. It seems to me that one of the reasons for the enduring popularity of melodrama is that the villain, whatever his class – and he ranged in class from wealthy peer to wretched outcast – and whatever his crimes, which were manifold – embodied a positive, active force for evil, to be hated and respected simultaneously, both repellent and attractive, frightening and magnetising.

From its inception as a popular stage form melodrama attracted burlesque and no character of melodrama attracted more burlesque than the villain. This burlesque can be found in stage plays, comic operas, prose satires, novels, comic magazines and caricatures. Nearly a century of it proves one thing, at least, that the villain was enshrined in Victorian culture as a figure of mythic proportions. We have Dracula and Frankenstein's monster to burlesque and laugh at, if we wish; the Victorians had the stage villain. But Dracula and the monster can also terrify and their very survival as icons of the popular mythology of horror is an indication both of their ambivalent position and of their hold over the imagination. So it was with the criminal of melodrama. He lived half on the stage, half in the imagination of audiences, a figure of fun to some but to many more a thing of moral darkness, a tempter to be respected, feared and execrated as he moved frighteningly through the deep shadows of his own criminality. The world of his foul exploits was not the actual underworld of Victorian crime, despite the techniques of verisimilitude that appeared at times to make it so. Melodrama does not work like that. What it presents, rather, are not social documents but images of crime, enactments of personal and social transgression in which the enactor is defeated and his crimes nullified. Melodrama often *seems* a superficial art, but it is not. Its complexities can surprise us. It tells us much about the life of Victorian England, but it also tells us about the Victorian imagination – never more so than when it treats of villainy and crime.

BOUCICAULT

True villainy and the old melodramatic character stereotypes are considerably diluted in the quality drama of the 1880s and the 1890s. In this respect the theatre made something of a jump, in a very few years, from the dominant and traditional melodrama of the 1870s, exemplified at its best in the work of Dion Boucicault, to the early serious work of Jones and Arthur Pinero in the 1890s. Boucicault,

whose *Corsican Brothers* fascinated Queen Victoria and the greater
public in the fifties, loomed even larger in the West End of the sixties
and seventies with *The Colleen Bawn* (1860), *The Octoroon* (1861),
The Streets of London (1864), *Arrah-na-Pogue* (1865) and *The Shaughraun* (1875). Many other melodramas of lesser stature were clustered
between 1865 and 1875, including *Rip Van Winkle, The Long Strike*
(an adaptation of Mrs Gaskell's novel *Mary Barton*), *The Flying Scud*
and *Formosa*, the last two being sporting melodramas centred on the
Derby and the Boat Race respectively. Prominent in this selection
are the three Irish dramas: *The Colleen Bawn, Arrah-na-Pogue* and
The Shaughraun, plays which featured romantic Irish settings, sensation scenes such as Myles-na-Coppaleen's header into the water to
save Eily O'Connor from drowing in *The Colleen Bawn*, shrewd and
resourceful comic men with heroic qualities like Myles and Conn the
Shaughraun, plenty of lively action, Irish patriotism and a skilful and
credible interweaving of comedy, sentiment, romance and physical
thrills.

Boucicault was an immensely popular dramatist in the sixties and
seventies, one who was to influence Shaw and particularly Sean
O'Casey. William Archer complimented him, backhandedly, for
being 'the great picker-up, or rather user-up of unconsidered trifles.
He knows every papier-maché property, every paste-board character, every threadbare phrase, every tough old ficelle of the theatrical lumber-room.'[13] Yet in 1882 Archer could call him a 'playwright
of yesterday', along with Taylor and Robertson, 'no longer a living
and effective influence in the dramatic life of the country' (p. 48).

The 1880s, indeed, mark a watershed in the English drama, a point
at which, while the drama of the past continued to flow into the
present, it perceptibly changed direction. Much of the change of
direction is related to the different composition of audiences and the
greater influence of an intellectual minority of critics and audience
members, and much of it to the impact of Ibsen. The trend toward
smaller theatres in the West End made certain kinds of broad and
extravagant efforts unacceptable in spatial terms, especially to the
relatively passive and well-dressed audiences of the orchestra stalls.
One critic said of James Albery's *Duty* at the Prince of Wales's in
1879 that the plot could under no circumstances 'be unfolded to less
advantage than here, where the occupants of stall and box are not
prepared to digest strong meat, and where a highly emotional
performance is not expected'.[14] There was still no shortage of critical
lamentation about the state of the drama and the alleged mindlessness

[13] William Archer, *English Dramatists of To-Day* (London, 1882), p. 39.
[14] *Theatre* (November 1879), p. 230.

of audiences, a strain of complaint that lasted into the Edwardian period. The *Theatre* pointed out in 1894 that the average playgoer 'does not go to the theatre to discuss the graver issues of life. You cannot induce him to regard a play as anything more serious than a figment for his amusement.'[15] To be entertained, to laugh and not cry, to avoid thinking about the sad world outside the theatre – this, critics claimed, is what the 'average playgoer' asked of the theatre. Some condemned him for his taste, others defended his right to ask for and receive what he desired.

IBSEN

Arguments over the taste of the audience and the extent to which the drama should satisfy it or advance beyond it came to a head in the debate over Ibsen. Intellectual interest in Ibsen was considerable before any of his plays were staged in England, through the advocacy of Shaw and the translations of Edmund Gosse and Archer. After *A Doll's House* and *The Pillars of Society* in 1889, nine more of Ibsen's plays were produced in the West End in the next ten years (not counting revivals), six of them in 1893. Many were given only in matinées; one or two, like *Hedda Gabler*, received brief but respectable evening runs; *Ghosts* was performed by the private Independent Theatre. They attracted great attention and aroused bitter controversy, playing to larger and socially more representative audiences than one might think, and they changed the face of the English drama. They also forced critics to redefine the purpose of theatre. Some, chief among whom was Clement Scott of the *Daily Telegraph*, vigorously defended the right of the average playgoer to pleasant entertainment and furiously rejected Ibsen; Scott offered this advice to dramatists:

> There is a public, a great public, an honest public, a playgoing and play-loving public, that deplores this consistent and obstinate preference for the base instead of the beautiful in art. Go to average human nature for your subjects, not to the experience of the specialist in moral disease ... Go out from the moral leper house, and hospital and society dissecting-room, reeking with the smell of dissolution and tell us something of the cleanliness that is next to Godliness: something of the trials and struggles of the just, the sorely tried, the tempted, and the pure.[16]

As for Ibsen himself, the Examiner of Plays, Piggott, offered his considered opinion to the Select Committee:

[15] 'Our Stage To-Day', *Theatre* (September 1894), p. 95.
[16] Clement Scott, 'The Modern Society Play', *Theatre* (January 1895), p. 10.

The Music-hall   Screaming Farcical Comedy

A Melodrama at the " Surrey "   A pathetic " Comedy-
                                          Drama "

Plate 20–22   The audience reacting. *Mr Punch at the Play*.

Another

The Opera

A patriotic Drama at the
" National Theatre "

And

Three acts   of Henrik Ibsen

The deplorable issue

I have studied Ibsen's plays pretty carefully, and all the characters in Ibsen's plays appear to me morally deranged. All the heroines are dissatisfied spinsters who look on marriage as a monopoly, or dissatisfied married women in a chronic state of rebellion against not only the conditions which nature has imposed on their sex, but against all the duties and obligations of mothers and wives; and as for the men they are all rascals or imbeciles. (1892 *Report*, p. 334)

Notwithstanding such powerful condemnation, the opponents of Ibsen were fighting what proved to be merely a strong rearguard action. In the theatre the 1890s were, Pinero believed, 'a period of analysis, of general restless inquiry', which created a new spirit that 'permits to our writers of plays a wider scope in the selection of subject, and calls for an accompanying freedom of thought, a large freedom of utterance'.[17] Other European plays were also performed in London in the 1890s, both by foreign companies and by the Independent Theatre, a private theatre society founded in 1891 by J. T. Grein with the express purpose of performing new European and English plays. The impact of this avant-garde work upon a theatre still conservative and socially timorous in subject matter was considerable. It forced dramatists to think freshly about their art, encouraged new playwrights like Shaw and Harley Granville-Barker to write in their own way, enlarged the thematic material of the stage in the direction of family tragedy and social corruption, allowed for subtle and unstereotyped characterisation and finally made the unhappy ending in domestic drama acceptable to audiences – a real achievement in the Victorian theatre. A sign of changing times was George Alexander's acceptance for the St James's of an unhappy ending to Pinero's *The Second Mrs Tanqueray* in 1893 (she kills herself) four years after John Hare at the Garrick refused to accept his original ending to *The Profligate*, in which the philandering husband poisons himself; Hare imposed a happy ending.

Despite the influence of Ibsen and the more socially adventurous drama of the 1890s, however, the old melodrama still held out in West End citadels like the Adelphi and Drury Lane, the latter specialising, as did the Standard in the East End, in huge, ponderous and spectacular melodramas of high society, sporting life, natural catastrophes and colonial wars. In the East End the Britannia successfully maintained its policy of melodrama and pantomime until nearly the end of the century. The Elephant and Castle in Southwark and the Lyric, Hammersmith were local melodrama strongholds in the 1890s, and one must remember that much traditional melodrama

[17] 'The Modern British Drama', *Theatre* (June 1895), p. 348.

Plate 23   The hero *in excelsis. At Duty's Call,* 1898. Touring poster.

co-existed in London with Ibsen, the first plays of Shaw, and the
work of Jones and Pinero. Its decline in the metropolis did not occur
until about 1905, when the popularity of the new cinema began to
drain away audiences from theatres in working-class districts; it
survived longer in the provinces, especially in the small touring
companies.

JONES AND PINERO

The two dominant serious playwrights of the eighties and nineties,
Arthur Pinero and Henry Arthur Jones, were not radical or avant-
garde in the European sense, and neither experimented with the *form*
of the drama. Nevertheless, they were regarded by conservative
circles as socially daring, although not daring enough to offend their
substantial middle-class audience.

In *Saints and Sinners* (1884) Jones introduced onto a stage which
had long been kept clear, both by natural inclination and the edict of
the Examiner of Plays, of religious subjects, savage portraits of
hypocritical members of a Dissenting congregation, who drive their
minister from his chapel because of his daughter's sin; the fact that
they are also grasping tradesmen touches upon one of Jones's obses-

sions, a hatred of the shopkeeping class. However, this theme, which caused controversy, is worked out in an otherwise conventional melodrama about villainy and seduction that followed by only two years his enormously successful melodrama *The Silver King*. Indeed, whatever the social content of his serious plays, Jones started from a strong base of melodrama, especially in the highly romantic dramas *The Dancing Girl* (1891) and *The Masqueraders* (1894). *The Middleman* (1889) is another in the long line of plays about capital and labour and the exploitation of the worker; showing that this theme was anything but exhausted, especially as it occurs in several other plays of the nineties, including George Moore's *The Strike at Arlingford* (1893), and reaches an Edwardian climax in John Galsworthy's *Strife* (1909). In Jones's drama, the exploited potter turns the tables on his employer by inventing a wonderful new glaze and himself becoming the capitalist. The religious interest of *Saints and Sinners* is continued in *Judah* (1890), in which an idealistic minister saves a fraudulent but beautiful faith-healer from rightful exposure and then resigns his ministry, and the unsuccessful *Michael and his Lost Angel* (1896), in which a minister who has compelled a young girl, the victim of a seduction, to confess her sin before his own congregation, then goes through the same process himself during a church service on stage (to which many objected) because of his own adultery with a married parishioner. He too leaves his ministry. Jones's boldness of theme is often more than compensated for by his timidity of execution. The previously unrepentant Michael is overcome by a fit of atonement in the last act, which discovers him in a monastery. The seductive parishioner dies of a fever; thus both parties are judged guilty, at least theatrically, and are punished. Similarly, Mrs Dane of *Mrs Dane's Defence* (1900), who is loved by the young Lionel Carteret and guilty of nothing more than concealing a dubious past, is exposed and denied her chance at marital happiness by a ruthless cross-examination conducted by Lionel's father, an eminent judge. Yet Jones was only expressing the mores and social concerns of his day, and it is unfair to criticise him for not fearlessly rejecting them. His own increasing conservatism, his initial opposition to Ibsen and his ambivalent attitude to socially risky themes also mark him clearly as a dramatist of the eighties and nineties.

Pinero shared some of these characteristics, although his work became thematically stronger in the Edwardian period while Jones retreated from earlier, somewhat radical positions. A master of farce and the author of many comedies before he came to writing dramas, Pinero shows a better sense of plot construction than Jones, an art Victorian playwrights had on the whole cared little about. Thematically, the sterner *The Second Mrs Tanqueray*, which despite Pinero's modernism owes much to an inheritance of melodramatic stock character types, is sandwiched between a compromised *Profligate* and an eventually conforming *The Notorious Mrs Ebbsmith* (1895). In this play the resolutely atheistic and politically leftist Agnes Ebbsmith, who takes a married radical politician as a lover and flouts all social norms, recants at the end, gives up her lover to his wife, and snatches out of the fire a bible which she has just flung into it – a clear borrowing from *Hedda Gabler* (seen in London in 1891). The difference between Ibsen and Pinero in this case, however, is that Hedda lets Lovborg's manuscript burn. *The Benefit of the Doubt* (1895), a bitter play, is an altogether weightier drama than *The Notorious Mrs Ebbsmith*, although it was called a comedy. The comic elements are, however, cruelly ironic, and the portrayal of failed marriage powerfully emotional. It is not surprising, given the current West End taste for mildly challenging but essentially safe drama, that it failed (though according to Shaw it was poorly acted).

SHAW AND WILDE

George Bernard Shaw himself was an iconoclast and violator of social taboos well to the dramatic left of such mainstream West End dramatists as Jones and Pinero. As a result his plays barely received a hearing in the 1890s; he had to wait until the twentieth century and particularly until the Stage Society seasons at the Royal Court from 1904 to 1907 to come into his full glory as a significant dramatic author. Most of Shaw's plays of the nineties, from *Widowers' Houses* (1892) to *Captain Brassbound's Conversion* (1900), were first given by private societies, in obscure locations outside the West End, or in copyright performances – a legal device whereby the author's rights in an acted play were assured provided a single performance (usually without scenery and costumes, with the actors reading from scripts) had been given before publication. In the nineties Shaw had no popular success and was better known as the drama critic of the *Saturday Review* than as a playwright. The tone of his 'dramas', like *Widowers' Houses* or *The Devil's Disciple* (1897) can be strongly comic, usually in an ironic and satirical fashion. The trial scene in *The Devil's Disciple* is in part taken from Boucicault's *Arrah-na-Pogue*, and it is interesting to see Shaw – as he himself freely admitted – using and adapting Victorian comic forms and the conventional material of melodrama, including its character stereotypes, to his own purpose. In *Widowers' Houses*, for example, these stereotypes are readily identifiable: hero (Trench), heroine (Blanche Sartorius) walking gentleman (Cokane), comic man (Lickcheese). But they do not behave as do the stereotypes of melodramas. Like Mrs Tanqueray, who is a richly complex character, quite different from the woman with a past of earlier Victorian drama, yet clearly descended from that stereotype, Blanche, with her selfishness and vicious temper tantrums is a nasty piece of work as a heroine, although that is clearly her ancestry. In fact Shaw plays off conventional expectation all the time, setting up a situation or a character in a particular way and then reversing audience assumptions about the outcome. His ironic comedy is frequently a device to mask a serious purpose; at least in the 1890s Shaw believed that 'problem' was 'the normal material of the drama' and that 'only in the problem play is there any real drama', since drama was 'the presentation in parable of the conflict between man's will and his environment: in a word, of problem'.[18]

Insofar as the drama of the 1890s dealt with ethical, moral and social issues that caused a serious dislocation in the domestic and emotional life of the principal characters, then Jones, Pinero and Shaw certainly practised the problem play, Shaw in *Widowers' Houses* and *Mrs Warren's Profession* (1898) especially. The immediate father of the problem play in England is Ibsen, although the earlier domestic melodrama is sometimes concerned with social problems. In the nineties it became the fashionable kind of play for a West End dramatist to attempt and many dramatists besides these three wrote it, including Haddon Chambers in *John-a-Dreams* (1894), in which Kate Cloud, the daughter of a prostitute and a prostitute herself in former hard times, is faced with revealing her past to her poet-fiancé and his clergyman father.

Among the authors of problem plays might be enrolled the name of Oscar Wilde. This is not as improbable as it seems. Although his four well-known plays have the reputation of comedies and were called comedies in their day, only *The Importance of Being Earnest* (1895) is purely comic. The others are essentially heavy social dramas disguised as comedies by a great deal of elegance and more wit. The problem play is most evident in *An Ideal Husband* (1895), in which the parliamentarian Sir Robert Chiltern faces a moral choice between the public exposure of his unsavoury past betrayal of a cabinet secret (his whole fortune is founded on this betrayal), thereby keeping his high-minded wife, or losing his wife and what private honour is left to him if he does not denounce a fraudulent speculative scheme in which the blackmailing adventuress Mrs Cheveley is

[18] *The Complete Prefaces of Bernard Shaw* (London, 1965), p. 228.

involved. Like many a Victorian dramatist before him, Wilde evades the issue: his friend Lord Goring traps Mrs Cheveley into giving up Sir Robert's incriminating letter revealing the secret, and Sir Robert – quite unlike an Ibsen character – avoids the consequence of his actions, retaining wife, wealth and position and being further rewarded by a cabinet post.

The social climbing tendencies of the middle-class drama in the late Victorian period are supremely exemplified, not only in the glittering public persona of Wilde the playwright and socialite, but also in the plays themselves: nine of the characters in *Lady Winder-mere's Fan* (1892) are titled, six in *An Ideal Husband*. In spite of this fashionable and aristocratic colouring, Wilde, like Shaw, was not above stealing from the conventions of humble melodrama, and more obviously. In *An Ideal Husband*, for instance, the heroine Mabel Chiltern is, physically at least, a classic stereotype. She is described on her first appearance as '*a perfect example of the English type of prettiness, the apple-blossom type ... There is ripple after ripple of sunlight in her hair.*' Mrs Cheveley, on the other hand, bears all the signs of the typical villainess (and behaves accordingly), her lips '*a line of scarlet on a pallid face. Venetian red hair ... She is wearing heliotrope, with diamonds.*' When at the end of Act III she apparently gets the better of Lord Goring, '*her face is illumined with evil triumph*'.

Wilde's essential comic style is certainly new in the Victorian drama, consisting largely of enigmatic flippancies about life, Society and the men and women both inside and outside that sacred domain. When these alternate, as they do in *A Woman of No Importance* (1893), with bursts of intense emotion, the consequence is disharmony of tone – something, however, that never worried Victorian dramatists. Significantly, the only Wilde play regularly performed today is *The Importance of Being Earnest*, the play least encumbered with the usual emotional weight of Victorian drama. The other three plays – *Salome* was first performed in Paris, not London, for obvious reasons – are very much of their time, notably in that terrible fear of social discovery and exposure, of loss of reputation and consequent social disgrace, that can also be found in Shaw's *The Philanderer* (1898) and permeates the Mayfair dramas of Jones and Pinero. This, indeed, is one of the main themes, spoken or unspoken, of the drama of the 1890s, and it is very prominent in Wilde.

COMEDY

The Philanderer is a comedy, and both Taylor's *Still Waters Run Deep* and Pinero's *The Benefit of the Doubt* were called comedies, despite their emotional weight, their essential seriousness of tone, and their obvious similarity to the 'drama'. Among the non-lyric comic forms of the Victorian stage – comedy, farce, extravaganza, burlesque and pantomime – comedy is the hardest to define, since it so often contains much of the pathetic and melodramatic freight with which the 'drama' is loaded. This is true even of the light comedies of Tom Robertson, and a mixture of strong pathos and emotions with low and eccentric comedy runs right through Victorian comedy, making distinctions between one genre and another difficult. Indeed, the Victorian theatre is a veritable potpourri of dramatic forms, and it is no longer possible to make the sort of clear genre definitions for the nineteenth century that were still applicable late in the eighteenth century. Comedy also carries much of the thematic burden of melodrama and drama: the sanctity of marriage, the ideal of the domestic hearth and domestic harmony, the idealisation of women and filial relationships and rural virtue, class conflict, social ambition, money and the proper use of wealth. All these themes are also explored in the Victorian novel.

Bulwer's *Money* (1840) includes several of the significant themes and techniques of Victorian comedy, as instanced by the antagonism between the poor dependent secretary Alfred Evelyn and his patronising cousin and employer Sir John Vesey, fuelled by the proud poverty of the one and the social arrogance of the other. When Evelyn suddenly inherits a fortune, everybody who previously ignored him fawns obsequiously over him. The play alternates between ironic satire in scenes such as the reading of the will and the heavy emotion of passages between Evelyn and his loved one, Clara. The final triumph of Evelyn over betrayers and sycophants alike, and his assumption of a position suited to both his wealth and integrity, is naturally accompanied by the hand of the devoted but financially disinterested Clara. Many a hero of melodrama is rewarded by sudden and unexpected wealth as well as by the person of the heroine, and *Money* is not the only Victorian comedy where this happens; Robertson's *Society* (1865) is another example.

Money is thus an important play that looks forward and establishes theme and tone for much succeeding comedy. On the other hand its popular contemporary, Boucicault's *London Assurance* (1841), looks backward, modelling itself on the wit, style and characterisation of an older comedy. Its success at Covent Garden owed a great deal to a splendid cast that included Vestris and Mathews. Such lines as these, spoken by the heroine about another character, well illustrate the unquenchable rhetorical tendency of early Victorian comedy and its equally prominent straining after literary effect (the same tendencies are pronounced in early Victorian melodrama). 'Who is she?' someone asks, and the reply is, 'Glee, glee, made a living thing. Nature in some frolic mood, shut up a merry devil in her eye, and, spiting Art, stole Joy's brightest harmony to thrill her laugh, which peals out sorrow's knell.'

London Assurance touches on no important themes, but the period's obsession with wealth and financial solvency is developed by many comedies. Money in association with class hostility is socially negative: in Jerrold's *Retired from Business* (1851) the retired grocer Pennyweight is told that 'the gentry of previous wholesale life do not associate with individuals of former retail existence. The counting house knows not the shop. The wholesale merchant never crosses the till.' Jerrold satirises such attitudes, and Victorian comedy is full of contempt for the *nouveau riche*, for the tradesman who has made money and now wishes to elevate himself socially above his station and ape the manners and life style of his betters. The vulgar Chodd Jr of *Society* is one such character, a man who thinks everything he wants in life can be obtained by waving a cheque-book; two others are Bodmin Todder of Todder's Original Patent Starch and Isaac Skoome (the anti-Semitic overtones are clear) in Robertson's *Play* (1868) and *M. P.* (1870) respectively. All this material is developed in the context of a middle-class and occasionally fashionable and aristocratic world. Whether urban or provincial, comedy was – unlike farce, melodrama and pantomime – entertainment for the middle class only, and appeared infrequently in the repertory of the East End and transpontine working-class theatres.[19]

Two plays that encapsulate much of Victorian comedy in style, characterisation and content are George Henry Lewes's *The Game of Speculation* (1851) and Tom Taylor's and Augustus Dubourg's *New Men and Old Acres* (1869). Lewes claimed that the former, adapted from Balzac's *Mercadet* and produced under a pseudonym, took him less than thirteen hours to write and was given only two rehearsals at the Lyceum. Charles Mathews played the principal part of Affable Hawk, a speculator of immense charm and extraordinary powers of persuasion who struggles frenziedly but always with perfect poise to outwit his creditors and obtain a wealthy marriage for his daughter. Eventually he is saved from ruin by a *deus ex machina*, the arrival from India of his now rich but previously absconding partner. The play is suffused with the spirit and values of the Stock Exchange, and

[19] There were exceptions. Squire Bancroft records a successful four-week visit in 1873 of the Prince of Wales's company in *Caste* to the Standard Theatre in Shoreditch, with its seating capacity of 3,400, four times that of the Prince of Wales's.

in that respect can hardly be considered dated. Hawk dupes his gullible creditors easily, and speaks ironically of prevailing attitudes to money. 'Here lies modern honour', he declares, holding up half-a-crown. Credit, he says, is everything, 'the wealth of commerce, the foundation of the state ... Now, nothing but selfishness exists. Everyone places his future in the Three-per cents. There lies our paradise ... All our morals lie in dividends.' In a longer speech he discourses to his wife upon debtors and creditors:

> What is life, Caroline, but one enormous loan? A perpetual borrow, borrow, borrow. Moreover, there is some skill required to get handsomely in debt – it is not every one that can get trusted. Am I not greatly superior to my creditors? I have their money – they must wait for mine. I ask nothing from them – they pester my life out with importunities. Think, my dear – a man who owes nothing, what a solitary, miserably incomplete being! Nobody cares for him; nobody asks about him; nobody knocks at his door. Whilst I am an object of intense and incessant interest to my creditors. They think of me in going to bed; they think of me in rising every day – their lips grow familiar with my name; their hands love my knocker.

Something of the financial fever and the money mania of *The Game of Speculation* also attaches to Boucicault's *The School for Scheming* (1847) in which several characters intrigue for a fortune and cheat and deceive each other to get it. The low comedian of the play, who styles himself The Macdunnum, speculates frantically in the stock market and abandons the girl who loves him in pursuit of wealth.

New Men and Old Acres is quieter and more restrained than either of these early Victorian pieces; it shows the influence of Robertson, especially in the gentle love scenes between the heroine, Lilian Vavasour of Cleve Abbey, descended from ancient stock, and the Liverpool merchant Brown. The worthy but impecunious Vavasours are contrasted with the vulgar parvenu Bunters (Buckstone played Bunter), who own a handsome but flashy house nearby, patronise the Vavasours, and attempt a bit of financial double-dealing to secure the heavily mortgaged Abbey estate. The Bunter attitude to tradition and beauty is made clear in Act I:

> LILIAN. Yes, I like ruins.
> MRS BUNTER. So I see, by the furnitur'. I like things that look like the money you've put into them.
> BUNTER. (*Sententiously.*) Everything has its place, Mrs B. Old families and old furnitur', like theirs – modern hopulence with modern elegance, like ours.

Bunter is frustrated in his scheme by the honourable Brown and the lucky find of valuable ironstone beneath the estate, a discovery that Bunter was secretly trying to exploit by getting hold of Cleve Abbey.

Brown is a new hero, a respectable man of business who is not satirised, a throwback, as it were, to the dignified merchant figure of eighteenth-century sentimental comedy. He agrees with Lilian that the future does not belong to the Bunters – or to the Vavasours, he adds. 'I rather think it belongs more to those whose brains and hands shape the world about them, than to those who stand on the dignity of old names.' Like most Victorian comedy, *New Men and Old Acres* is deeply conservative in outlook. The older values are best, unless they are pushed to foolish extremes; social climbers and the vulgar rich receive their comeuppance; the landed gentry are superior to 'the upstart class' if their views are tempered with a sensible modernity.

ROBERTSON

Tom Robertson was another dramatist whose comedies affirm the social order rather than challenge it. Of all Victorian drama, only the occasional melodrama and the early plays of Shaw do the latter. The brief flowering of Robertson's Prince of Wales's comedies, from *Society*, in 1865 to *M.P.* in 1870 (he died in 1871), obscures the fact that he had a long and hard apprenticeship as an actor, stage manager, scene painter, songwriter, prompter and unsuccessful playwright, both on his father's declining Lincoln circuit and in London. He knew the theatre inside out, and the Bancrofts were glad to entrust him with the stage management of his own plays. All the significant thematic material and much of the style of a previous generation of Victorian comedy (which inherited much of it from pre-Victorian dramatists) was contained in Robertson's comedies: the animosity between a new upthrusting moneyed class and an old aristocracy or land-owning gentry, money, social aspiration, romantic love, the co-existence of the pathetic, the melodramatic and the comic, the idealisation of Victorian womanhood, and a marked reluctance to explore social and moral issues with any real depth or seriousness, despite the ambitious titles of some of the plays: *Society*, *Caste* (1867), *Progress* (1869), *Birth* (1870) – these last two not produced by the Bancrofts. What *was* new in Robertson was a delicacy and restraint in the handling of the inevitable love scenes and in much of the dialogue, although he could write a wildly emotional passage with the best of them. Also novel was his simple domesticity and the attractive goodness of perfectly ordinary characters. Stylisti-

cally, Robertson had a knack in dialogue of juxtaposing a quarrell-
ing couple with a tender couple in the same scene, as well as a
traditional affinity for strong curtains. His *School* (1869), the most
successful of the Prince of Wales's comedies with an initial run of 381
performances, is a romantic fantasy, a fairytale treatment of Victorian girlhood. In fact the play begins with Bella, one of the two
heroines, telling the story of Cinderella, the opening lines coming
after the curtain rises on a scene straight from a mid-Victorian
painting: '*Music from "La Cenerentola" before the Curtain rises. A
Glade. All the* GIRLS *discovered in various positions.* BELLA *standing. The*
GIRLS *have wild flowers, ivy, &c, in their laps.* NAOMI TIGHE *has a long
string of wild flowers in her lap, which she is engaged in weaving together.*
BELLA *has a small branch, which she uses as a wand.*' And of course Bella
meets her prince, in the person of Lord Beaufoy.

Such romantic sweetness can also be found in James Albery's *Two
Roses* (1870), with idealised portraits of young Ida and Lotty, the
roses in question, and would be overpoweringly syrupy if not
balanced by a rich vein of comedy in the seedily dignified Digby
Grant. *Two Roses* is another example of Robertson's immediate
influence.

The emphasis on romantic love and the ideal view of womanhood
caused problems for comic playwrights as well as offering them
many possible variations on basic material. Love went wrong, of
course, and women had faults – some were even villainesses – but
such things did not change the essential premises. Naturally a plot
motivated by romantic love had to end happily, and therefore
almost all early and mid-Victorian comedies are concerned with one
or more relationships that are successfully concluded, at whatever
cost to reality. In a sense Victorian dramatists were imprisoned
within both conventions, romantic love and the happy ending,
which could severely but cosily limit thematic freedom and boldness
of approach.

Like many a dramatist before and after him, Robertson avoided
resolving or even properly developing the interesting social problems raised at the outset of several of his comedies. Instead, he
retreated into pleasant but utterly conventional romantic
entanglements. In *Progress*, for example, the engineer Ferne arrives at
Mompesson Abbey eager to demolish it and drive his new railway
line straight through the estate, to the horror of its deeply conservative heir Arthur Mompesson, a declared enemy to all forms of
modern progress. In *Birth* Paul Hewitt, the prosperous owner of a
new factory which has despoiled the rural environment, confronts
the values of the Castle as represented by the penurious Earl of

Eagleclyffe. However, this promising subject matter is frittered away after the first act of each play, which then develops in the direction of romantic sentimentality. Ferne falls in love with Mompesson's niece; Hewitt becomes engaged to the Earl's sister and the Earl to Hewitt's sister. These are but two examples of many. The thematically significant *School for Scheming* suffers a sentimental collapse in the last act, and *Retired from Business* sinks its social conflicts in a welter of love affairs among the younger set.

BYRON

Another mid-Victorian playwright whose comedies and dramas avoid the issues they raise, preferring instead requited love or marital reconciliation, was H. J. Byron, briefly the joint manager of the Prince of Wales's with Marie Wilton. Byron was a prolific author of burlesques, extravaganzas, pantomimes and melodramas, as well as comedies. His melodrama *The Lancashire Lass, or Tempted, Tried, and True* (1867) is strikingly colourful, one of several plays Byron wrote for his Liverpool management. *Cyril's Success* (1868), *Partners for Life* (1871), and *Married in Haste* (1876) all deal, interestingly, not with young couples headed for the altar, but with marital problems and marital estrangements. In *Cyril's Success* a flourishing writer neglects his lonely wife; in *Partners for Life* a husband leaves his wife because he finds that her wealth corrupted his independence; in *Married in Haste* a young painter is jealous of his wife's artistic talent, which is greater than his own. The first acts are convincing and thematically powerful; after that, however, Byron abandons all pretence of working out these problems with any sort of dramatic credibility, and resorts to an improbable series of misunderstandings, mistaken identities, coincidences and, of course, happy reconciliations between husbands and wives that ignore the issues raised.

At least marriage and not courtship becomes the focus of comedy, and this is a significant thematic advance, delightfully heralded by Buckstone's farcical *Married Life* (1834), in which the marital difficulties of four couples, three comic and one serious, are amusingly resolved. *Married Life* is a companion piece to the later *Single Life* (1839), in which five men with quite different attitudes to marriage eventually espouse five quite different women. The two plays together comprise an unusually extended and at least partly serious stage discourse upon marriage.

Byron's best-known and most popular comedy, *Our Boys* (1875), which broke the long run record of *The Ticket-of-Leave Man*, concerns not a marriage but a romantic relationship between two

young couples, which concludes successfully, despite the obstacles, in
the last act. These obstacles include class hostility between the
uneducated and good-hearted retired butterman Middlewick and
the snobbish aristocrat Sir Geoffrey Champneys, and parental plans
for their sons, who are themselves also sharply contrasted. Talbot
Champneys, Sir Geoffrey's son, first appears as a mid-Victorian
eccentric comedian. '*He is a washed-out youth, with yellow-reddish hair
parted down the middle; a faint effort at a fluffy whisker and moustache;
dreadfully over-dressed, and has a limp look generally; an eye-glass, and a
soft namby-pamby manner.*' By Act III, however, he undergoes a
Robertsonian transformation from a potential Lord Dundreary into
a quietly resolute, decent and somewhat ordinary young man –
rather like Captain Hawtree in *Caste*, whose manly and restrained
behaviour belies his eccentric comedy appearance. 'I'm about the
average standard sort of thing', he appealingly informs the middle-
class Prince of Wales's audience. It is no wonder that with characters
like Talbot Champneys and the warmly compassionate Middlewick
the critic for the *Daily Telegraph* could write of a revival of *Our Boys*
in 1881 that Byron 'has deliberately appealed to the great bulk of the
middle classes, from whom the staunchest playgoers are drawn ...
Best of all the play was kind-hearted and pleasant' (3 June).

GILBERT

Generally speaking, Victorian dramatists were soft-centred: a warm
bath of sentiment, good deeds and true love cleansed any impurities
of deceit, bad dealing or hard-heartedness from their plays.
However, one author of mid-Victorian comedies, W. S. Gilbert,
was in his best comic work an exception to the general kind-hearted-
ness and pleasantry, especially in *Engaged* (1877). Gilbert had been
previously noted for his 'fairy' comedies *The Palace of Truth* (1870)
and *The Wicked World* (1873), plays which indicate the Victorian and
particularly the Gilbertian fascination with fairies, and which exploit
the dramatic potential for transformation and social subversion in a
fairy world. In the former a king and his court are compelled to
speak only the truth within the walls of a mysterious royal palace;
they are enchanted. Not only must the characters speak the truth;
they are also unaware that they are speaking it. Given these premises
Gilbert misses no opportunity for the satiric exposure of deceitful-
ness, hypocrisy and pretension. Things are patched up at the end of
The Palace of Truth, but not at the end of *The Wicked World*, whose
central theme is the ultimate destructiveness of love. The fairy cloud
world of the play, all beauty and innocence at first, is slowly

darkened and poisoned by the intrusion of human love, as two knights are introduced from the earth below. The fairies who fall in love with these two mortals cannot bear the burden of this love and fall into selfishness, jealousy, recrimination and despair. A third fairy comedy, *Foggerty's Fairy* (1881), treats of the intrusion of misguided fairy benevolence into the human world, and *Iolanthe* (1882) is the Savoy opera in which the impact of humanity upon the fairy world is comically painful.

Despite ironies, the weight of the pathetic and sentimental is clearly evident in *The Wicked World*. The Savoy operas carried this softening process further; although the collaborative force of music elevated Gilbert's familiar themes – romantic love, money, social status – to a new realm of fanciful satiric power, Sullivan's music somehow makes the satire kinder and gentler. This is not true of *Engaged*, whose young men and women, totally preoccupied with money to the exclusion of genuine affection and thus quite unlike their forebears in Victorian comedy, are not even agreeable. The plot, too complicated to explain in a brief summary, centres upon one Cheviot Hill, a young man with an over-careful sense of the value of money, who because of a fatal attraction to women becomes engaged to three of them simultaneously, despite the preventive efforts of his sinister friend Belvawney, whose income depends upon keeping Cheviot single. Also present are the mercenary father of one of the women and a virtuous Scottish peasant who wrecks railway trains for profit and sells his loved one to Cheviot for two pounds. The satiric treatment of money and money's sufficiency or insufficiency, its effect on domestic happiness and love relationships, and the way it affects individual and social attitudes – this was theme material by no means new on the comic stage when Gilbert took it up, as we have seen. What *was* new was the logical thoroughness with which he used this material, the iconoclastic nature of its application, the absence of sentimental and romantic compensation and the fact that the supposedly sweet, tender, modest and domestically inclined young woman is financially even more ruthless than the man.

The tone of *Engaged* is well caught in two speeches, the first by Belinda in Act I in response to Belvawney's proposal of marriage:

> Belvawney, I love you with an imperishable ardour which mocks the power of words. If I were to begin to tell you of the force of my indomitable passion for you, the tomb would close over me before I could exhaust the entrancing subject. But, as I said before, business is business, and unless I can see some distinct probability that your income will be permanent, I shall have no alternative but to weep my heart out in all the anguish of maiden solitude – uncared for, unloved, and alone!

The second speech, in Act III, is addressed to two of Cheviot's ladies by a Belvawney in danger of losing his income by Cheviot's marriage and desperate to marry *somebody* with money:

> One of you will be claimed by Cheviot; that is very clear. To that one (whichever it may be) I do not address myself – but to the other (whichever it may be), I say I love you (whichever you are) with a fervour which I cannot describe in words. If you, whichever you are, will consent to cast your lot with mine, I will devote my life to proving that I love you and you only (whichever it may be) with a single-hearted and devoted passion, which precludes the possibility of my ever entertaining the slightest regard for any other woman in the whole world.

Linked as it was to the common themes of Victorian comedy, *Engaged* nevertheless departed from the accepted practices of this comedy sharply enough to be a truly revolutionary play. Several contemporary critics reviewed it violently. It did not take them and the first audiences of *Engaged* long to realise that their cherished ideals of romantic love, marriage, the home, selflessness and filial relationships were under attack; by Act III these ideals lay in little bits and pieces all over the stage. Rural virtue, the dominant but protective male, the loving and domestically inclined female, the loyal friend, the tender father, the obedient and doting daughter – all these character types were familiar from generations of drama, fiction and painting. Gilbert tore them to shreds. *Engaged* offended against the general Victorian belief – and this was well before the appearance of Ibsen in London – that the theatre was principally a place of entertainment, a place to relax in, a place to have a good evening out – not a place in which to think or be troubled by the serious side of life, above all not a place in which to be *disturbed*.

1890S COMEDY

No Victorian dramatist after Gilbert possessed his ironic and condemnatory power; only Shaw came close, and Shaw did not have Gilbert's decidedly bilious view of human nature. Comedy turned again to the sweet and sentimental, as in Pinero's *Sweet Lavender* (1888) and Sydney Grundy's fairytale-like *A Pair of Spectacles* (1890), an adaptation from the French. Clement Scott praised *Sweet Lavender* – the story of the romantic union in spite of all difficulties of a young barrister and the daughter of his laundress – and said that life is sad as a rule, but 'let us sometimes, even in a despised theatre, dream how happy and ideal and beautiful it *might* be. Rose-coloured spectacles are so much more soothing than the bare white glass.'[20] In

---

[20] Clement Scott, *The Drama of Yesterday and To-day* (London, 1899), vol. II, p. 189.

Grundy's play a kindly philanthropist turns nasty when he breaks his spectacles and borrows his miserly brother's, but regains his good nature when he puts on his now mended pair. Even the brother reforms, and the play ends in a glow of benevolence and good deeds. Nevertheless, *A Pair of Spectacles* is a charming and skilfully written comedy. Pinero did *his* most charming work in *Trelawny of the Wells* (1898), the affectionate portrait of a theatre company of the sixties some distance from the West End and of the courtship of Rose Trelawny, its leading vocalist-comedienne, by Arthur Gower of the formidably old-fashioned Gowers of Cavendish Square. Much of the interest of the play comes from the contrast between the lively but vulgar creative energy of the Wells company (Pinero carefully observes the distinctions between stock company lines of business as reflected in the characters' behaviour) and the arid, stultified routine of the aristocratic shut-in Gowers – a little reminiscent of the contrast between school and circus in *Hard Times*. *Trelawny of the Wells* is easily the best of the many plays about theatre written in the nineteenth century.

Of the Mayfair comedies of the 1890s the two most entertaining are by Henry Arthur Jones: *The Case of Rebellious Susan* (1894) and *The Liars* (1897). Both contrive to use the mid-Victorian notion of concentrating thematically upon an unhappy marriage rather than a romantic if obstacle-strewn courtship. The former deals with Lady Susan's revolt against the continued infidelities of her husband and her refusal to play the role expected of her by her family, friends and Society and 'patch things up'. She embarks upon a romantic adventure with the handsome young Lucien Edensor, a relationship which appears by the textual evidence to have been consummated, although Jones fudges the matter. There is no *Doll's House*-like ending, however, no final closing of the door upon Susan's dim husband. The play's spokesman for Society and morality, Sir Richard Kato, lectures Susan at length on her marital and social obligations, and she returns reluctantly to her husband only because Edensor has suddenly married another woman – a dubious plot trick by Jones to increase the pressure on her and load the moral dice. If Kato's view of the role and duties of women is indeed Society's – it was certainly Jones's – she has no choice. 'There is an immense future for women as wives and mothers, and a very limited future for them in any other capacity', he tells a repellent feminist (another loading of the dice), 'Nature's darling woman is a stay-at-home woman, a woman who wants to be a good wife and good mother, and cares very little for anything else.' A more stylish, witty and elegant play, *The Liars* contains the same sort of character dispensing the same sort of advice to another woman tempted to leave an even more unpleasant husband for an even more attractive alternative. The outcome is the same: she is unwillingly reconciled to her repentant spouse. The play is masterfully plotted, especially Act III, in which character after character becomes comically involved in the wife's cover-up story. The aforementioned fear of exposure, loss of reputation, social disgrace and ostracism that can be found in plots like *The Second Mrs Tanqueray*, *Lady Windermere's Fan*, *Mrs Dane's Defence* and other dramas of their time is a powerfully motivating force for much of the action in *The Liars*.

FARCE

While a comedy was a major item on the evening's bill, farce functioned as a one-act or two-act afterpiece and, until the advent of the single mainpiece on the playbill in the West End, was ubiquitous in middle-class and working-class theatres alike, often timed to begin about 9 p.m., or half-price time. On the Victorian stage acting in comedy was divided into the usual lines of business, prominently featuring light comedians, low comedians and – by the 1860s – eccentric comedians. Farce focussed on low comedy, although the rest of the stock company had to be employed, and is in many respects close to comedy as a dramatic form, notably in the earlier Victorian period with a strong vein of morality, sentimentality, serious matter and domestic idealism. By the 1840s farce had mostly discarded its eighteenth-century inheritance of middle- and upper middle-class romantic intrigue and the gulling of foolish parents, guardians and rivals by a pair of lovers and their clever servants. It had become far less genteel, much more domestic and lower class in its settings and characters, especially for theatres like the Adelphi whose audiences were not in the least genteel or fashionable. This period, in many ways a golden age of English farce, lasted from the forties to the sixties, and was marked by a plethora of servants, tradesmen and journeymen as characters; of attics, third-floor backs and cellar kitchens; by a special kind of comedy arising from the preparation, serving and consumption of food; direct address to the audience in asides and explanatory monologues; and a great deal of amiable and homely charm.

Dominating all other farceurs at this time was John Maddison Morton, who took many plots from the French but made them (as did all the best adapters, no matter what the dramatic form) into a thoroughly and seemingly original English product. Morton wrote for a variety of West End playhouses over a long career and well knew how to adjust his work to the different audiences of different theatres, moving up and down the social scale in settings, characters and language whenever necessary. The best of his farces is the still performed *Box and Cox* (1847), in which the scheming Mrs Bouncer rents a single room to both Cox the hatter and Box the printer without either being aware of the deception, since Cox is employed by day and sleeps in the only bed at night and Box is employed by night and sleeps by day. Of course they confront each other early in the piece (when Cox is given an unexpected holiday), each discovering after a fierce territorial dispute over the room that the other is also pledged to marry the fearsome offstage widow Penelope Ann; each tries desperately to yield her to the other. To their enormous relief the imminent arrival of Penelope Ann is averted by news that she is marrying the equally offstage Knox. *Box and Cox* is written in a wonderfully elegant style expressing the most mundane materiality and is full of splendid climaxes and anti-climaxes.

It is also a parody (as its sub-title 'A Romance of Real Life' indicates) of melodrama, done with a light and delicate touch typical of Morton. At the end of the play Box is about to embrace Cox in hearty reconciliation, but suddenly steps back, seizes his hand, and *'looks eagerly in his face'*:

> BOX   You'll excuse the apparent insanity of the remark, but the more I gaze on your features, the more I'm convinced that you're my long-lost brother.
> COX   The very observation I was going to make to you!
> BOX   Ah, tell me – in mercy tell me – have you such a thing as a strawberry mark on your left arm!
> COX   No!
> BOX   Then it is he! (*They rush into each other's arms.*)

Other good farces by Morton are *Slasher and Crasher* (1848), *A Most Unwarrantable Intrusion* (1849), *Grimshaw, Bagshaw, and Bradshaw* (1851), and *Drawing Room, Second Floor, and Attics* (1864), a play in which a considerable amount of physical business suggests one direction in which farce was heading.

This kind of humbly domestic and energetically jolly farce flourished in the East End as much as it did in the West, if anything taking on an even more plebeian tone and character, and lasting longer on the stage. Edward Stirling's *Dandolo* (1838) is set in a boarding school in Hackney and an oyster shop in the City. Two of the main characters of Hazlewood's *Going to Chobham* (1853) are Mr and Mrs Sneezum. A great deal of physical business, running about, bumping together and digging each other in the ribs (known as 'sly dog' business) marks Meritt's *Chopstick and Spikins* (1874), which is set in a villa in Clapham.

The wives of Sneezum and Scratchley in *Going to Chobham* hold distinctly feminist views and make their husbands repent for their neglectful behaviour. In William Suter's *A Quiet Family* (1864), a Surrey farce, Benjamin Bibbs tyrannises over his wife while his brother Barnaby is in terror of *his* wife, the sister of Benjamin's wife. Their house is a battleground, the war being carried so far as endless squabbling between a male and female servant, Grumpy and Snarly. Mrs Benjamin finally rebels and brings her husband to a recognition of his tyranny and to an equal marital partnership. Barnaby drinks champagne to find the courage to bring *his* wife to a reluctant promise 'to be dutiful'. Speaking the last lines of the play, a triumphant Barnaby declares,

> I love Mrs B., but I will have my own way,
> We'll both *love*, we'll both *honour* – but she must *obey*.

Thus domestic peace and harmony are restored. The domestic ideal shines as brightly in farce as in comedy; sometimes it involved an assertion of the husband's authority and the wife's submission, but always domestic excesses had to be curbed, and domestic wrongs righted.

One aspect of early and mid-Victorian farce that distinguishes it from comedy, in addition to its relative brevity and its emphasis on low comedy, is the intense and cumulative pressure brought upon an individual who is helpless at the storm centre of domestic events entirely out of his control. The best Victorian farce works in this way. What is hilarious to the audience is deadly serious for the characters, who have no sense of humour. *Box and Cox* are frantic with fear at the approach of Penelope Ann, but this is merely climactically amusing for spectators. The wretched tailor Widgetts of Coyne's *How to Settle Accounts with Your Laundress* (1847), under the impression that the sweetheart he has rejected has drowned herself in his water butt out of frustrated love, is humiliated when, disguised as a waiter in order to hide from a detective (actually the 'drowned' laundress, also in disguise), he is forced to serve the 'detective' and a ballet dancer a delicious supper at his own table – a supper, furthermore, designed to advance his own romantic affair with the dancer. In another Coyne farce, *Did You Ever Send Your Wife to Camberwell?* (1846), the unfortunate attorney's clerk Honeybun is convinced that he has accidentally squashed a baby to death, and is assaulted by a seeming madman who declares that Honeybun has seduced his wife, whom Honeybun has never met. As in all good farce, misunderstandings and coincidences accumulate, audience expectations are either richly fulfilled or surprisingly denied, time is shortened, exits and entrances follow quickly upon one another, characters encounter other characters whom they should by *no* means encounter, and so forth.

By the 1870s farce was changing its content and increasing its length, moving from afterpiece to mainpiece on the bill and from one or two acts to three. This was initially a West End development caused by the popularity of adaptations from full-length French farces concerned with sexual peccadillos and adulterously minded but thoroughly bourgeois husbands (and wives) plotting to consummate affairs, usually failing, and frantically trying to escape the consequences of discovery and domestic and social exposure. Naturally, such adaptations had to be laundered for the English audience and the Examiner of Plays. Even then they were severely criticised by many, including Shaw, for their alleged heartlessness, immorality, and subversion of the family:

> The plot, nine times in ten, is the attempted invasion of married life and disregard of its obligations, the construction conducted with a view to many doors and mistaken rooms ... Whether this is the outcome of the high-pressure times in which we live, and which are opposed apparently to deliberate thoughtfulness, or comes of a taste depraved by a too close study of the dramatic works of our French neighbours and their views of domestic life, it is difficult to say.

Such farce dealt with 'the worthless side of life'.[21]

Trying to avoid being found out increased the pressure on the individual (who in English farce makes mistakes but is commonly innocent of sexual wrongdoing) that distinguished the farces of an earlier generation. If Gilbert's *The Wedding March* (1873), a version of *Un Chapeau de Paille d'Italie* and Albery's *Pink Dominos* (1877), an adaptation of *Les Dominos Roses*, started the trend to three-act farce – or 'farcical comedy', as it was called – of this kind, Pinero was its undoubted master. The 1880s, which saw three of his farces performed at the Royal Court Theatre, was, after the 1840s, another golden decade for Victorian farce.

Les Dominos Roses and several of its French and English imitators adopted a pattern of bringing their principal characters together, in the second act, in a hotel or restaurant of dubious reputation, the French farces with specifically adulterous intent, the English for a jolly night out and a mild flirtation. Pinero used this pattern in *The Magistrate* (1885), in which the fussy and scrupulous Posket finds

---

[21] C. Penley Newton, 'Frivolous Comedy', *Theatre* (December 1881), pp. 268–69.

himself, at the instigation of his far too mature stepson, in the restaurant of the shady Hôtel des Princes, hiding – at the end of the second act – under a table while the police search the room. His wife is hiding under the same table, but neither party knows the other is there. Posket flees onto a shaky balcony which collapses, falls through glass into the kitchen, runs miles in the pouring rain to get away, with the chase in hot pursuit, and arrives in a dreadfully battered and humiliated condition at his own magistrate's court the next morning, where he has to administer the law and sentence malefactors – including his own wife, whom the police *have* arrested.

When the hero – or rather anti-hero – of this kind of farce is a pillar of the establishment and eminently respectable in the most proper middle-class way, his frightful predicament is more extreme and the farce that much funnier for the audience. Posket is a magistrate; Dr Jedd of *Dandy Dick* (1887) is a mild-mannered rural Dean of the Anglican Church who, in order to restore the steeple of St Marvell's and improve his own financial position, bets heavily on a horse race. In attempting secretly to administer a stimulant to his horse on the night before the race, Jedd is nabbed at the stable and thrown into a cell – with his identity as yet unknown. The contrast between the awful new world in which he finds himself and the gentle, even tenor of his former ways has exactly the same function and comic effect as that in *The Magistrate*; the content of such farce is philosophically absurdist and not superficially comic. The third of the Royal Court farces of the eighties is *The Schoolmistress* (1886), which deals with the double life as headmistress and comic opera singer of Caroline Dyott and the complicated subterfuges which her schoolgirls engage in to give a party, under the protection of their 'uncle' – actually the headmistress's new husband – to celebrate the secret marriage of one of their number, subterfuges which become more difficult when the hostile father of the bride (a blustering Admiral) turns up at the party. The school burns down and further plot complications ensue too lengthy to summarise, save that they involve the sheltering of all the girls and the men in the Admiral's house while it is still dark, the return of Miss Dyott from the theatre in full opera costume – and the consequences. *The Schoolmistress* is one of the few Victorian plays in which women clearly assert their authority and superiority of wit over men; even the downtrodden wife of the irascible Admiral turns on him at the end. In these three plays the domestic ideal and domestic harmony are carefully restored by the end of Act III. Technical ingenuity and the assimilation of French models did not affect the friendly English humanity and ultimately cheery optimism of Pinero's farces.

PLANCHÉ AND EXTRAVAGANZA

Also cheerful and ingeniously crafted was another Victorian comic form, the extravaganza, which flowered at Madame Vestris's Olympic in the 1830s and held the stage until it was ousted by its cruder cousin, the burlesque, in the fifties and sixties. Its great practitioner was J. R. Planché, who, in collaboration with Charles Dance, first started writing genteel classical extravaganzas for the Olympic, such as *Olympic Devils* (1831), a merry send-up of the myth of Orpheus and Eurydice, and then, beginning with *Riquet in the Tuft* (1836), a long series of fairy extravaganzas for Vestris at the Olympic, Covent Garden and the Lyceum. These were frequently adapted from the French fairy stories of Madame d'Aulnoy and Charles Perrault. A fairy extravaganza was essentially a pantomime with the harlequinade omitted, written (if by Planché), in graceful couplets, the plot concerned with fairy intervention in the human world, a strong element of contemporary social and domestic reference blended in with the fantasy, transformations of characters and scenery and increasingly elaborate spectacle. New lyrics were written to music from popular airs and English, Italian and German opera, not to mention the songs from the black-faced minstrel craze that swept London in the 1840s and was a strong influence on popular music and entertainment for two generations. Extravaganzas were obviously for the educated, the scripts alluding to and frequently quoting from Shakespeare and other poets and dramatists. For instance, in Planché's *The Island of Jewels* (1849), the King of Pharitale, Giltgingerbread the Great, goes mad in a storm in the manner of Lear:

> I tax not you, ye elements, you pay
> No duty under schedules D or A

and declares during a heavy burst of rain,

> A thought has struck me, rather entertaining,
> I am a king more rained upon than reigning.

The authors of extravaganzas were also punsters, and often witty ones, as in this example from Planché's *Fortunio and His Seven Gifted Servants* (1843) – produced with great enthusiasm by Macready at Drury Lane – when the daughter of Emperor Matapa the Merciless accuses him of levity in a tight spot:

> Aye, joke, that's right, whilst ruin's o'er you hovering;
> You'll change your note, sir, when they change their sovereign.

The fundamental character of fairy extravaganza may best be conveyed by a brief plot summary. In *The Island of Jewels* the allegedly ill-favoured Princess Laidronetta is rejected by her family because she was cursed with ugliness in her cradle by the malevolent Fairy Magotine. However, a mysterious green serpent implores her aid, and a beautiful fairy boat appears to take her and her devoted companion Fidelia (played by Vestris) over the sea, in a storm, to a rocky cavern in which the serpent again appears, bearing Laidronetta to safety. The cavern *'changes to a magnificent palace composed entirely of the precious metals and stones'*, and a splendid company of guards and courtiers arrives – *'all composed of Jewels'* – carbuncle, onyx, topaz, pearl, ruby, sapphire, turquoise, amethyst, garnet, etc. – bearing the closed litter of King Emerald. From inside the litter Emerald begs the Princess to become Queen Diamond, in order to break Magotine's spell over him and enable Laidronetta to regain her own beauty. She reluctantly accepts; a *'crystal proscenium rises'* and the ballet of Cupid and Psyche is performed to reinforce the court's warning not to lay eyes on the King before the marriage ceremony. Prompted by fears that the unseen Emerald may be a monster or a pig, Fidelia and Laidronetta peep into the litter and discover the serpent. The litter and the scene vanish in thunder, lightning and wind that bring on a triumphant Magotine to take Laidronetta as her prisoner for seven years, imposing upon her impossible tasks like spinning a tangled spider's web strong enough to catch salmon and climbing a steel mountain in a pair of iron shoes to bring back well water with a cracked pitcher. However, the good Fairy Benevolentia intervenes to make sure that Laidronetta can fulfill these tasks with ease. The magic water from the well restores the serpent to his former manly shape; the scene changes to *'a magnificent Fairy Garden and* KING EMERALD *appears surrounded by his court'*. Magotine and her attendant elves are despatched shrieking to the regions below; Laidronetta is reconciled to her unpleasant family and, for the final transformation, the scene changes to the *'Brilliant Discovery of the Crown Jewels in the Palm of Success. Tableau'*. There are also thirteen songs, the newly fasionable Row Polka danced by the ballet, and pretty scenery.

Planché's work in extravaganza was both appealing and imaginative. In *The Golden Fleece* (1845), an adaptation of Euripides' *Medea*, the stage was constructed 'after the approved fashion of the revived Greek theatre' – a reference to Covent Garden's recent quasi-Greek staging of *Antigone* – and Charles Mathews played the Chorus, introducing the play, explaining matters to the audience in verse and song, and expostulating with the characters. Planché was expert in the technical aspects of production, and the directions for scene and costume changes in his extravaganzas are a veritable compendium of Victorian theatrical effects.

In a related form, the topical revue, Planché was also without peer. These revues, basically spirited accounts of what was going on in the London theatre and entertainment world and laudations of the producing management, were written for the Olympic and the Haymarket in particular, and they ranged chronologically from *The Drama's Levée* (1838), for Vestris and Mathews, to *The New Haymarket Spring Meeting* (1855) for Buckstone. Not only do they review contemporary entertainment in a lively manner, but also contain a great deal of theatrical information. *The Camp at the Olympic* (1853), for example, written for Alfred Wigan's new management, presents, at the '*Camp of the Combined British Dramatic Forces*', characters representing Tragedy, Comedy, Burlesque, English Opera, Ballet, Melodrama, Pantomime, Hippodrama[22] and Spectacle, each character claiming dramatic superiority over the others.

BURLESQUE

Arising out of extravaganza was the mid-Victorian burlesque, which dominated West End light entertainment in the 1850s and 1860s, especially at the Strand Theatre under the Swanborough management. Burlesque was a part of the Victorian cultural phenomenon of parody. In cartoons, in prose and poetry, in comic journalism, comic opera and in plays Victorians relentlessly parodied any possible and well-known target they could find. Stage burlesque existed well before 1837, however, with melodrama and Shakespeare providing popular material for spoofing. Shakespearean burlesque was almost an industry of its own, from John Poole's *Hamlet Travestie* of 1811 through William and Robert Brough's *The Enchanted Isle* (1848), a parody of *The Tempest*, to William Yardley's *Very Little Hamlet* of 1888. Gilbert contributed a *Rosencrantz and Guildenstern* (1874). Here the dramatists' intention – particularly in the early and mid-Victorian period – was to reduce Shakespeare's plots and characters to a low level of grotesque domestic comedy and to write ingenious comic paraphrases of the verse, as in Hamlet's address to the Ghost in a *Hamlet Travestie* of 1849:

---

[22] Hippodrama was the mounting of plays on horseback in theatres with circus rings. It flourished for many years at Astley's, where in the fifties William Cooke staged four Shakespearean productions on horseback, including *Richard III* and *Macbeth* in 1856, and several spectacular military melodramas.

O all ye ministers of state, defend us!
(Alas! that ministry's too drunk t'attend us!)
Yet will I speak to thee! I'll call thee Pa!
Dad, Faythur, Guv'nor, tell us what you are!
Say why, without the usual month's warning,
Your situation you have left this morning?

Almost every popular melodrama and opera had received burlesque treatment by the 1880s, Gilbert being a leading parodist of Italian opera in his early burlesques as well as of nautical and Gothic melodrama in *H.M.S. Pinafore* (1878), *The Pirates of Penzance* (1879) and *Ruddigore* (1887). English history, classical legend, novels, star acting performances and even Ibsen – J. M. Barrie's *Ibsen's Ghost* (1891), with J. L. Toole – were all energetically burlesqued.

An element of parody is certainly present in Planché's extravaganzas – 'burlesque' and 'extravaganza' became almost interchangeable terms – but it was considerably enlarged for the benefit of an audience that thought Planché's wit and grace old-fashioned. Topical allusions increased in number and puns multiplied to excess. Although we would dismiss many of them as atrocious, Victorian audiences found them hugely enjoyable. Better than most are two from William Brough's *The Field of the Cloth of Gold* (1868). A seasick Henry VIII disembarks in France:

Yesterday was fair – a glorious Sunday,
But this *sick transit* spoils the *glory o' Monday*.

(So that readers would not miss the point, puns were carefully italicised in the printed play.) Anne Boleyn complains of Queen Katharine's rudeness:

Such language she employs, I'm grieved to state,
Queen Kate gets *daily* more *in-daily-Kate*.

The strengths of burlesque lay not only in its sometimes clever use of language and occasionally imaginative parody, but also in its performance style. The influence of the minstrel show was very marked, in the eccentric and grotesque dancing as well as in the songs, and the clothing of shapely actresses in tights was *de rigeur*. Tom Robertson said of burlesque, 'We go express pace now, and we want singing, and dancing, and acting, and personal beauty, and pink boots, and puns, and gauzy nymphs, and nigger melodies, and classic fables, and apt allusions, and coloured fire all at once.'[23] This is

[23] 'Chambermaids, Soubrettes, and Burlesque Actresses', *Illustrated Times*, 23 April 1864. Robertson's description of the arts of the burlesque actress reveals much about the dramatic and musical eclecticism of burlesque, an extraordinary amalgam of style and content. 'Burlesque Writers', 16 January 1864, is also very informative about burlesque.

as good a brief description of burlesque as any, and conveys an often expressed Victorian belief that the fast pace of life was changing the nature of the theatre. Another description is from Robertson's *M.P.*, where one character states that only burlesque is to the taste of the present day, explaining that 'it's an entertainment crammed full of fun and singing, and dancing, and tumbling, and parodies on popular songs, and – it's written in verse.' By 1880 John Hollingshead was producing three-act burlesques at the Gaiety and burlesque was becoming more elegant and more musical. As the rage for parody diminished and West End audience taste grew more refined, burlesque was gradually displaced by the new musical comedy, importations of European comic opera, and the continued popularity of the Savoy operas of Gilbert and Sullivan.

PANTOMIME

The last Victorian dramatic form to be considered here, pantomime, was unlike extravaganza and burlesque in that it appealed to all classes of society, being even more widely played in the provinces and the working-class London theatres than it was in the West End. During the Regency, pantomime had a distinct and formal structure: an 'opening' of two to four scenes in verse in which an authoritarian guardian or father, assisted by his servant, opposes the heroine's wish to marry her young man; sometimes the father figure plans to marry her to a rival of his own choice. The plot comes from history, legend, folk story or fairy tale; the tone is serious, and the staging offers an element of tasteful spectacle. A benevolent spirit, usually female, brings the opening to an end by taking the young lovers under her protection and transforming them into Harlequin and Columbine, while father and servant become Pantaloon and Clown. She also awards Harlequin a magic bat with power of transforming objects. The almost wordless harlequinade that followed consisted of the pursuit of Harlequin and Columbine by Pantaloon and Clown and constituted the bulk of the pantomime. It was set most often in the streets and shops of London and was made up of low comedy physical knockabout, topical satire, dancing, scenic trickwork, the occasional song, extensive musical accompaniment and specialty acts, all culminating in the final intervention of the benevolent spirit, a chorus and the triumph of true love.

After a pre-Victorian interval in which the opening lengthened

These are nos. VIII and II respectively in the 'Theatrical Types' series. Substantial excerpts from both articles are printed in T. E. Pemberton, *The Life and Writings of T. W. Robertson* (London, 1893).

and the harlequinade shortened, in part because the great Clown Joseph Grimaldi had retired in 1823, the content and character of pantomime became fairly well set in the forties and fifties. The opening became more and more dominant and the harlequinade of less and less importance, until by the end of the century it was merely vestigial. Long before that the comic business of the harlequinade had ceased to have any relationship to the plot of the opening and the main harlequinade characters were played by specialists who did not appear in the opening at all. The mid and late Victorian pantomime, then, was essentially the opening, which absorbed the low comedy and physical business of the Regency harlequinade and grew even more scenically elaborate and spectacular, concluding in a splendidly lavish transformation scene that took fifteen or twenty minutes to unfold. The supernatural component of the earlier pantomime was extended; the old fairy stories and folk tales were used again and again as plot material – Aladdin, Cinderella, Dick Whittington, the Babes in the Wood and many more – and the fairy realm of the extravaganza, juxtaposed once again with a comic and eccentric domestic actuality, became the operative world of pantomime.

The fact that the pantomime of the forties stressed the fairy element and lengthened the opening to accommodate it was cultural in origin, European as well as English, and by no means an isolated theatrical phenomenon. Victorian pantomime at Christmas was mainly for children and their families, and Victorian children – and many adults – believed in fairies. Pantomime was not the only form of contemporary culture which they inhabited in large numbers. The cult of the fairy developed from 1820 to 1840 and in the 1840s was at its peak. This was the decade in which the fairy tales of Hans Christian Andersen were first translated into English; Grimms' fairy tales had been translated in the 1820s. The great fairy ballets, *Giselle* and *La Sylphide*, were products of the thirties and forties; in the fifties and sixties there are Ruskin's *King of the Golden River*, Thackeray's *The Rose and the Ring*, Kingsley's *The Water Babies* and Carroll's *Alice's Adventures in Wonderland*. At the end of the century all those fairy books by Andrew Lang – Blue, Green, Red, Yellow, Crimson – thirteen in all – the book illustrations of Arthur Rackham (who illustrated Barrie) and Edmund Dulac – and, of course, *Peter Pan* in 1904. The Royal Academy exhibited generations of fairy painting. Productions of *The Tempest* and especially *A Midsummer Night's Dream* stressed the fairy element and these two plays were the subject of many fairy paintings. The fairy cult also entered popular music and endured well into the twentieth century.

This fairy culture in the pantomime was made visually and

splendidly manifest by production methods, particularly by the transformation, a romantic but concrete physicalisation of a fantasy world. This scene – the Fairy Boudoir, the Glittering Region of the Silver Star, the Opal Throne of Happiness in the Golden Hall of Pendant Gems and so forth – required elaborate lighting and scenic methods and the suspension high above the stage of numerous fairies; many of their sisters also rose from below. There are several descriptions of a transformation, which became increasingly spectacular in the big theatres of the eighties and nineties – perhaps the most vivid is Percy Fitzgerald's, quoted in the second chapter.

Scenic effects also served the overt morality of pantomime, which was prominent in the early and mid-Victorian years. This was quite appropriate, since pantomime's story line often involves a largely comic struggle between good and evil in which supernatural agents, the demon and the good fairy, take sides. E. L. Blanchard's *Aladdin* (1865) at Drury Lane opens in a *'romantic cavern'*, the headquarters of the wicked magician Abanazar:

> *Invisible chorus, which commences with the rising of curtain ...* KAZRAC *the dumb Slave of Magician is seen stretched in slumber. As chorus continues, huge bats and enormous moths fly into cavern, and are seen hovering over the sleeper, whilst a large Owl appears flapping its wings over* KAZRAC *... [he] starts up, in terror and increase of alarm at seeing six Efreets or Spirits of Darkness take the place of the Bats, and preserving in appearance their winged form.*

Thus evil assumes a visually felicitous aspect, as does good. In Byron's *Robinson Crusoe* (1860), the second scene is laid in the *'Abode of Tyranny'*, who has resolved to destroy Crusoe: *'The scene is heavy, dismal, and dark.* TYRANNY, *who enters, is dressed completely in black, and no colour of any kind is visible in the scene or its adjuncts.'* However, Liberty *'rises in an illuminated bower, her dress is of shining silver, and stands out in marked contrast to the darkness of the scene'.* She ticks Tyranny off in song and doggerel couplets, takes Crusoe under her protection, and changes the scene to the Lucid Labyrinths of Liberty Hall, *'a shining silvery scene in which everything is dazzlingly brilliant, except the black form of* TYRANNY'.

The extensive comic business of *Robinson Crusoe* is strongly physical, with much fun arising from Crusoe's and Friday's disastrous attempt to make a meat pie, seriously hindered in their clumsy efforts by the interference of Crusoe's dog, goat and parrot and the involvement of uninvited cannibals – the same sort of comic use of food abundantly available in Victorian farce. This kind of business is continued in the four brief 'Comic Scenes' appended to the opening, a good illustration of the amiable and unplotted chaos

Plate 24 Nellie Reed of the Flying Grigolatis: *Blue Beard*, Drury Lane, 1901.
The Playgoer.

of the Victorian harlequinade. In Blanchard's next *Aladdin* (1874),
the business of the first comic scene occurs in front of the entrance to
a railway station, and concludes in this fashion:

> *A gipsy party now enter: a* LITTLE OLD MAN. *a* FAT WIFE, *about three or four*
> BIG GIRLS *and* BOYS, *also a chaise with two* CHILDREN *drawn by the father,*
> *followed by a* SERVANT *with a large hamper which is placed on stage.* CLOWN
> *tickles the* OLD LADY; *she screams.* LITTLE MAN *shows fight;* CHILDREN, *all*

> cry. Business. LADY *knocked into hamper* – 'Oh, the pastry!' LITTLE MAN *is*
> *upset into chaise;* CLOWN *runs him off in it, the other* CLOWN *picking up all*
> *the articles.* FAT LADY *shouts,* 'Where's my husband? Police, police!'
> CLOWN *enters with chaise, trips* BOBBY *into it.* Children cry, 'Oh, oh,
> oh!' BOBBY *gets the hamper over his head. Business. Wheels come off chaise*
> *and eventually they are all whacked into the station, squeezing in,* CLOWNS
> *pelting them, &c. &c. Bell rings loudly.* HARLEQUIN *bats; scene changes.*

Increasingly luxurious and expensive, and populated by hundreds of dancers, supers and children, pantomimes lumbered towards a *fin-de-siècle* apotheosis in such vast and lengthy works as Drury Lane's *Cinderella* in 1895 and *The Sleeping Beauty and the Beast* in 1900, a combination of two fairy tales written by J. Hickory Wood, a respected and competent author of pantomime openings in an age where a pantomime really did not have an author in the traditional sense, but a librettist, who collaborated with manager, stage manager, gasmen, limelight men, machinists, singers and low comedians to get his work on stage. That work consisted of the opening alone, since the harlequinade was almost invariably the responsibility of stage management, the machinists and the artistes playing Clown and Harlequin.

Of all Victorian dramatic forms only pantomime has survived today, changed but genuinely popular all over the provinces and still preserving, except for the long-departed harlequinade, its basic Victorian structure, combining character and spectacular fantasy. Other Victorian plays are sometimes revived, although revivals tend to keep to the farces and comedies, managements today being unwilling, with occasional exceptions, to undertake the financial risk of large-scale melodrama or the presentation of a *passé* Victorian morality and rhetoric to modern audiences. Yet the immensely rich and complex life of the Victorian theatre deserves performance as well as study; it is not only our immediate theatrical ancestor, worthy of attention and respect, but also a lively old soul in its own right whose multitudinous activities successfully entertained many millions of people, from the highest to the lowest, during the long reign of its most eminent devotee.

Sources

The intention here is not to provide a comprehensive bibliography of the Victorian theatre and drama, which would take a great deal of space, but to offer a selection of books that might be helpful for further reading. Of course many articles on the subject have been published in scholarly journals; these can mostly be found in specialist theatre journals of an academic nature, especially in *Theatre Notebook*, *Theatre Survey*, *Theatre History Studies*, *Theatre Research International*, *Essays in Theatre* and *Nineteenth Century Theatre* (and its predecessor *Nineteenth Century Theatre Research*). *Victorian Studies* also publishes the occasional article in this field.

Selected bibliographies of nineteenth-century drama and theatre are contained in several books: a listing of contemporary works in George Rowell, *The Victorian Theatre 1792–1914* (London, 1956; 2nd edn 1978); a chapter on the nineteenth century by Michael R. Booth in the bibliographical guide *English Drama*, ed. Stanley Wells (Oxford, 1975); a bibliography of melodrama in Michael R. Booth, *English Melodrama* (London, 1965); and a selection of books and articles published in the 1970s in the same author's *Prefaces to English Nineteenth-Century Theatre* (Manchester, 1981). *English Drama and Theatre 1800–1900: A Guide to Information Sources*, ed. Leonard W. Conolly and J. P. Wearing (Detroit, 1978) is more concerned with dramatic literature than the theatre. *English Theatrical Literature 1559–1900*, ed. James F. Arnott and John W. Robinson (London, 1970) contains only contemporary items and has a large nineteenth-century selection. Diana Howard, *London Theatres and Music Halls 1850–1950* (London, 1970) is a directory of theatres, music halls and pleasure gardens, with a listing of London libraries and collections holding relevant archival material. Russell Jackson, *Victorian Theatre* (London, 1989) is a valuable collection of documentary material relating to audiences, actors, authors, production and management, accompanied by helpful and informed commentaries at the beginning of each section.

1 Theatre and society

Queen Victoria's devotion to theatre is fully and pleasantly recorded in George Rowell, *Queen Victoria and the Theatre* (London, 1978). A great deal of contemporary information about the theatre and music hall is available in the three parliamentary Select Committee *Reports* bearing on these subjects: *Dramatic Literature* (1832), *Theatrical Licences and Regulations* (1866) and *Theatres and Places of Entertainment* (1892). These were originally official publications of the House of Commons, and have been reprinted by the Irish University Press (Shannon, 1968–70).

The journal *Victorian Studies* publishes, in its summer issue, an annual bibliography of items relating to the social and cultural history of the period and David Nicholls, *Nineteenth-Century Britain 1815–1914* (Folkestone, 1978) is a basic bibliography with sections on culture, economics and society. Also useful for publications before 1970 is Lionel Madden, *How to Find Out About the Victorian Period* (Oxford, 1970). An encyclopedia, *Victorian Britain*, ed. Sally Mitchell (New York, 1988) contains a great deal of information about the life of the Victorians, with a general bibliography and brief suggestions for further reading after each entry. *The Victorian City*, ed. H. J. Dyos and Michael Wolff (London, 1973), 2 vols., includes chapters on population, urbanisation, the image of London on stage, the growth of suburbs, the railway, prostitution, housing, poverty, the East End and many others. David Thomson, *England in the Nineteenth Century* (London, 1950) is a Pelican introduction; two useful paperbacks are J. F. C. Harrison, *Early Victorian Britain 1832–51* (London, 1979) and Geoffrey Best, *Mid-Victorian Britain 1851–75* (London, 1979); more specialist studies are Michael Flinn, *British Population Growth 1700–1850* (London, 1970), Rosalind Mitchison, *British Population Change since 1860* (London, 1977) and John R. Kellett, *The Impact of Railways on Victorian Cities* (London, 1969).

The East End at the end of the nineteenth century is thoroughly documented by Charles Booth in the *First Series* (London, 1902) of his monumental *Life and Labour of the People of London* and by Walter Besant, *East London* (London and New York, 1901). Booth is far more statistically minded than Besant, who is more of an impressionist. A. E. Wilson, *East End Entertainment* (London, 1954) is an unscholarly but entertaining account, with chapters on several important East End theatres; there is, unfortunately, a dearth of scholarship in this area. John M. East, *'Neath the Mask* (London, 1967) contains much information on working-class neighbourhood theatres, which are specifically placed in a social context.

Almost every edition of *Who's Who in the Theatre*, which started life as the *Green Room Book*, ed. John Parker (London, 1906), includes lists of important West End productions and their dates, long runs on the London stage, plans of West End theatre auditoriums and working dimensions of West End stages, actors' family trees and much other factual material relating to the Victorian period. *British Music Hall 1840–1923: A Bibliography and Guide to Sources*, ed. Lawrence Senelick, David Cheshire and Ulrich Schneider (Hamden, Conn., 1981) is an essential reference in a field overflowing with anecdote but dry of scholarship. However, a new and welcome academic rigour characterises two collections of essays: *Music Hall: The Business of Pleasure*, ed. Peter Bailey and *Music Hall: Performance and Style*, ed. J. S. Bratton, both published in a popular music series by the Open University (Milton Keynes, 1986).

There is no single book on the Victorian provincial theatre, although Kathleen Barker, *The Theatre Royal, Bristol 1766–1966* (London, 1974) is a substantial and detailed study of one of the most important provincial theatres, possibly the best and most scholarly of the books on various Theatres Royal and provincial circuits; many of these are listed in the Conolly–Wearing bibliography.

International touring is the subject of two books. *Emigrant in Motley*, ed. J. M. D. Hardwick (London, 1954) is a readable compilation of letters home by the Keans on their tour of Australia and North America, 1863–66. David Holloway, *Playing the Empire* (London, 1979), is a striking narrative of the problems facing the Holloway family tours to South Africa, India and the Far East between 1895 and 1913.

2 Management

The only general book on West End theatre management is John Pick, *The West End* (Eastbourne, 1983), which has a special case to argue against the managers, as the subtitle *Mismanagement and Snobbery* indicates. Half the book concerns the Victorian period. Leo Waitzkin's curiously titled *The Witch of Wych Street* (Cambridge, Mass., 1934) examines Madame Vestris's staging reforms at the Olympic; William W. Appleton, *Madame Vestris and the London Stage* (New York, 1974) is the most scholarly recent study. *The Diaries of William Charles Macready*, ed. William Toynbee, (London, 1912), 2 vols., are necessary for an understanding of their protagonist. *Macready's Reminiscences and Selections from His Diaries and Letters*, ed. Sir Frederick Pollock (London, 1875), 2 vols., covers similar material, but includes diary entries and autobiographical recollections before 1833, which is where the Toynbee *Diaries* begin. William Archer, *William Charles Macready* (London, 1890), is a most useful and compact summary of Macready's career; Alan Downer, *The Eminent Tragedian* (Cambridge, Mass., 1966), the only significant modern study, focusses more upon acting than management. *Bulwer and Macready*, ed. Charles Shattuck (Urbana, Ill., 1958) is a record of the practical collaboration between the two men on the production of the former's plays; it is an interesting account of how a leading actor-manager shaped a text for performance. The only Victorian account of Samuel Phelps is by his nephew, with the aid of a future manager who had acted with him: W. May Phelps and J. Forbes-Robertson, *The Life and Life Work of Samuel Phelps* (London, 1886). The only twentieth-century book on such an important actor-manager is Shirley Allen, *Samuel Phelps and Sadler's Wells Theatre* (Middletown, Conn., 1971), which looks carefully at the relationship between Phelps and Macready and pays particular attention to Phelps as an actor and producer of Shakespeare. In terms of scholarship, Charles Kean and the Bancrofts have fared worse than Phelps. No monograph has appeared on any of them in this century. J. W. Cole, *The Life and Theatrical Times of Charles Kean, F. S. A.* (London, 1859), 2 vols., although offering valuable descriptions of Kean's archaeological conceptions and productions of Shakespeare, is nevertheless the work of an adulatory fellow actor and manager. Squire and Marie Bancroft are jointly responsible for *Mr and Mrs Bancroft On and Off the Stage* (London, 1888), 2 vols., chiefly useful for the story of the acquisition of the Prince of Wales's, the production of Robertson's plays, and the move to the Haymarket.

The late Victorian actor-manager is represented by two books, Hesketh Pearson, *The Last Actor-Managers* (London, 1950) and Frances Donaldson, *The Actor Managers* (London, 1970). The former includes essays upon Forbes-Robertson, Tree, Alexander, Benson and Martin-Harvey; the latter upon the Bancrofts, Irving, Alexander, Forbes-Robertson and Tree. Pearson had the advantage of knowing the actor-managers he discusses; Frances Donaldson takes her material from secondary sources. The two together supply much information, and both extend their accounts into the Edwardian period. Irving is the actor-manager who has generated more contemporary writing, biography and modern scholarship than any other. The massive biography by his grandson Laurence Irving, *Henry Irving* (London, 1951) is still the 'official' story; it suffers from being uncritical but is a detailed survey of his life and work. Bram Stoker, *Personal Reminiscences of Henry Irving* (London, 1906), 2 vols., is a diffuse and more than respectful account by the business manager of the Lyceum, but Stoker knew Irving intimately and comments very specifically upon production and the Lyceum company. George Rowell, *Theatre in the Age of Irving* (London, 1981) is a gracefully written recital of Irving's career, placed in the context of actor-management from the 1860s to the 1890s. *Henry Irving and The Bells*, ed. David Mayer (Manchester, 1980) shows Irving at work on one of the best-known Victorian melodramas; it contains Irving's text of the play, the music for it, a reminiscence of the production from an eye-witness, notes, reviews and illustrations.

3 Playhouse and production

Several modern architectural histories of the playhouse contain sections on nine-teenth-century English theatre. The best of these for the Victorian period are Richard Leacroft, *The Development of the English Playhouse* (London, 1973) and Richard and Helen Leacroft, *Theatre and Playhouse* (London, 1984). The former is an authoritative study with a substantial Victorian component; the latter is a shorter work with two chapters on the nineteenth century. Both are especially helpful for isometric drawings of stages and auditoriums and accounts of stage machinery. Richard Southern, *The Victorian Theatre* (Newton Abbot, 1970) is useful for many illustrations of production methods, stages and auditoriums; Victor Glasstone, *Victorian and Edwardian Theatres* (London, 1975) offers splendid illustrations, some in colour, of auditoriums, notably those of the late Victorian and Edwardian years. There is also a section on music hall. Edwin O. Sachs and Ernest A. E. Woodward, *Modern Opera Houses and Theatres* (London, 1896–98; repr. New York, 1968), 3 vols., is an exhaustive survey of the architecture and stage construction of selected English and European theatres.

On the subject of stage production, one can profitably consult M. J. Moynet, *L'envers du théâtre* (Paris, 1873) or its English version *French Theatrical Production in the Nineteenth Century*, trans. Allan S. Jackson with M. Glen Wilson (New York, 1976). Moynet documents the exact operation of spectacle production and stage machinery and, although he writes of Paris theatres, much of what he says is also applicable to English staging. There are many helpful illustrations; the English version also includes illustrations from later editions of the work. The only English Victorian to write a substantially informative book on production technique was Percy Fitzgerald. His *The World behind the Scenes* (London, 1881) has a section on spectacle and staging mechanisms. In this century Terence Rees, *Theatre Lighting in the Age of Gas* (London, 1978), is indispensable for an understanding of the development and refinement of Victorian theatre lighting systems, including the advent of electric lighting and special lighting effects. It is handsomely illustrated. Michael R. Booth, *Victorian Spectacular Theatre* (London, 1981) discusses spectacle production and its social and cultural origins; there are chapters on Shakespeare, melodrama and pantomime and reconstructions of Irving's *Faust* and Tree's *King Henry VIII*. *Victorian Theatrical Trades*, ed. Michael R. Booth (London, 1981) is a reprint of an interesting series of articles in the *Stage* for 1883 and 1884 on the suppliers of theatrical materials such as hosiery, wigs, fabrics, boots and shoes, and furniture. Two articles are about gaslight and limelight.

Two collections of essays by different contributors could be mentioned here as well as anywhere else: *Nineteenth Century British Theatre*, ed. Kenneth Richards and Peter Thomson (London, 1971) and *Shakespeare and the Victorian Stage*, ed. Richard Foulkes (Cambridge, 1986). The former contains thirteen articles on the theatre, the drama and Shakespearean production; the latter twenty-one articles on various aspects of Shakespearean production, acting and the provincial repertory.

4 The actor

The social position and status of the actor and something of his training and the demands of his job are examined in Michael Baker, *The Rise of the Victorian Actor* (London, 1976) and Michael Sanderson, *From Irving to Olivier* (London, 1984); about half of each book pertains to the Victorian era. Sanderson virtually ignores the actress; Baker spends a chapter on her. Both tend to concentrate upon the upper echelon of the profession and the social recognition it received, largely disregarding the mass of ill-paid and drudging actors who experienced no 'rise' whatever in condition or status.

The reminiscences of a portable theatre proprietor in the north of England are the content of *The Original, Complete, and Only Authentic Story of 'Old Wild's'* (London, 1888; repr. 1989). This is complemented by Josephine Harrop, *Victorian Portable Theatres* (London, 1989), which focusses on the north. Jerome K. Jerome, *On the Stage and Off* (London, n.d.) is a humorous and instructive narrative of a novice actor's experiences around 1880.

The only general study of nineteenth-century acting is George Taylor, *Players and Performances in the Victorian Theatre* (Manchester, 1989), which traces the development of acting style from the Romantic concentration on the passions to the emphasis on psychology and motivation. The best Victorian accounts of acting are George Henry Lewes, *On Actors and the Art of Acting* (London, 1875) and Westland Marston, *Our Recent Actors* (London, 1888), 2 vols. Lewes, a perceptive judge of acting, writes of Macready, Charles Kean, Mathews and other aspects of acting; Marston writes at greater length about Macready and the Keans, and upon Phelps, Vestris, Mathews, Buckstone, Fechter, Alfred Wigan and others. In terms of substance and information, Marston's is the more useful book, Lewes's the more philosophical and theoretical.

In modern scholarship, *Victorian Actors and Actresses in Review*, ed. Donald Mullin (Westport, Conn., 1983) is a dictionary of excerpts from critical reviews of over 200 performers, both major and minor. It is prefaced by a thoughtful essay upon the organisational structure and nature of Victorian acting. E. B. Watson, *Sheridan to Robertson* (Cambridge, Mass., 1926; repr. New York, 1963) considers acting and theatrical conditions as well as management and the drama, including the acting of Fechter and the managerial reforms of Vestris and Macready. It is, in fact, a pioneer work of modern scholarship in this field. Alan Hughes, *Henry Irving, Shakespearean* (Cambridge, 1981) discusses the acting and production at the Lyceum of eleven of the twelve Shakespeare plays put on there between 1878 and

1901. John Stokes, Michael R. Booth and Susan Basnett, *Bernhardt, Terry, Duse* (Cambridge, 1988), contains a chapter on the acting of Irving's co-star, Ellen Terry.

5 Dramatists and the drama

Modern collections of English nineteenth-century plays offer a fair selection for the reader. *English Plays of the Nineteenth Century*, ed. Michael R. Booth (Oxford, 1969–76), 5 vols., comprises thirty-three tragedies, dramas, melodramas, comedies, farces, extravaganzas, burlesques and pantomimes. Nine of these are pre-Victorian. Each volume has a substantial introduction and a short preface to each play; there are several appendices relating to acting, production and criticism. *The Magistrate and Other Nineteenth-Century Plays* (London, 1974) is a selection of nine plays from the first four volumes of this edition, with an introduction. The introductions to the original five volumes have been collected in *Prefaces to English Nineteenth-Century Theatre*. Nine volumes of English plays, almost all of them Victorian, edited by different scholars, are available in the series *British and American Playwrights 1750–1920* (Cambridge, 1982–87). Each volume includes an introduction and notes and is given over to a single playwright: Planché, Boucicault, Taylor, Robertson, Byron, Reade, Gilbert, Pinero and Jones – a total of thirty-seven plays altogether. Robertson has also been anthologised in *T. W. Robertson: Six Plays*, ed. Michael R. Booth (Ashover, 1980). The texts, prefaced by a biographical and critical introduction, are *Society, Ours, Caste, Progress, School* and *Birth*. *Nineteenth Century Plays*, 2nd edn (Oxford, 1972) and *Late Victorian Plays 1890–1914* (Oxford, 1968), both edited by George Rowell, together contain sixteen plays, eleven of them Victorian. J. O. Bailey, *British Plays of the Nineteenth Century* (New York, 1966) is a textbook of unattractive appearance, but it does offer sixteen stage plays, twelve of them Victorian, and several unavailable in other collections. *Hiss the Villain*, ed. Michael R. Booth (London, 1964) is a selection of six English and American melodramas, four of them performed after 1837, with a goodly introduction. Finally, *Nineteenth-Century Shakespeare Burlesques* (London, 1977–78) is a collection of thirty-three plays, eight of them American, printed in facsimile. Each volume is admirably introduced by Stanley Wells.

The nature and exercise of the Lord Chamberlain's powers of censorship are considered in J. R. Stephens, *The Censorship of English Drama 1824–1901* (Cambridge, 1980), and the various attempts to abolish the monopoly powers of Drury Lane and Covent Garden are documented in Watson Nicholson, *The Struggle for a Free Stage in London* (Boston, 1906; repr. New York, 1966), still the standard work on the subject.

A major general history is Allardyce Nicoll, *A History of English Drama 1660–1900*, 2nd edn (Cambridge, 1955–59), 6 vols. In vol. IV, 1800–1850, and vol. V, 1850–1900, Nicoll writes about theatrical conditions and staging as well as the drama and is perhaps most useful now for the lists of theatres, authors and plays at the end of each volume. Two volumes of *The Revels History of Drama in English* cover the nineteenth century: vol. VI, 1750–1880 and vol. VII, 1880– (London, 1975–78). Vol. VI, by Michael R. Booth, Richard Southern, Frederick and Lise-Lone Marker and Robertson Davies, contains, as well as a long section on the drama, chapters on the social and literary context and theatres and actors, a guide to

London theatres, a chronological table and a bibliography for each chapter. Vol. vii, by Hugh Hunt, Kenneth Richards and John Russell Taylor, follows the same format and comments on the later Victorian period. The standard introduction to the nineteenth-century theatre and drama has for many years been Rowell's *The Victorian Theatre 1792–1914*; the second edition adds an 'Afterword' chapter touching on several subjects not developed in the earlier edition. Victor Emeljanow's *Victorian Popular Dramatists* (Boston, 1987) is a perceptive analysis of Jerrold, Taylor, Robertson and Jones with an introductory chapter on dramatic forms and their theatrical contexts. A usefully large number of plays by these four authors are discussed or summarised.

Genre studies of Victorian drama are few in number. Booth's *English Melodrama* is one of them; it concludes with a chapter on the acting of melodrama. About a third of Frank Rahill, *The World of Melodrama* (University Park, Penn., 1967) is about English melodrama; the rest of the book is concerned with French and American melodrama – this last being the subject of David Grimsted, *Melodrama Unveiled* (Chicago, 1968). James L. Smith, *Melodrama* (London, 1973), a brief summary and analysis in Methuen's Critical Idiom series, focusses principally upon English melodrama. Jeffry H. Huberman, *Late Victorian Farce* (Ann Arbor, Mich., 1986) concentrates on French-influenced farce and Pinero and his contemporaries; it has the merit of bringing to our attention many good but now forgotten plays. Jessica Milner Davis, *Farce* (London, 1978), another in the Critical Idiom series, is a helpful introduction to the genre and gives examples from Victorian farce. J. R. Planché, *Recollections and Reflections*, 2nd edn (London, 1901) conveys information about Planché's extravaganzas, as well as about his other work in the theatre, especially in the movement toward historically correct costumes and properties. W. Davenport Adams, *A Book of Burlesque* (London, 1891) summarises the various kinds of stage burlesques and their subject matter. There is no scholarly monograph on Victorian pantomime, but David Mayer, *Harlequin in His Element* (Cambridge, Mass., 1969) is essential reading for an understanding of pantomime in the nineteenth century; it focusses on the period 1806–36 and the prime of Joseph Grimaldi as Clown. A. E. Wilson, *Christmas Pantomime* (London, 1934) is a popular and colourful account; most of it is about the Victorians.

Index

act drop, 75
acting space, 124
acting: approaches to, 133–36; traditional
nature of Victorian, 119; approach to
character, 134, 139; authority of, 123–24;
casting, 109–10; character, 127; family
dynasties of, 100; loss of influence, 139;
melodramatic, 129–30; memorising of
parts, 105, 110; moral prejudices against,
22, 101; portrayal of emotions, 133–34,
151; procedures for a novice, 101–2;
provincial, 100–1, 112; Romantic, 134;
star 99, 106–7, 124, 127, 131;
supernumerary *see* supers; touring, 127,
129, 131; tragic, 120–21; wages, 109,
117–19; walk-on parts, 108–9; West End,
111–12; working day of, 102–4
actor-manager 31, 36, 43, 55–58, 80, 106–7,
112
Actors' Association xvii, 111–12, 117
actresses 112–13; difficulties for, 113, 114;
hazards in work, 114
Adelphi Theatre, xiv, 7, 41, 51, 54, 63, 90,
92, 109, 128, 145, 173
advertising, 37–38, 102
Albery, James, 183, 192
Albion Theatre, 5
Alexander, George, xvii, 23, 41, 55–58,
104, 173
Alexandra Theatre 49
Alhambra, xvi, 11
Alma-Tadema, Lawrence 95
Almar, George, 130
amateur dramatic society, 111

America, touring of theatre to, 54, 56, 57
American copyright law of 1891, xvii, 145
Anderson, Hans Christian, 199
animals on stage, 1, 196
Appleton, William W., 34
archaeology, 95–97
Archer, William, 168–69
Arliss, George, 103, 109
Arnold, Samuel, 152
Astley's Theatre, 12, 61, 69, 107, 152, 196
attitude, 134, 151
audience, 1, 2, 95, 97
audience: behaviour, 9, 22, 62, 146, 168–72;
composition of, 2–3, 6–13, 15, 17–18,
163, 168; increase in size of, 15, 25,
59–62, 63; melodrama, 162, 166; box,
pit, stalls and gallery, 17, 125, 150; taste,
12, 141, 145–47, 169
auditorium, 58–66, 70–71, 75; design
features, 59, 62–66, 83, 85, 117; lighting
of, 59, 62, 83–84, 87–88, 90; of Regency
theatre, 59; of Restoration and
eighteenth century theatre, 2, 4
author's role, 104, 107

Bain, Alexander, 137
balcony, 59–60, 62
Ballanytne, Evelyn, 20
Balzac, 180
Bancroft, Squire, xvii, 52–54, 63, 71, 103,
112, 180
Bancrofts, the, xvi, xvii, 35, 40, 48, 51,
53–54, 63, 107, 119, 142, 182
Barker, Kathleen, 22

210